Dena Blatt

The Artist and the Alien

Guidance, Warnings, and Hope from an ET Living Among Us

2/24/08

To Anne —
All the Very Best
to you!,
Dena Blatt

Outskirts Press, Inc.
Denver, Colorado

Acknowledgments

I wish to thank

Shirlè for her patience and trust in me; her willingness to let me dig, even to the point of tears.

Martha Collman, writer, for her constant encouragement; her belief in me and in the cause of disseminating UFO information.

Cindy Owens, my efficient "Girl Friday" for taking care of things other than writing, and without whom I would never have had the time to finish the book. Her good nature, praise, helpful advice for my writing, and her interest in UFOs made it so much easier.

Scott Mandelker for his time, kind attention, advice, and his books *From Elsewhere—Being ET in America*, and *Universal Vision –Soul Evolution and the Cosmic Plan* from which I was educated on "wanderers."

Warren Aston for his thoughtfulness, good advice and precious time, which I truly appreciated.

Timothy Conway for his kindness, and for taking time to give helpful ideas and encouragement, no matter how busy or involved.

Leo Sprinkle for his easygoing attitude—his "anything is possible" attitude which I love—and for his helpful critique.

Table of Contents

PART I: The Alien Frank and the Artist Shirlè

Chapter

Preface

Shirlè—"Indigo" and "Wanderer"

I had seen all I wanted to see and heard all I wanted to hear. It was the last hour of the last day of Seattle's Whole Life Expo. All lectures were over, and the exhibits on health, ecology, and related subjects were being taken down. As I was passing the last booth near the exit, an attractive woman with a warm, friendly smile was telling passers-by about her *two-year platonic relationship with an extraterrestrial— looking like us— living and working here on Earth.*

Something happened to me at that moment. I smiled at her, and I just knew she was telling the truth. It was like being told that the world was round when you are taught it is flat; something inside me resonated with her truth. At the same moment I knew I was supposed to get to know this woman. Her card said: Shirlè Klein-Carsh. We exchanged phone numbers and soon she invited me to her home in Surrey, British Columbia.

***

I arrived at the Carsh home on a sunny afternoon. Shirlè welcomed me in a warm embrace. The house, in a neat middle-class neighborhood, was beautifully landscaped. The flowering bushes and fragrant roses, Shirlè said, were the result of the loving ministrations of her husband Fred. She took me out through the kitchen to the backyard. Fred looked up from tending his vegetable garden, now ready to be harvested, and came over to greet me. Tall, broad-shouldered, and tanned, his strong handshake was almost too much for my fragile hand. Proudly, he gave me a tour of his garden.

I was impressed. Every vegetable had its place in neat rows that he had weeded, watered, and labeled with delicate and loving care. Along the back fence grew bushes loaded with raspberries. Vines with dark grapes and a tree laden with figs stood alongside a tall apple tree bent with the weight of many huge apples. A swinging bench, patio table, and chairs were a few steps away. I sat down and watched as Fred went into his little painted and decorated toolshed for a spade, picked some green beans, dug up some new potatoes, and picked the makings of a salad to go with the wonderful roasted chicken Shirlè had already made.

Inside, Shirlè gave me a tour. The living room was a work of art in the layout of furniture and art objects, with each area of the room a three-dimensional "picture" begging study and reflection. Though it was called the living room, it was obvious that the room that was actually lived in was the family room next to the kitchen. It held a fireplace, TV, stereo, comfy couch, and a coffee table covered with a mass of papers that invited visitors to put up their feet and relax. In the garage that led to it was a small workshop area. Shirlè told me there wasn't anything that Fred the handyman couldn't fix.

Shirlè's paintings and various collections adorned the walls of every room except Fred's model train room. Down the hall from the bedroom was Shirlè's art studio. The room was warm and sunny, perfect for painting in. With its high ceiling and large window it looked more like a loft than a regular spare room. Paintings of all sizes covered the walls from floor to ceiling; more canvasses circled the huge center table. Like Fred's garden, everything was orderly. Paint cans stood neatly lined up, a work-in-progress ready for her on the easel. I noted almost every picture had a rendering of male and female figures, and I pondered its significance. I was mesmerized not only by the vivid color combinations, but also by the unique patterns, which gave me the odd sense that her inspiration was not of this time and place. "I make my own colors," she said quietly, "and I think of myself as a futurist."

I wanted to know more about her art, their subject matter, their meanings, her exhibits, and so on. She gladly obliged. Her art resume was impressive—155 paintings from 1987 to 1997, all on the subject of cosmology, listed with interpretations and comments—and 33 international exhibits from 1965 to 2003.

From that day Shirlè and I became friends. We found we had similar backgrounds, similar interests, and enjoyed being together, going on little trips, laughing at our own jokes.

One day I received a call from Shirlè; a screenwriter was interested in her story and after hearing the details, had faxed his synopsis of a TV show with a note that said: "There's money in this. People are interested in psychic stuff these days."

Shirlè faxed it to me. I was shocked; the synopsis did not bear even a passing resemblance to her story. Only one thing was true in this fictitious psychic episode: her name. It was obvious he didn't believe a word of Shirlè's story. What I uttered then was spontaneous and involuntary: "Even I could do better than that!"

I was taken aback at what came out of my mouth. I had no intention of writing someone's story since I already had too many projects going on and it would be a very demanding undertaking. Yet I knew it had to be written—the *truth*, not fiction.

Silence on the other end—then in a soft clear voice "I knew you were going to do it..."

***

At the start of the book I wondered, could I just stick to my original idea: demonstrate the similarity of Shirlè's traits with that of Indigo, Wanderer and Star children; show what led up to Shirlè's contact with aliens; and explain the two missions Frank the alien had given her—along with his warnings for mankind?

But could I really exclude how this woman became an artist in a man's world? How she survived growing up being "different," sometimes doubting her sanity? How her spiritual search and her metaphysical experiences seemed to be both a cause and effect of her alien contact? No, I realized, I couldn't. It's all connected. In addition to the psychological and spiritual growth stories—throughout which Shirlè had a sense of being guided by God, angels, extraterrestrials—perhaps by all three, there is the "Shirlè Klein the artist" story (her unique work alone would fill a book). Finally, there is, outstanding by itself, the alien story and the alien message: that we on Earth must learn to get along with each other. I was intrigued by the interrelationship of all these forces.

I began with Shirlè's childhood. Not satisfied with the superficial answers she gave, I kept digging. The more I heard, the more confused I became. At one time I interviewed Shirlè's daughter, a nurse. She talked freely, with respect and admiration for her mother, aware of her mother's sometimes contradictory and puzzling personality. "My mother's an enigma," she said, finally, confirming my feelings.

A few days later, I introduced Shirlè to my friend Elke Siller Macartney as we met for lunch in a charming little café in the small town of La Conner, Washington, just a few miles away from where I lived. Elke, who sees whole body auras and paints them for clients, took one look at Shirlè, smiled and said, "I can see you're an Indigo."

Shirlè nodded her head knowingly. Now, finally I had something to grasp onto in order to understand this strange, fascinating woman and what motivated her.

With only superficial knowledge of so-called "Indigo" children, I began to look for books and talk to people familiar with Indigos. The book *Indigo Children* by Lee Carroll and Jan Tober had caught on all over the world as many people recognized their children, or even themselves in it. However, it was about very young children and Shirlè was in her mid-seventies, though she looked much younger. *Indigo Celebration* which followed *Indigo Children,* discusses older Indigos believed to be the precursors of the Indigos. And in the book's "test" for Indigos, Shirlè scored near the top.

Yes, I thought, Shirlè could well be a forerunner of the present Indigo; she matched many of their characteristics. I gathered together her childhood stories and listed them under traits to see how well they fit the Indigo type. They fit only too well.

Who are these Indigos? What are they like? The following are some characteristics from an abridged version in *Indigo Children* by Lee Carroll and Jan Tober:

> Super-sensitive, they feel dysfunction, and the lack of love much more than other children. Psychologists and teachers have been hearing more about these children—some diagnosed ADD and given Ritalin. They cannot be intimidated, controlled by shame, guilt, physical restraint, or punishment. They understand spiritual concepts such as reincarnation, may tell of a past life, hear voices, see lights and auras, do astral travel, have invisible friends, see into other dimensions, or have pre-birth experiences.

These traits can also be found in children and adults called "walk-ins" and "wanderers."

A walk-in is a soul who exchanges with another in a human body who voluntarily departs and the newcomer takes over. "Wanderers" on the other hand, are ETs who volunteer to incarnate on Earth to help in some way. Born of human parents, they forget their ET identity and suffer severe alienation until they pierce the veil and remember their non-human origins.

Both are described in Scott Mandelker's *From Elsewhere—Being ET in America*. In his book *Universal Vision--Soul Evolution and the Cosmic Plan* that followed, Shirlè scored 90 out of 100 for "wanderers." Another good book is *Star Children* by Jenny Randles. These books, together with the Indigo literature, finally helped me to better understand Shirlè and appreciate what she had experienced.

***

Introduction

This is the true story of how one woman's life and art developed and changed as a result of her two-year contact with an extraterrestrial looking like us—living and working here on Earth. Her experiences illustrate the UFO-metaphysical connection, and reveal her to be what is called a "wanderer"—with a mission. My brief analysis of the UFO phenomenon and its implications, in the last part of the book, is an attempt to make her story more understandable to the general public less familiar with the subject.

I am not a trained psychologist or a UFO researcher, so I don't claim to have all the answers. In the end, you will naturally deny or discard any information that does not fit your particular worldview or philosophy—you will simply take what fits.

For me, Shirlè's story reveals the need to bring the existence of extraterrestrials living among us into the open so that we can face any fear we have of them. While the so-called "negative" aliens teach us what we should not do, the more spiritual aliens impress on us the necessity of getting along with one another—to work on our spiritual evolution. This progression, of which we are mostly unaware, is natural and inevitable, they tell us, and is the destiny for Earth and its inhabitants. It seems from my studies that all aliens give the same warnings: Earth and We are heading for physical (natural) and man-made (warfare and ecological) catastrophes—unless we make some changes.

***

This book is not to prove that UFOs exist, or that Shirlè's alien was a real extraterrestrial living and working among us, for there simply is no proof. Rather, it is for those who are open to UFO and metaphysical subjects, but want to learn more, especially about the spiritual aspect.

It is to be noted that while some abductees have had negative experiences with aliens who have their own agenda—contactees on the other hand, have reported positive experiences with aliens of a more spiritual nature who respect our free will and do not interfere with our earthly decisions. Fortunately, Shirlè's experience was with a caring alien who guided her along her spiritual path. My hope is that in the telling of one person's strange journey into other dimensions, other worlds, you will want to investigate—perhaps gain the courage to go where you had always feared to tread.

The question of ET identity, which has rarely been addressed, might be a starter. Scott Mandelker PhD, author of *From Elsewhere: Being ET in America,* interviewed and researched these contactees, sometimes called "wanderers"[1] or adult "Indigos" (about a hundred million world-wide today. One quote from the book,(and it applies perfectly to Shirlè):

> They were far from being flaky, naïve faddists. Most were serious, reasonable in thought and speech, definitely not fanatics, and not particularly bedazzled by beliefs of being 'From Elsewhere.' They were generally mild and well spoken, gentle and peaceable—far more accepting and tolerant than many leaders and followers of conventional religious groups. Unfortunately, the experiences of those with non-Earthly origins often gets lost in a medley of strange and fascinating tales, while their *personal conflicts, struggles and accomplishments—their confusion to confidence*—all that has been given far too little attention by academics or the mainstream public.

***

In *The Artist and the Alien* I have attempted to fill that gap. In the process I have been learning about myself and the universe, for we are all on a journey to find the truth. In my search, I was very impressed with "The Greatest Story Never Told," a UFO video by Robert Dean[2], who claims this is really the biggest story in human history, and I agree. I am

---

[1] ETs who volunteer to incarnate on Earth to help in some way. Born of human parents, they forget their identity and suffer severe alienation until they pierce the veil and remember their non-human origins.

[2] Robert Dean –SHAPE 1963—secret NATO reports on UFO and alien involvement with Earth.

simply using Shirlè's story to make the public aware of it—aware of the truth that aliens are real and are here among us. In Part IV, I try to bring attention to the political, financial, religious, and spiritual implications of this knowledge, and how it pertains to us *personally*.

***

Somehow I feel *compelled* to tell the UFO story—and I don't have time! I had a dream the other day. I was with a group who were to embark on a ship to some final destination. No one talked about it. All went about unconcerned. I, however, rather than make final preparations for embarking, ignored the people milling about, and sat down to write. I felt I *had* to get it done, before the call to sail, before it was *too late*—for the essence of my book is essentially the aliens' message—a message for all of mankind: we must realize our destiny—and it is *spiritual* evolution. We must understand and develop our innate metaphysical abilities that allow us to experience the spirit world. Most important of all, we must save Earth from deterioration and develop the practice of compassion.

PART I

The Alien Frank
and the Artist Shirlè

Chapter One

The Strange Man
in the Secondhand Store

"They're not of this world"

T he book started out clear-cut; the story of my artist friend Shirlè Klein. Simple enough. But as I listened to her tales of psychological and spiritual searching, I realized that I too was on the path. I too, am learning and seeking, and I couldn't exclude my own thoughts and feelings. So bear with me. This is not a biography in the normal sense. I have used Shirlè's experiences not only for the examination of my own life, but also for the study and analysis of the UFO phenomenon.

And I can't help it… It's written from the view of a UFO *believer*.

The following story—a turning point in Shirlè's life—eventually became mine as well.

***

The year was 1970, the place an apartment in Vancouver, B.C.

Shirlè laid down her paintbrush and slowly picked up the ringing phone. "My name's Mike," the caller said. "It may sound forward, Shirlè, but a friend of mine suggested I ask you for a date."

Moments passed as she hesitated. It had been three years since her husband Hymie had died. Her children were grown; there was no excuse. She knew she should get out more. Oh, she had had dates—she was a warm, attractive widow of forty-eight, but no one, absolutely no one, could measure up to Hymie. She was only half listening.

"I'm a mathematics professor at UBC[3], a respectable person," he went on. "You can call the university."

"Okay," she found herself saying. But why, she wondered, and to a blind date, yet; her heart really wasn't in it. She pictured him, staid, rule-bound, with no imagination—what would she have in common with him?

Yet the very fact that he was a mathematician was crucial to what followed; it was to change her life forever. At the time, however, it was simply a dinner date, made for his day off.

The day came. In late afternoon she wondered what to wear, tried on various outfits, and studied herself in the mirror.

She certainly didn't look forty-eight. No one would give her more than thirty. She had shapely curves, soft wavy brown hair, an ivory complexion, and dark sensitive eyes. She was considered beautiful—she had heard it said often enough. But what she yearned for was a man who would appreciate her for her mind and soul, not just looks. She chose a simple skirt, blouse, and jacket—took one last look at her reflection, and was ready.

Mike arrived. She was pleased to see he was good looking and neatly dressed in a suit and tie. About half an hour later, they were driving to the restaurant along Fourth Avenue and making small talk. Suddenly Shirlè felt a powerful "pull" to go into a thrift shop they had just passed. It was so strong and definite, she felt compelled to obey the urge. She had never experienced anything like it in her life.

"Mike," she said, "please stop. I want to go in there." Annoyed and mentally writing her off, he parked the car.

---

[3] University of British Columbia

"You're kidding," he said dryly, as they faced the shop. "What would you want in there? The stuff in the window is just junk."

"If you won't go in with me," said Shirlè, quietly, "I'll go by myself."

Grumbling, Mike followed Shirlè into the secondhand store. A man in a blue shirt sat at a desk near the electronics section. Shirlè looked him over. Mid or late forties, she figured. Shoulder length dark hair, sallow complexion, straight nose, thin lips—and the eyes, unremarkable except for the large, dark irises—Italian perhaps? She wandered about, looking at housewares. What had drawn her here, she wondered—and so powerfully!

Meanwhile, Mike headed for the electronics section, more to his interest. He had to pass the man at the desk, who kept working at his papers. As a mathematician teaching at a university in Vancouver, Mike couldn't help noticing strange writing and what were obviously equations.

"What are you doing?" he asked, fascinated. "What are those equations?"

"They're not of this world," the man said without looking up from his papers.

Shirlè, now close by, overheard. "Dear God, a nut," she said to herself.

The man seemed to have read her thoughts. He turned, faced her, and smiled. While Mike probed the man for explanations of his mathematics, Shirlè went looking for something, anything, to buy. When she finally settled on a knickknack, the man was at the counter, waiting. She put down a bill.

"What's your name?" she asked.

"Frank."

"So Frank, when are they going to take me?"

The man kept a straight face. "I'll find out," he said, and handed her the change.

As they left the shop, Mike could contain himself no longer. "Good God," he said. "The math he was doing, made my knowledge look primitive. I feel I know nothing now."

But Shirlè was not hearing him. She was lost in thought. She had asked that question half jokingly. Now she wondered—could it be possible? A real alien? An extraterrestrial?

Fast forward to 2003. The place—my home in Washington State:

It was a dreary foggy day. From my dining room window, Lopez Island looked a blur. Dreary days are good for writing and one reason I came to Washington—no sunny California to distract me. We were now both in our seventies, but Shirlè looked fifteen to twenty years younger, could manage with only three or four hours of sleep each night, and still have boundless energy.

Earlier, we had gone into town to do some garage sales. Giggling like teen-agers, we prided ourselves on our finds: exactly the right frying pan for me, a unique piece of jewelry for Shirlè. Everywhere we went, there was not a person or child that did not respond with warm smiles to Shirlè's exuberant greetings, and I thought of how practically every painting she has done includes human figures or faces. She is definitely a people-person. Relationships and friends are very important to her.

As Shirlè gradually related the details of her two years with Frank and the mission he gave her, now and then I'd interrupt with questions:

"Are there any witnesses to the alien Frank—who are they—where are they? Have the artifacts been examined by any authority? Did you keep a journal?"

"Look," she said, "it was about thirty years ago. I moved a few times—Montreal, Australia, Vancouver. I kept notes, but most got lost. The names of some witnesses I've forgotten, others I can't locate. And If I knew then what I know now, I'd have asked Frank different, better questions. I didn't know enough to ask the right questions, and he wouldn't offer what I couldn't understand."

But I had so many more questions. Why was *she* chosen—of all people? What was it about her? Was she really an adult Indigo, a "wanderer"? And the "guidance"—what, who was guiding? What did her art have to do with her mission?

And what was operating when Shirlè was drawn to Frank—Hypnosis? Mind control? And Frank's message—his answer to natural and man-made catastrophes—*we* must act and we must have *compassion*. And what was all this about moving from the third to fourth and fifth dimension—what did it really mean?

Finally synchronicity… How does it operate? I marveled at this force that could bring together three strangers—for a *purpose*—a mission only revealed to Shirlè at the close of their contact—when she was finally deemed ready to receive it.

Of course there were steps—incidents leading up to her meeting with the alien in the secondhand store. There were many, from childhood on, as the tape recorded.

***

"Okay," I said, "you've told me about your relationship with Frank. But what led up to your feeling that he really might be an alien—what had gone on in your life up to that point—what influenced your thinking?"

"It was an incident," she said, "twelve years earlier—in 1959."

"Missing Time" With "Scuba Divers"

> "Time and space are modes by which we think, not
> conditions in which we live." –Albert Einstein

She was thirty-three, attending college at night. She had been sitting at her kitchen table one afternoon, studying for exams, when two figures simply appeared before her in scuba gear, complete with flippers, masks, and tanks on their backs. They were men, she noted, for they were flat-chested. Strangely, she wasn't frightened, though she knew instinctively they were spacemen. Was the disguise to lessen her fear of what they really looked like? She stared, engrossed.

"Shall we take her?" she heard telepathically.

The other eyed her intently. "No, not yet," he replied.

The next thing she knew, the "scuba divers" were gone and she was lying on top of the blankets of her bed with her head pillow-less at the foot of it. She sat up. How could this have happened? She had no memory of leaving the table and much time had elapsed, for it was now dark.

She told no one but her husband Hymie. "Don't dare open your mouth, Shirlè" he said. "With two small children and you going back to school they'll think you've flipped out."

He didn't doubt that she actually had such an experience; he simply understood that in 1959 people would think she was losing her mind. As to whether the scuba divers were real aliens or not, he was open. He went to UFO meetings with her, and helped her find books and articles on space. With his encouragement, she went to the library and asked for books on spacemen and "flying saucers." As the term "UFO" or "aliens" had not yet been coined, she was guided to the Science Fiction section. Though little was available at that time, she continued to search. Finally, in a little bookstore, she found George Adamski's[4] 1952 book *Inside the Spaceships* that detailed his contact experience with an alien who, he claimed, looked, acted, and talked like us.

***

"Do you think you were abducted?" I asked. "And how come you were not frightened?"

"Years later," she said, "when I heard of 'missing time' episodes and their meaning, I wondered if I had actually been abducted not only by the 'scuba divers' but when I was about three years old. I was sitting on the living room floor and a beam of light came down and enveloped me. I remembered nothing after that. No, for some reason it didn't scare me.

"And when I was five, I awoke suddenly in the middle of the night. While my parents slept, I dragged my blanket down the stairs with me. Suddenly I was back on my bed with no memory of having returned. I was lying on top of the blankets, not under them, and my parents were still sleeping soundly. Now I think, maybe I was abducted."

***

I wondered what transpired between the age of five and the appearance of the "scuba divers"—a span of twenty-eight years. There had to be more incidents leading up to the meeting with the alien, and there were: glimpses into other dimensions, voices in her head, experiences of telekinesis of an auto while inside it; interaction with the dead in solid and astral form; entering the past, experiencing another's experience, and the viewing of her first UFO. Furthermore, she was searching spiritually, believed in other inhabited worlds and was aware

---

[4] Much has been written about Adamski. He was the son of Polish Catholic immigrants, author of many books on his experiences with UFOs and aliens. Interested in astronomy and philosophy, he lived at Mt. Palomar making a living as a lecturer. He claimed that in 1952 an alien who looked human had contacted him, a month after he had seen his first UFO in New Mexico, and five witnesses saw the UFO from which the alien had emerged. For years he was treated with credibility and respect by the public and the press. Then he was discounted as a fraud, as conflicting data appeared about the case.

of synchronicities.

So all these factors, and especially her ability to enter into and receive from other dimensions, prepared her for the "scuba divers" incident; it didn't shock her.

Finally, the "scuba divers" had mentally and emotionally prepared her for Frank, the man in the secondhand store. *But to look like us? Living among us?*

It was weird. She needed to know more. She had to see Frank again.

Chapter Two

Getting to Know Him—to Final Acceptance
Frank the Alien, Frank the Teacher

"When the pupil is ready the teacher appears."
–Anonymous Chinese proverb

"**D**escribe him a little more," I said. "Did he have any mannerisms, a peculiar walk, a way of talking,? What did he usually wear, eat? Any habits?"

"I told you he looked completely ordinary," she said. "Even his shoulder length hair would not draw attention. Only his large dark irises stood out. He was quiet and easy-going. I never saw him eat anything, and he smoked. He always wore a simple ordinary patterned shirt and loose-fitting brown pants. He would be indistinguishable in any crowd."

"Then what made you feel he could be an alien?"

"It wasn't because of the way he looked or acted," she replied. "It was his answer when Mike asked about his equations. He said, and I can never forget it: '*They're not of this world.*'

The very next day Shirlè set out to see him with the intent to converse with him as though she accepted him as an alien, while still needing proof. After all, she already had been going to UFO meetings and had attended a lecture by a scientist who spoke of aliens helping the U.S. space program. She knew what she would ask—her previous question.

She entered the shop expecting a reaction from him to her coming. But his manner was casual, as though he were expecting her. His lack of surprise jolted her, and her question "When are they going to take me?" eluded her. So she began with the usual questions.

"Where did you come from, originally?"

"Saskatchewan," he replied.

"How long have you been in Vancouver?"

"A few months."

"What other places have you been to?"

"I'm around. I don't always stay in one place."

"How long have you worked here?"

"Not long."

Days would go by with small talk, then one day she came out with it. "Are you an alien?"

No answer.

"Which planet did you come from?"

With a laugh, as if teasing, "A planet[5] far, far away."

"Where, far, far away?" Silence.

Why, she wondered, did she not insist that he answer? Then it occurred to her that perhaps she was putting words in his mouth and his answer would have no meaning.

"What do you like to eat?" she asked another day.

When he didn't respond, she went out and bought two hamburgers, and gave him one. Engrossed in conversation, she realized later that she did not see him eat it. She checked the room, the wastebasket, and the garbage. It had simply disappeared.

She had no photo of him. Every time she would bring her camera, he would say, "Not now, later." Half way home on the bus, she would realize she hadn't taken his picture. Once she "took" his picture only to discover she had no film in her camera. But maybe it wasn't *her*, she mused. He had a way of distracting her, diverting her, when he didn't

---

[5]Much later Frank told her that he came from the planet Sirius.

want to answer or do something, and she would forget.

They would have lengthy philosophical talks on the meaning of life, but only in answer to her questions. She didn't ask about his personal life. She felt it would be an imposition. If he wanted to tell her, he would. So if he was an alien and had a wife and children on his planet or ours, he kept it to himself. Though he appeared to be single, sleeping in the back of the shop, and Shirlè a widow of a few years, their relationship was purely platonic. He didn't ask personal questions of her and didn't initiate conversation. But this was fine with Shirlè. She felt his reticence showed a certain respect.

Each time she would see Frank, she made notes either at the shop or when she came home. He never offered her any information, unless it was asked for, except telling her of his concerns for the future of the planet. However, one day, after a few months, he did more than just answer questions. A nice-looking couple entered the store.

"Terrible vibration," he said, shaking his head.

"How can you be sure?" asked Shirlè. He just smiled. Therefore she knew she couldn't ask what she wasn't ready for. But once, she simply rephrased and rephrased her question.

"Do you want to get me in trouble?" he said finally. "I have superiors. I cannot divulge some things you cannot yet understand." But she wouldn't give up. She tried to trick him, to see if he would repeat the same story, hoping he would say something different. It didn't work.

At times when they were completely alone, Frank would be more responsive to her questions. He seemed to know everything about her—certain events in her life; personal things he could not possibly have heard of—the fact she couldn't get along with her mother and how she always felt like an outsider.

But what finally convinced Shirlè that Frank was an alien wasn't any one thing in particular. It was a gradual process over six months' time, entailing many situations. However, it was the owner of the shop who finally cemented her belief.

One day while Frank was attending to a customer, Shirlè approached the graying, casually dressed owner who appeared to be in his mid-fifties, as he was putting away some merchandise.

"Where'd you find this guy?" she asked. "He's a strange one."

"Sure is," he replied. "He comes in one day and says he wants work. He can repair things—wants no pay, just a bed in the back to lie down on. I didn't know what to make of it, but if you look into Frank's eyes, you know he's sincere. He's a genius in electronics. There isn't anything he can't fix. I don't know what I'd do without him. Real strange, though. I watched him for days. He smokes, but I never saw him eat."

"Maybe he's an alien," said Shirlè laughing.

"I think so," he said, and his face was serious. She wondered... Could it be that the owner was chosen for the role he was to play, and that it was some kind of prior arrangement?

Shirlè had been going to the shop three or four times a week to see Frank, and he was always there, sometimes with the owner, more often running the store alone. She always came alone. She had only gone out with Mike the one time and wasn't that attracted to him; he was too negative. Fortunately, Mike didn't ask her out again. He had brought Shirlè to Frank and had played his part as a scholarly witness. Twelve or so years later, she met him on the street.

"That strange man we met in the second hand store," he said. "I wanted to see him again, but I couldn't find the shop. I went a few times to Broadway and it simply wasn't there. Did it close?"

"But the shop was on Fourth Avenue, Mike."

"I know where we went that day, and it was Broadway!"

He was insistent. Only later did Shirlè understand that Frank had the ability to call a person to him (as he did Shirlè) as well as repel a person. For whatever reason, he caused Mike to be confused and go to another street. Was this hypnotism, she wondered, or a form of mind control?

When Shirlè had finally accepted him fully, Frank acknowledged it by initiating conversation more often. He knew the right way to impart knowledge to her. He fed her little bits, inklings only. It was the perfect way for her to learn. She would go home, mull it over, then go back and ask him the same question. And always, in answering, he would appear sure of himself, like he had a goal and he would achieve it, like nothing bothered him, like he couldn't care less what customer was in the store. When she was with him, he ignored the customer unless they came to him and asked for help. He gave all his attention to her as if she were his only mission.

As time went on he began to talk more freely on spirituality and contact with the dead. At first she thought his knowledge was from books he had read. But she knew he was no ordinary being, when, before her very eyes, on an unplugged television, he "changed channels" to another planet.

Looking in on a Neighbor: Life on Other Planets

"Time travel might be within our capabilities. Any advanced form of space travel would require faster-than-light travel, which automatically means going back in time."-- *The Physics of Star Trek*, Stephen Hawking

Inhabitants on some planets may not be human in your sense, yet they are far ahead of earthlings in understanding and spirituality.—the Alien Frank.

He didn't say if it was his planet or another. The city he showed her on the unplugged TV had tall, crystal-like buildings with many connecting passageways. Both men and women walked about outside. They all wore capes of various colors and slipper-like shoes that turned up at the toes, so it was difficult to distinguish their sex from their apparel alone. The few children she saw looked like neatly dressed miniature adults.

The view switched to the inside of a home, where she saw separate rooms for dining, reading, and music, all circular-shaped, and all facing a round sunken livingroom. The walls shimmered in "rainbow" colors. A diamond-shaped chair and a round table seemed to float just slightly, giving the impression the furniture could move if gently blown upon.

Frank zoomed in so Shirlè could see people up close. She noted their slightly slanted Egyptian-looking eyes. They appeared to be friendly, gentle people.

Shirlè sat with her notepad and Frank patiently answered her questions. "They limit the number of births to avoid overpopulation," he said. "They are continually studying, learning. To avoid boredom they change jobs or workplace. Finance is by the barter system."

"But this is only one planet," he said, as he switched the channel to another scene. "There are others with dwellings and transportation underground, and services on top. Residences are compounds or separate homes. There are no tall buildings."

He shut off the TV with a small gadget held in his hand, and took a seat facing Shirlè. "On still another planet," he said, "one small card serves every need. You do "x" amount of labor of your choice. You know exactly whom you will marry, and you marry only once.

"Schooling is to the age of seventy, and you live hundreds of years. If you want to live longer, you get cloned and your essence put into the new body."

Shirlè's eyes widened. "When ill," he continued, "you can be regenerated. You step into an apparatus and through it into another, and you are rejuvenated. Your structure and molecules are made younger."

"Wow!" exclaimed Shirlè.

"But unfortunately," said Frank, "they will not give this rejuvenation machine to Earth, because they are convinced that only a few would get it and not the masses.

"On one planet," he went on, "some houses float, anchored somehow to the ground. When you want to move, you remove the anchor and it flies to where you want it to go. You don't own a car, but if you want one, it's available. Everything is made so well it lasts a lifetime. No street people. No drugs."

"Tell me about *your* planet," begged Shirlè.

"To begin with," he said, "my planet, Sirius, is technologically and spiritually evolved, with no prejudice towards different races or types, and no wars. A card is used for money. Nobody has a steady job in only one place. If you worked "x" amount of time you are given what you earned, and you can buy what you wish from various stores. Everything manufactured lasts, so no replacement is ever needed—so the economy is based on need rather than want. Liquid from flowers produce a plentiful staple food, so there's no hunger."

It sounded too good to be true. But he had more good news. "People on my planet marry only once, are not promiscuous, and do not divorce." She wondered about sex on his planet, but didn't ask.

"People live over a thousand years," he went on, "and have time to mature. Here on Earth, due to your shorter life span, you have to hurry, making for superficial values."

He didn't say if such a thing as mental illness or physical disabilities occurred on his or other planets, and at the time Shirlè didn't think to ask. Also, he didn't name the planets he showed Shirlè; however, it wouldn't have made a difference to her. She knew nothing of solar systems outside our own.

One day she heard Frank speak in a foreign language into a gadget he held before him.

"Who are you talking to?" she asked.

"The crew of our craft," he said, grinning. "It's right above us, but invisible to you."

He tapped a small instrument attached to his belt and on an unplugged broken TV, a picture appeared. A pilot in goggles and helmet, with an insignia on his form-fitting uniform, was at the controls, apparently conversing with a member of the crew.

Today, with wireless, it isn't farfetched. But in 1972?

Another time, again on an unplugged TV Frank let Shirlè see the image of a saucer-shaped UFO in a wooded mountainous area near Harrison Hot Springs, B.C. "It's mine," he said, "one of our earlier models—there's something wrong with it—I've been going there every so often, trying to fix it. When it's ready I'll give you a ride in it."

It was her birthday and Shirlè was sitting and reading. Suddenly she heard a buzzing in her ears and she knew it was a sign that UFOs were nearby. She went outside, looked up and saw five UFOs, in different colors and shapes—gold, silver, square, bell-shaped, and oblong with antenna. She told passersby to look, but they saw nothing (a common phenomenon). Thrilled, she drove to tell Frank.

"They came to say Happy Birthday," he said.

"Why can't others see them?" she asked.

"They were meant only for your eyes," he said. "We wanted you to see our various spacecrafts. Every so often there are new models, just like your cars here."

Apparently in some cases one person sees vividly, while another sees nothing or only minimally. It depends not only on whether or not the alien wishes the viewer to see the UFO, but on the ability of the viewer to "see."

An interesting note: Orlon, Adamski's alien contact who claimed to be of the Ashtar Intergalactic Command, gave this explanation to Adamski in 1968: UFOS are really aggregates of consciousness that can be in the third or fourth dimensions. When they are in both simultaneously, UFOs will be seen in the skies when not seen before. They are always there, but it appears they have suddenly come in great numbers. Instead it is we who see with new eyes.

Once, on her way to Frank, Shirlè saw a bell-shaped craft and sensed that Frank was in it.

As she entered his shop he was at the door. "Did you come in a UFO?" she asked.

"Yes," he said with a smile.

She then showed him an article she had seen in a regular newspaper. It stated if anyone wanted to meet an alien, the writer could arrange it. He stopped, looked at her, turned away, and she could feel him fuming.

"What a down-right lie," he hissed. "It's not true."

"Then why did he advertise it?" asked Shirlè.

"Not for the purpose you think," said Frank.

He sat down and picked up a pen and paper. "If he's an alien," he said scribbling, "he'll know what I'm writing."

She put it in an envelope and sent it off as Frank had directed with no return address. In the early seventies, photocopiers were hard to find. So she didn't even think of having the letter copied. She didn't think of taking a photo of it, either. But maybe this was again Frank's doing. He had a way of making you forget or not even think of something if he wanted it that way. Was it because it wasn't yet time for aliens to be revealed, she wondered—or were we Earthlings not psychologically and emotionally ready for it?

She continued to take notes as he touched on world affairs. "I'm worried that Earthlings are tinkering with nuclear energy," he said, moving to a more comfortable chair, "like one planet that had already blew itself up."

She wondered if he was referring to his[6]. "But the worst," he said, "was that some people mutated into strange forms as a result." He paused. "I'm afraid Earth people are on the verge of doing the same."

He got up and looked out the window. "My planet," he continued, "is in contact with other planets—like the Pleiades. Together we're helping Earth by influencing Earthlings spiritually and by floating ideas to scientists so that medicine and technology can advance at a faster pace."

"I have trouble lying," said Shirlè one day. "I can't purposely lie."

"That's because the place you come from," he said, "is the place of only truth."

She took it to mean her higher-self or conscience. She didn't realize that he may have been referring to a planet of telepathic people.

"Also," he went on, "part of you came from somewhere else."

Did he mean, she wondered, that her soul came from another planet? She didn't understand, knew nothing of hybrids or "wanderers" at the time, and said nothing in response.

"Frank," she said one day, "do you know my past lives?"

"Well," he said, "most of your lives have been spent on other planets, but you've had a few reincarnations on Earth—they were mostly in the arts—you were a leader of an orchestra in Russia and played many

---

[6] Sometime later he told her his planet was Sirius.

instruments… and you were wealthy most of your lives."

"Anything else?"

"Well," he said, pausing as if debating the release of information, "there's one that I *can* tell you. You were one of the Masters."

"Which one?"

He turned and looked at her squarely. "Bottecilli."

"Bottecilli?"

"Well, look at the eyes in his paintings. You do the same in your portraits."

***

She asked Frank if he would like to visit her at home.

"I visit you all the time."

"But I haven't seen you."

"But I see *you*."

"Well then," she said, "have you checked my body? I'm sure there is something wrong with it."

"We have a special instrument," he answered, "and we can know a person's health in a few moments. We've been continually checking your body, and there's nothing wrong with it. It's fine."

So, she figured, they do it while she's sleeping. How else if it's physical? It never occurred to her that perhaps she could have been "taken up" (abducted), physically or in her astral body, and then her memory of it erased. She said nothing. She knew she wasn't ready; she didn't know the right questions.

However, as time went on, she noted that he was more and more willing to share his knowledge.

One day Shirlè brought up the book she was reading, *The Keys of Enoch.*

"Jesus," said Frank, "was Enoch when he came to Earth at that time."

The Bible entered the conversation. "How come the Jews came out of Egypt with gold?" asked Shirlè. "Enough to make the golden calf?"

"Not only Jews left Egypt," replied Frank, "but many Egyptians and high officials of the pharaoh went with them, and they took with them much gold. But the Jews themselves had no gold." (Later her temple's rabbi, who had studied old texts of the Old Testament, confirmed it.)

They discussed reincarnation. She was already aware that reincarnation was part of the Jewish faith, especially of the Kabbalists and the ultra Orthodox, though most modern Western Jews were unaware of this fact. It was also in the faith of the early Christians, he told her; much later it had simply been deleted from the writings.

The discussion moved to world problems: people starving, wars, and politics. Frank looked away, his countenance in deep sadness. "All problems," he said, "are man-made. There's enough food for everyone. The people in power are ego-driven. The government and religious leaders have taken over. You must think for yourselves, have more love—*give* more love."

Frank was an excellent teacher. He did more than lecture. Seeing that Shirlè had come from a rather sheltered life, he proceeded to give her during her next visits, various tests with lessons to learn.

Tests and Lessons to Learn

"To understand and love God, and at the same time feel fear,
is mutually impossible."—Alien Frank
"Be suspicious of gurus; many are dishonest. No one can decide for you."
—Alien Frank

It was three years since her husband Hymie's death, and there were still things she had to learn—simple spiritual truths, as well as everyday know-how for the real world. Wouldn't you like to have your own private guru teaching you, guiding you? I sure would. Shirlè didn't know it then, but Frank was preparing her for her mission.

There were times when they were completely alone, that Shirlè had the eerie feeling Frank was looking right through her, that no secret could be hidden from him. At the same time he was like a protective father watching over her, secretly checking up on her. She had known Frank for about a year when she planned a trip to Montreal to visit her family. Before leaving Vancouver, she went to the shop to say goodbye.

"I have something to protect you," he said. He attached a metal disk to the inside of her purse with a device that prevented it from being removed manually. She then left on her trip.

While in Montreal, Shirlè met a man at a dance. She was lonely, she wanted to be taken out, and he wanted to take her to a wonderful concert and dinner. But she was to sleep with him—he made that perfectly clear. She really didn't care that much for him, but she acquiesced.

When she left his house, she noticed that Frank's disk was gone from her purse. When she returned to Vancouver, she stayed in a girlfriend's house overnight, planning to see Frank the next day. As she walked out of the house, she was accosted by fiercely barking dogs. One, a Doberman, bared his teeth.

Shirlè also growled and showed her teeth. "Go away," she said, "I'm not frightened of you." Immediately they stopped barking, moved aside and let her through.

The moment she entered the store, Frank greeted her with a smile. "You did a good job with the dogs," he said. "You showed no fear."

"How do you know that?" He smiled, but said nothing.

"Frank," she said, "I'm sorry. I lost the protective disk you gave me."

"You didn't lose it; I took it from you."

"How?"

"I can't say how, but I can tell you why. Your liaison with that man in Montreal was not a good one."

"I know," she said. "I made a mistake."

She was ashamed; it was a lesson for her. He smiled and was quiet.

Then she realized the dogs didn't bother her even though the protective disk was gone! Why should one need a piece of metal for protection, she realized, when one is protected by the Creator? And if you believe that God is within you, you can be fearless and strong. Did Frank remove the disk to teach her that lesson as well?

***

She was in Vancouver, waiting for a bus, when a man in a car driving in the opposite direction to the bus, waved to her, then turned his car around.

"I'm sorry," he said as he came up to her, "I thought you were one of the nurses. I thought I knew you. Where are you going? I can give you a lift."

Shirlè accepted and he dropped her off at her destination. He asked for her address and phone number, and she gave it to him. He said he'd call her and drove away.

As she opened the shop door, Frank was there to greet her.

"Don't ever do that again!" he said, his voice quiet but firm.

"Do what?"

"Take a lift from a stranger."

"But he said he thought he knew me."

"He didn't know you. It was a pick-up."

So...she was a naïve widow. After all, she had married Hymie, her first boyfriend, at seventeen. She looked at her watch; she was late. She had said she'd be at the store at three. She wondered if he had gone out-of-body to find her. At that moment he smiled. She took it as a "yes." He had read her thoughts.

Then Frank looked squarely at her. "And in the future," he said, "when you have a lot of money, and you will, don't you dare let someone swindle you like before."

"No, I won't," she meekly promised. "I'll be very careful now." She had not told him of having lost Hymie's inheritance. She didn't need to.

"Hymie was your soul mate," Frank continued. "He's helping you from the other side, and I'm in contact with him."

Shirlè then related an incident after Hymie's passing. She had awakened with a start, calling "Hymie, Hymie." The clock read 2 a.m. Twenty minutes later the fire alarm blasted. With smoke in all floors of the ten-floor apartment building, it was difficult getting down to the ground floor. In the hallway, she bumped into another tenant, Patrick O'Hoolihan[7]. The stairs were crowded with people trying to get down. Though taking the elevator was against fire safety policy, they took it, got outside, and waited it out in a nearby restaurant.

She and Patrick had met at a spiritualist church. When he happened to need a chest of drawers, Shirlè had recommended Frank's shop, and had introduced him to Frank. "He's taking a different road," was about all Frank would say of him.

Finally, the fire out, they returned to their apartments. Only then did she realize that there must have been an entity in her room before the fire, watching and protecting her, waking her twenty minutes before the alarm went off. She felt it was Hymie.

"Yes," said Frank, "it *was* Hymie. He and I have been working on your psychological and spiritual growth. We can work with departed souls who have reached a high 'vibration.'"

So it was clear Frank knew all about Hymie—as well as Shirlè.

---

[7] We cannot locate this witness.

Chapter Three

To Be a Serious Artist
"It's alive, it moves"

"Art is a kind of innate drive that seizes a human being and makes him its instrument. The artist is not a person endowed with free will who seeks his own ends, but one who allows art to realize its purpose through him. As a human being he may have moods and a will and personal aims, but as an artist he is 'man' in a higher sense—he is 'collective man'—one who carries and shapes the unconscious, psychic forms of mankind."
--Carl Gustav Jung (1875-1961) Modern Man in Search of a Soul–1933

Yes, Frank seemed to know all about Hymie and Shirlè; how they met, how he died—what he meant to Shirlè,—how he had encouraged and supported her in her art work—how she had bloomed as a woman and an artist. And how important this was for her *first future mission.*

Fifteen years earlier, in 1955—Shirlè was sitting at her canvas, Hymie's hand on her shoulder.

"You're good," said Hymie. "You have great ideas." He drew a chair beside her and looked at her squarely. "Why not learn some good techniques—take some lessons. I'll pay for everything."

She enrolled in an art class at Sir George Williams Evening College, (since renamed Concordia University). But at the age of thirty-two, still unsure of her artistic capabilities, she knew she would have to really apply herself. And she did. By the end of the year, her work showed great improvement and she passed with high grades.

Classes at Arthur Lismer's Art gallery followed. After four or five months, she received the encouragement she so badly needed. "Don't ever change," the teacher said. "You're good."

Next was a once-a-week art class with artist Leslie Shock. He looked at her chalk forest scene and started to touch it up.

"Leave it alone," said Shirlè and erased his strokes in anger.

Disturbed by the remark, he left abruptly, but came back later. "I'd like you to be my protégé," he said. "I'll give you private lessons."

"Does protégé mean I copy your way?"

"Yes."

"No thank you," she said. "I want to be *me*. I'm working hard at being me. And it's not easy. Nobody lets you."

He looked at her, shrugged his shoulders, and walked away. He called her "the primadonna" and she knew her classes with him were over. She told Hymie and he just smiled.

Hymie went further. "You want to learn about everything, Shirl? Then go to college," he said. "Get a foundation. I'll support you. I'll take care of the kids while you study."

She appreciated his generosity, but was afraid. Her esteem, though improved, was still shaky. "I don't know if I have what it takes," she said. "I don't know if I'm intelligent enough."

"Okay," said Hymie, "take an IQ test."

A psychologist gave her the tests. After that she had no more excuses; she applied to the college. It meant three or four nights a week away from the family. She asked her sister Mary if she also wanted to attend.

"I'd love it," said Mary.

"How dare you!" shouted her mother on the phone. "Just because *you're* crazy, don't make everyone else crazy. Leave her alone! She has a husband and family."

As for Shirlè, she wanted to see life from a broader perspective, be part of the larger world. She wanted to experience life, taste life—not just her immediate surroundings. But she lived in an era when she had to endure the laughter of "friends" behind her back, while they spread gossip that her marriage was on the rocks. Nevertheless, she went.

As Shirlè related this, I thought—if she had been born a *man*, not a woman, "he" would have been *admired* for his yearning to achieve, his desire to accomplish what he felt he had come here to do. He would have had a wife to take care of all his needs as well as those of his children. How many women are serious artists—wish to be serious artists? How many women are Nobel Prize winners? How many women do you see in important political gatherings? You can pick out the rare woman by her red or white tailored suit against the mass of black, blue or brown of the men. So it is still our culture that wishes to relegate women to the position of helpmate rather than an equal. And strangely, it is usually women who dislike women who do not act in the role society prescribed for them.

But Hymie was unlike other husbands of the time. He backed her in every possible way, encouraging her to get her B.A. degree, which took from 1955 to 1961. She took classes in art, elocution, and drama, and performed in plays. He was a true helpmate husband, doing housework and acting as mother and father to the children while she was away. More than that, he was her soul-mate, always there for her, protecting her, showering her with love.

With Hymie's encouragement, Shirlè entered a Montreal art contest with a pastel of flowers in a vase. As directed, the contestants placed their canvases on a table and left the room. Shirlè's name was called out and she came forward.

"Why the short brush strokes along the stem of the flowers?" one judge asked.

"It's alive," she said. "It moves; it shows motion."

That's what they wanted to hear. Others were more beautiful, but it was her work that spoke to them.

"You are going to be a very special artist," said one of the judges. "You have something in you dying to be brought out." He paused and then continued. "It is something that may not be understood by others in this lifetime. You may not sell anything, but keep at it, because you will discover something. You will be different from any other artist here today."

The other judge was listening and nodding his head. Shivers ran down her spine. They made her sound so talented. Could she really become that good? She had only two years of training. At the age of thirty-four she was merely a novice!

Pleased with Shirlè's progress, Hymie felt she needed one-on-one lessons. So she and four of her friends got together with a private teacher, who told them she would coach the pupil of her choice.

"Show me what you can do," she told all five. "Pick a subject or any idea. You have one hour, then I'll tell you if I take on one of you."

She chose Shirlè. "You have something," she said. "With my help you have the ability to be great. If you move in with me, we will work hard every day. I'll work you to death, but I promise you, you will make it as an artist in one year."

Here she was being offered what she had wanted all her life, the chance to be an artist. Any man would have jumped on it. But she had a man's drive in a woman's body.

"Thank you kindly," she answered. "I appreciate your offer, but I can't. I can't leave my family, and I'm still taking classes at evening college. I'll have to make it in ten years, instead of one."

About this time, she met Paul David, a French photographer in his late forties, who was giving an exhibit on Montreal's Mt. Royal. He recommended places to study and people to know, and one day, she and Hymie invited him over for dinner.

"Hymie," he said, "like I've told Shirlè, she will have to work night and day to get where she should be. She's a futurist, a visionary—she has the ability to become great."

Scared, she didn't paint for a couple weeks. Then she became determined. Paul David would pick her up from home and bring her to a community center for free lessons. Hymie, as always, was supportive.

"Shirl, you're so lucky," he said, "to have such a good friend." And later "He likes you, Shirl." She understood. He trusted her and she trusted herself.

One day Hymie and Shirlè were out driving when they were caught in a sudden downpour. They decided to wait it out. To pass the time, Hymie sat in the front and read a book, while Shirlè sat in the back and painted. In a short time she had completed her work.

"My God, Shirl," said Hymie, eyes wide with amazement, "you have such talent. Promise me you'll never give up painting." He made her promise again the night before he suddenly died of a heart attack.

At different times Shirlè would ask Hymie if he would like to go for his dream of becoming a doctor or a pianist. Each time he would simply say, "No, it's not for me in this lifetime."

Husband Hymie, and Father Pass Over

One day Hymie's defective heart suddenly gave out. Shirlè, in denial about his condition, went into shock, and never completely recovered.

The funeral parlor was jammed, with standing room only. Hymie was well known and loved. He received two medals from the Queen, one for starting the first Jewish Division of St. John's Ambulance, which taught life-saving techniques. The other was for getting incorrigible Jewish boys to do voluntary work in hospitals after school. The boys were the pall bearers, and they cried as they carried his coffin.

The rabbi said something about Judaism and life hereafter, recited the *Kaddish*, the Jewish prayer, the casket was lowered, and each family member threw a handful of earth over it. Shirlè stood there, in shock, seemingly unmoved. It was not her Hymie, being placed in the grave, cold and rigid. It was only the remains of the man[8] she loved so much.

It was bad enough to lose Hymie. Soon after, Shirlè lost her father. He was in his seventies, had a stroke, and was in a convalescent home. She knew her father loved her and was proud of her, especially of her art, but he never told her.

Why couldn't he have been more demonstrative? God forbid he should come over and hug her. But, she had to admit, there were those warm peaceful times. Her father would come home from work and sit in his big comfortable armchair. "Shirlèy," he would say, "play for me Schubert's Serenade." And she would sit down at the piano and play his favorite piece, and he would sit with his eyes closed, and he'd be happy.

Alone with her father, Shirlè pleaded with him to "let go." Her mother then entered, and in her presence he let go. It was over. Shirlè's held in emotions broke and she let the tears flow.

And as she grieved, she painted and painted, and it was a life-saver for her.

***

By this time Shirlè knew she wanted to be a *serious* artist; she was passionate about it. My own story about "passion" comes to mind. I was about forty, working as a medical laboratory technologist, and had taken adult education classes in art, music, and sculpture—for the fun of it, to see what I could do. The teacher said excitedly that I had talent as a sculptress, and it was not too late to make it my career. Strangely, I felt only sadness, and never returned to finish the "head" that only needed to be fired in the kiln. I wrapped the sculpture in a pillowcase and put it

---

[8]One month after his passing, Hymie came to her in the astral plane as she dreamt. Another time, while awake, he was invisible to her, but she knew it was Hymie; when he walked, his shoes always made a snap, and she heard the same sound.

under my bed. Each time I relocated, that's where it went.

One day, years later, I realized why. I simply did not want to be a sculptress. I wanted to be a psychologist. I wanted to work with people, though I had little talent or education for it. However, I did have the *passion* for it. From then on, when I did vocational guidance through graphoanalysis, I always told my clients to go where the *passion* is, not necessarily the talent, if you want to be happy and successful.

As for Shirlè, she seemed to know from an early age that she wanted to be an artist and kept her dream alive growing up. She had *focus*. But within that focus she changed direction.

But what makes one go in one direction and not in another? Are we really thinking it through as we suppose, or is there something else like fate operating? And what really is fate? Are we being guided?

"But I See Them Now"—A Turning Point

> "The real voyage of discovery consists not in seeking new landscapes, but in having new eyes."--Marcel Proust

It was still a couple of years before meeting Frank. Shirlè's work was coming along—landscapes, portraits—she was learning different techniques. In addition, she began surrealistic paintings. She showed her first to a fellow woman artist, and she was stunned. "You were painting so *beautifully*," she said. "Why are you doing *this*?"

Soon after, however, it was *Shirlè* herself who questioned her work. Somehow she wasn't satisfied. Something seemed missing in her art. It just wasn't quite what she wanted to convey.

And then it happened—while vacationing in Nova Scotia. How she loved the town St. John's. She could paint in peace, with no obligations—at least for awhile. The kids were grown; the time was hers.

She stood at the seashore in awe...in awe of the rugged terrain, the mountains, the rocks jutting out of the water, the waves receding from the shore. "My God," she said aloud, "the things You create—such unbelievable beauty!"

She ran to the water's edge, put up her easel and with all her heart and soul she painted. And it flowed. She stood in amazement, in wonder. Unbelievable, she mused, how in nature, every piece, every color fit together in the right place.

Her thoughts raced. She couldn't help but reproduce well, from what she saw. And that's what she was doing, attempting to reproduce God's work. And what God has done is so overwhelming. Why try to copy? God put her on this earth to do something... She had to find it—leave a little bit of herself behind that was unique, and paint it, express her feelings in it.

Her landscapes, still life, and portraits—even these common subjects didn't look ordinary to her when she painted them—her personality was struggling to come through. No two snowflakes are alike; no two people are alike, she mused.)

Eight-year-old cousin Frances, sitting quietly beside her, was feeling Shirlè's total absorption. A moment later, Shirlè laid down her brushes, and stepped back. "I'm done," she said, took out her camera, and photographed it. **(See photo of painting in center of book.)**

Frances scrutinized the canvas, then the view. "I never saw the scene in those colors before," she said, "but I see them now."

Suddenly Shirlè, not knowing what possessed her, took a rag and began wiping it out.

"Don't!" pleaded her cousin—"It's so beautiful, don't!"

But Shirlè couldn't stop. "This is *it*," she said, *"No more."* And the scene was no more.

She methodically picked up her paints, easel and canvas and headed for her cousin's house, ignoring Frances trailing behind her with her plaintive "Why? Why?"

"I must do my own thing," she kept repeating to herself. "But what *is* it?" She no longer wanted to paint only what she *saw*. Frances' remark had triggered something in her. It was what she *didn't* see, she must paint. But what? She was stumped.

Still lost in thought, she washed the dishes, and put them away. Well, what could she do—she'd just have to start from scratch!

Then it came to her. The embryo, the beginning of life! For life is continual change, ever evolving—first, evolution of the physical, then the spiritual. Without realizing it, she was longing for the knowledge of spiritual evolution. **(See painting of embryos in center of book.)**

In her new way of painting she could express herself while being in the fourth dimension. In it she would be at "home" where she was a whole being, where she could relate to everything—inanimate objects, animals, or people. It was the beginning of expressing her art through what she calls "cosmic surrealism." Only years later did she come to realize that **she was being led in this direction; she was being readied**

for Frank and her painting mission.
***

Three Years Later, 1972—The Thrift Shop in Vancouver B.C.

HER PAINTING MISSION
Show Other Dimensions and Paint Other Civilizations such as Atlantis, as a Warning

"If men understand God, love follows inevitably. The key to understanding is in the heart."—*UFOs--Keys to Earth's Destiny.*
"More important than a work of art is what it will sow. Art can die, disappear. What counts is the seed." –Joan Miro

It seems her sensitivity to metaphysical experiences in her earlier life, her Indigo personality, and her strong focus on painting contributed to being contacted, and was preparing her for her first mission—her painting mission. But of course she was unaware of all this at the time. She just wanted to know why Frank had come for her, and one day she simply asked.

"Well," he said, "I'm here because God loves you." A slight pause. "As He loves us all—and because you love God so much."

"And which God is that?" shot back Shirlè.

"There's only one Creator," he answered. *"We all belong to the one Creator."*

At the time the "God" answer satisfied her. However, a second reason was about to be conveyed, and a third would be revealed much later.

Frank, sitting at his shop desk, motioned to Shirlè to sit down next to him. "There's another reason," he said. "I'm a teacher—a teacher from another galaxy, and I'm here on a mission for students who are ready. And you are ready for your *painting mission.*"

Shirlè was speechless.

He asked her to make some sketches. Pleased with her work, he rolled them up and slipped them into a cylindrical apparatus on the wall. That's strange, she thought. She hadn't noticed it before. Then, smiling mischievously, he pressed buttons on a gadget hooked onto his belt.

"Now," he said, as if it were a normal everyday thing, "I've sent on copies of the sketches to a gallery on my planet." (Today we take faxes for granted. So perhaps aliens in 1971 could fax things farther and faster?)

"Incidentally," he went on, "you work in many places, other planets." Shirlè was puzzled, but said nothing. At the time she didn't understand that perhaps he meant that while asleep on Earth, she sometimes goes astrally to other places on Earth or to other planets to paint or teach.

"From now on," he continued, "everything you make will be copied and reach my planet. You're a top notch artist."

Her mind reeled. Was he saying that just to boost her ego, or did he really mean it? But he wasn't finished. "Your paintings," he went on, "have a spiritual quality—they have messages regarding the spiritual evolution of Man.

Then he looked at her and his tone became serious. "Everything you will paint will be very important. They will show other dimensions, civilizations destroyed, planets before their destruction, planets that flourish—and how to paint them will be shown you." (Strangely, some years later, just after finishing painting the figure of an alien, an entity appeared before her in solid form pointing to stiff whisker-like protrusions in his neck she had apparently left out.)

"Eventually," he continued, *"you'll adopt a new way of painting, inspired by us. It'll come as an idea or a word, through your psychic opening, your third eye."*

But all this was too much for Shirlè to digest. She was longing for a mate, another Hymie, preferably. It was not long before she met Arne at a Singles Club and a new chapter in her life began.

Chapter Four

ARNE
"I'm supposed to do something for you"

"There are only two symptoms of enlightenment, and they are: you stop worrying—it just disappears from your life, and the other symptom is that more and more synchronicities start to happen."—Deepak Chopra

It's about being guided. But by who, why or how? I don't really know. All I know is throughout Shirlè's life the right thing happens at the right time for her advancement, though she may not like it at the time. A karmic mate unable to support her as she would like, gave her initiative, and as the saying goes, "Necessity is the mother of invention." She was learning to rely on herself.

It was Arne's birthday, and the owner of the club had introduced them. Together they helped him celebrate. He was tall, good-looking, soft-spoken, and gentle—"one of those tall Danish guys." And once more synchronicity came into play in the form of key words.

"I don't know what it is," he said as they danced, **"but I feel I'm supposed to *do* something for you."**

Boy, some line, thought Shirlè. The dance over, Shirlè went her way and he went his. A few days later he asked her out. But after a few dates she wanted to end the relationship.

"Arne," she said, "I have something to tell you. I know an alien. Would you like to meet an alien?" She figured it would finish their relationship.

"Oh, my God," he said. "Do you really know an alien? All my life I've wanted to meet one. You've no idea. I've read every book I could find on UFOs and aliens."

They dated. After some time, she brought Arne in to see Frank. Arne immediately began asking questions, "What's your planet like? What do you do there? On and on he went. And Frank didn't mind answering. He accepted Arne at once, and Arne accepted Frank at once. Strange, she thought, for it had taken her six months. Arne was so taken with Frank that he went to see him every chance he could get.

Shirlè and Arne continued their relationship. At the time, Arne worked as a stockbroker, and Shirlè sold Guatemalan clothes for her friend Irene. Her small apartment on Barclay St. in Vancouver, was shared with son Ronnie. There was a couch and pull-out bed in the livingroom, and a single bed in a small second room in which Ronnie slept, and where she did her painting. The apartment complex had a swimming pool and one day, after a swim, Arne came up to change clothes, and for the first time, they ended up making love. It was then he asked her to marry him.

She had known him now only about a month. She would think on it. True, they had a similar interest, his thoughtfulness reminded her of Hymie and she was always looking for a Hymie. Still…

She asked Frank's advice as he tinkered with a TV. "Marry him," he said, matter-of-factly, without even looking up.

His nonchalant attitude shocked her. "But I don't even know if I love the man!"

Strange too, that he never advised on important issues. She always had to make up her own mind. She mulled it over. She certainly liked Arne. Perhaps, in time, she would learn to love him. He was gentle, considerate, thoughtful and sensitive. Above all, he had the knowledge and interest in the subject she was interested in—aliens and the paranormal. Why argue? She trusted Frank. He had passed all of her tests. She would take his advice.

"Will you come to the wedding?"

"No," said Frank, "I can't. There will be someone there with a very high vibration. I must not be in contact with that person."

She wondered if he meant in the physical or spirit form, but he didn't elaborate and she didn't ask. To this day she wonders about it. Was it because he and this other person would clash? Would it have been bad for her, or was there some danger for him being there? Perhaps he didn't have the right clothes to wear? She would never know.

No sooner had her engagement been announced than her sister Mary called. She had something important to tell Shirlè. While in her waking state, Hymie's spirit had visited her, looking sad—then all at once, all the ten paintings Shirlè had given her fell off the wall.

Was it really telekinesis? Was Hymie trying to stop the wedding, she wondered, or was it just a scheme her family thought up to make her mother or Shirlè believe that Hymie was against her marrying a Gentile? Certainly her mother was against intermarriage. Her mother even sent Shirlè's brother-in-law Leonard to Vancouver to stop the wedding. But the fare she paid was wasted. He was unable to convince Shirlè. She would marry Arne because she believed in Frank completely.

Her mother still knew nothing about the alien called Frank. Just before the wedding, Shirlè brought her up to date.

"And I'm marrying Arne," she said, "because Frank advised me to. I believe he's a real alien. He's very spiritual. I believe in him."

Her mother stared at her, shrugged her shoulders and walked away.

It was a small wedding. The Unitarian Church performed the neutral intermarriage ceremony, and their Singles Club gave the reception.

Arne was kind, sensitive, and he made a living as a stock-broker. Shirlè worked at the boutique but only a few hours each day, so that she had free time for her art. They had things in common, and they got along. What could go wrong?

Giving Up Material Things, Learning Self Sufficiency

"The artist's life cannot be otherwise than full of conflicts, for the two forces are at war within him--on the one hand the common human longing for happiness, satisfaction and security in life, and on the other a ruthless passion for creation which may go so far as to override every personal desire."
—Carl Jung, Modern Man in Search of a Soul.—1933.

"Have all the beautiful things, the richness of material life, but do not be possessed by these things. They are yours if it's your destiny. But if necessary, you must be able to leave everything behind."—the Alien Frank

Completely unaware, Shirlè was being readied for her *next and most important mission. And Arne was to play a part.* A stockbroker, he was too honest to recommend stocks that weren't good, and it wasn't long before he lost his job. Shirlè's part-time job selling Guatemalan apparel was not enough to live on. As things went from bad to worse, she vented her anger and frustration on Frank.

Finally, Frank told Arne to go to a ranch in Surrey where farmhands were needed. Arne had grown up on a cattle ranch in Denmark and knew the life.

He took the job. They were given one hundred dollars a month plus a rent-free house with utilities paid. Still, it was not enough to live on, even in 1972. Two or three times a week, Shirlè commuted the sixty miles to her work in Vancouver. She was exhausted and frustrated. She was an artist and had to have time to paint, especially now that the children were grown and had lives of their own! Frustrated, she felt she was fighting for her life.

"Frank, I can't take this any longer," she said, finally. "I'm moving into town."

"But you have to be there..." he said, stopping himself from explaining why he could not interfere. Only much later did he tell Shirlè that it was her karma. She had to spend a certain amount of time with Arne in that area, that very environment. If she didn't, she'd have to make up for it in later lives.

While Shirlè worked, Arne looked for and found a place to live. Shirlè's son Ron, helped them move. With their belongings in the livingroom of the new apartment, they went out to eat. But everything went wrong. When they returned they couldn't get in. It appeared the locks had been changed.

"We can't rent to you," said the owner.

"Why?"

No answer. He simply shook his head and walked away. Was it because he had seen her palette and paints? Arne had not told him that his wife was an artist, and landlords were prejudiced against artists, their messiness and lifestyle. Or was this Frank's doing?

Now they had to wait for the manager to retrieve their belongings, rent a truck by the hour, load it up, and drive around looking for a "For Rent" sign. It wasn't until eleven that evening that they found a place. However, the apartment wasn't ready. They were forced to take another temporarily.

The next day, Shirlè rushed in to see Frank. "Everything went wrong!" she yelled.

He was silent for a moment. Then, quietly, "So why don't you yell at God?"

"What's God got to do with it!" she yelled back.

He looked intently at her. "You're not blaming God for this?"

She shrugged her shoulders. "I don't see what God has to do with it," she said, subdued.

From then on, his teachings were more subtle. They were on life situations, and at first she was unaware of being taught.

***

Though Arne did part-time jobs here and there, and Shirlè worked, they had barely enough to live on. By this time Shirlè was a resentful, unhappy wife. She hated that she had to take over, be a steady provider in the marriage. What was worse, she could see that the more she helped, the weaker Arne became.

Unable to find steady work in Vancouver, Arne decided to try his luck in Australia. Shirlè agreed to the move and would join him later. For one thing, she needed to be alone to sort out her thoughts, see what to do about her marriage.

She told Frank that Arne was leaving. "Good," he said. "That's where he's supposed to go."

Forced to give up her apartment, Shirlè moved in with her daughter Sharon. In two months time she would be joining her husband. She would need the time for last minute preparations and goodbyes. She had no idea how long she would live in Australia.

What they could not bring over, they had to sell. She thought back to the time she and Hymie had saved and saved for a particular piece of crystal. Parting with her beautiful things was painful. Every time she sold something it tore at her heart.

Little did she know that Frank had discussed it with Arne. "If she doesn't start to detach herself from her belongings," he told Arne, "I'm washing my hands of her. Either she does something about it, or...." And he pledged Arne to secrecy. They would not interfere.

But slowly Shirlè began to let go. Gradually the hurt of relinquishing things subsided and she felt better. Things weren't that important anymore. Frank was pleased with her newfound ability to somewhat detach herself from material things. He greeted her one day with a big smile. "Don't sell everything," he said. You'll need some of it."

Before Arne's departure, Frank gave him a disk similar to Shirlè's and a special belt with a tracking device. (He still has the worn-out belt with the buckle's tracking device.) With a blinking light in the shop, Frank would know his whereabouts at all times, and by astral projection observe what he was doing. Shirle wondered how he could not only watch over her, but Arne and others, in addition to whatever else he was doing. "I have others who help," he explained.

With the disk and belt Arne felt protected, cared for. Years later, he attended a lecture by a monk and showed him the disk.
"Where'd you get this?" he asked.
"A space person," Arne replied."
"Well," he said, "this space person is a very high entity."

For some time after Arne's departure, Shirlè did not hear from him, nor did Frank tell her how Arne was doing. One day as they were sitting and talking, Frank came out with something that really moved her.

"Since you feel so lost here on Earth," he said, "we want to help you. You've been hurt and you're so sensitive. We're going to protect you, but you still have some karma."
Shirlè was quiet, listening intently as he went on. "I had asked the group of seven who look after this planet to allow me to take on your karma, but they refused. They said you have to go through everything yourself. It's the only way you are going to learn."
Shirlè was stunned. "You would take on my karma? You care that much for me?"
"Yes," he said quietly, his eyes on her. "I do."
She was moved to tears. Some time passed before she realized the ramifications: being relieved of her karma meant she would be leaving this Earth—"passing over" or as some say, "going home." It would mean never seeing her grandchildren grow up. And it would mean she had failed her mission!
Furthermore, she wasn't quite sure what she had to *learn*. Frank said she had to experience everything so that she could help others, having gone through it herself. But it was more than that. She was being readied for her second mission — yet to be disclosed to her. The pre-requisites for it, apparently, were to achieve more self-worth, self-reliance, and self-sufficiency. She would discover those three—not by choice, but by necessity in Australia.

***

Temptations and Leaving for "Down Under"

> "A balanced life can only be reached by the mastery of mind
> using the body, not the body using the mind."—Alien Frank.

I included this next part because there are many ways to look at things, and I figured an alien's view about sex should be of interest.

The Guatemalan boutique in Gas Town, Vancouver, where Shirlè worked, was a very "arty" place. Next door to it was an African boutique, and a fellow named Bob was visiting a friend there. He noticed Shirlè and came over to talk. He returned night after night, and they had lively conversations about UFO's, aliens and spirituality.

"I have two tickets to the Vancouver symphony," he offered one evening.

"I'd love to," she said, "but I'm married. My husband's in Australia, and I'll join him some day."

"But he's not here now," was his reply.

He came for her, presented her with a rose, and the concert was wonderful. She had known him only a few weeks when he asked her to leave Arne, get a divorce and marry him. She told him that she had to first go to Australia and resolve her relationship with Arne. She was sexually drawn to Bob, but refused to sleep with him. What always attracted her, were men who engaged her intellectually and spiritually. She asked Frank if she should sleep with him.

"You make too much of sex," he said.

"But I'm married…"

"You earthlings make too much of sex," he repeated. "He's just a distraction right now." So shortly before she left for Australia, she slept with him.

Bob wanted to meet Frank, so she brought him to the shop. Immediately Frank was antagonistic towards him, saying they had enough teachers. Nevertheless he gave him a silver bracelet.

***

As I saw it, Shirlè felt guilty for breaking society's rules by committing adultery. Frank, however, seemed to be motivated by another standard of morality. When she was single and slept with a man she had just met, Frank "removed" the disk he had given her to teach her that the arrangement and her motives were insincere and as a result she felt a lack of self-respect. On the other hand, with Arne in Australia and Shirlè alone in Vancouver, Frank knew that Shirlè's heart and soul were not with Arne. Frank understood how she felt, and knew she would in time leave him.

"Should I go to Australia now?" she asked on each visit. He would never give her a direct "yes" or "no." She would have to decide for herself. All the while Arne was waiting for Shirlè, and Frank was in touch with him with his special tracking device.

Finally Arne wrote to her. It was beautiful there, she would like it, he had gotten a job—and he promised to send her money so that she could join him. She waited, but no money came. Here she was, a married woman, all alone, with men asking her out. She had to make a decision, straighten things out, one way or the other.

"Frank, I think I have to go 'down'" she said simply one day.

As usual he tried not try to influence her decision one way or another. He gave her a very special belt that contained a magnetic gadget, similar to Arne's, that would show her the location.

"You'll be protected all the way," said Frank. "If there's no spacecraft available to look after you, a fog will appear and you will not go. When you go, if something happens to the aircraft, we will beam it down and you will be protected."

Her son helped her ship things they would need in Australia. The rest had already been sold. She wondered how to bring over her art, and asked Frank.

"If you take all your paintings," he said with a smile, "I will sink the boat. You're only allowed to take four paintings with you."

"Where am I going to store the rest of them?" she asked.

"All your artwork is very important," was his illogical answer.

The next day Shirlè received a "coincidental" call from a friend who knew she was leaving. "Tell me," she said, "what are you going to do with all of your paintings?"

"I don't know," said Shirlè.

"Look, why don't you use my basement? Maybe for a year or so?"

Shirlè phoned Frank about it and it was as if he already knew. "Fine," he said. "I'll send a truck around and pick up everything, and we'll bring it there." And it was done.

Shirlè said goodbye to Sharon, her son-in-law Michael, and grandchild Heidi. Sharon seemed to take her leaving pretty well. Shirlè's father had already passed on, and her mother in Montreal had told her sister Nancy that she had washed her hands of her because she didn't approve of the marriage; she didn't even call to say goodbye. For some time Shirlè hadn't heard from her sister Mary in Vancouver, but Nancy with whom she had close contact, phoned to say goodbye.

It was her twenty-three-year-old single son Ron, who was feeling abandoned, thinking perhaps his mother was going for good. He had always been attached to her, and now he would be alone. She had conflicting feelings. She wanted him to be independent, yet she felt somehow guilty. With his father gone, he would need her more. She left him her car and other belongings, tried to cheer him up and suggested he go back to Montreal where he had more friends.

There was no goodbye party. By then, her friends had drifted away. As the time for her departure drew near, she went to say goodbye to Frank.

"Be sure to wear the belt wherever you go," he said, "so I'll know where you are."

It was awkward. They stood there and she didn't know what to do—they had never hugged. So she offered her hand and they shook hands. Emotionally it was so inadequate. She didn't know what to say, so she said nothing.

"I'll come every now and then, and see you," he said.

Astrally or telepathically? she wondered, but didn't ask. She felt comforted by his words, and headed for the airport, wondering what lay ahead.

***

Australia—Faith, Synchronicity, and More Tests

> "What is imagined in time becomes reality. Negativity, fear, causes illness. We can heal ourselves." Alien Frank

It's all about the little things we do as we live our daily lives without realizing that we are always being tested. I began to be more aware that those little things are really not so "little". It's all about the importance of initiative, having faith in oneself, and letting synchronicity do the rest. Though Shirlè was unaware, Australia was Shirlè's *test for self-reliance and integrity,* while Frank monitored her progress.

***

"I'm sorry, ma'am, your baggage is overweight," said the worker in a bored tone. She handed Shirlè back her baggage. The rules were strict in 1972. It would have to be left there and picked up on return if she couldn't pay the extra. And she couldn't.

Her first reaction was panic. She was used to being taken care of. Now she was alone, no Hymie, no Arne, and no Frank to rely on. But initiative took over. She turned and faced the man behind her in line, who by chance (?) carried only a briefcase. "You have very little luggage," she said. "Would you mind taking some of my poundage?"

He smiled good-naturedly. "Of course—glad to help."

She thanked him as her heavy luggage checked through. She did have a lot, but then Australia was far away, and she could be there for who knows how long. No matter. Arne would help her with the luggage when she arrived at the Sydney Airport. She had sent a cable advising him when and where to meet.

But Arne was not at the meeting place.

In a hotel room, her thoughts raced in sudden realization "Frank," she called out loud. "What's this all about? There must be a reason— what if I don't find Arne? How will I get back? I don't have enough money!

Then the telephone rang. "There's a man living here by the name of Arne Moller" said the apartment manager, "and he's usually home by five o'clock."

It was a tiny studio apartment, not big enough for two, let alone all the belongings she had brought and those yet to come. He found her a temporary place and they commuted. He was working at a menial job, making very little money.

Finding an Apartment Big Enough for Two

She had to do something. She went to the Jewish Community Center. A man there overheard her say she and her husband were looking for a place and didn't have the required three months rent to get in.

"I have an empty apartment," he said. "You can have it." (A coincidence?)

She thanked him. It was synchronicity again the following day. Her belongings, sent two months earlier from Canada, and which had been mistakenly (?) sent to Melbourne, were finally arriving. She wondered had Frank held it up until they could be together in an apartment?

It was an unfurnished one-bedroom basement unit, the living room merely an alcove. The manager gave them a single bed, a neighbor donated an old TV, and they bought an old refrigerator. Arne worked a split shift. When he worked nights, he slept on the bed during the day. On his day shift he slept on the floor at night and Shirlè had the bed. It was difficult and confusing for her. She came from a culture where the husband supported the wife completely, and she preferred it. She had already made up her mind to leave, not only Australia but the marriage. She figured she would tell Arne in a more caring way *later*. First she had to save the money for the airfare.

Finding Work

Despite the cramped space, Shirlè produced twenty paintings and took them to a gallery.

"We don't take foreign painters," the owner said curtly. "We have enough Australian painters."

"But I'm married to an Australian."

He looked at her sad face. "Okay," he said reluctantly, "let me see what you have."

She displayed her work. By "coincidence," a woman nearby, caught sight of it. "Wait a minute," she said excitedly, "I *like* that one."**(See painting in book center.)**

"Let me handle it," said the owner. The woman paid, and he turned to Shirlè. "If you like, you can work weekends."

Now she needed a full time job. She wandered down the street and stood before the largest shoe store she had ever seen. Although there was no "Help Wanted" sign in the window, she sensed she should go in, and followed her intuition.

"I'm a new Australian," she told the owner. "I think I could be happy working here. You have beautiful shoes; so you must have beautiful people coming here."

"Okay," said the owner. "It just so happens (coincidence again?) we could use a saleslady. However, there is one stipulation. You must sell fifty pairs a week to keep the job."

It was a good salary plus commission. She sold more than her quota. Customers asked for her by name. The manager took notice, and one day called her into his office. "The greatest thing you did for us," he said, "was walk into this store. We are giving you a raise and promoting you to our higher-class shoe shop. Italian shoes sell for $150 to $1000. We think you can handle it. No quota—just straight salary. And we'll train you!"

It wasn't until much later that she realized that in each situation she was not only being tested for self-reliance, but for honesty and integrity. One day while shopping, "they" left money openly and unguarded to see if she would steal. Another day the cashier in the supermarket handed her twenty extra dollars. Would she return it? Was this another test?

She was being offered a better position. It was enticing. But her boss was going to spend time and money to train her—and she planned to leave when she had enough money! Should she not say anything and take the position—or tell him the truth?

She couldn't resist. She took the job and loved it. The women entered with chauffeurs, and bought three or four pairs of shoes and handbags. Shirlè enjoyed meeting customers and being invited to their homes.

But she felt guilty. Her boss was even grooming her to become manager of the store. Three weeks into the new job, she decided it was time to talk to God. "Okay 'upstairs'" she said. "What should I do?"

The answer came in a dream. A tiny plane flew towards her. The front of the plane opened its "mouth" and chewed on her finger. She understood she must make plans to leave Australia. The following day she told her boss the truth, thanked him for all he was doing for her, and asked for her old job back.

He sat, stunned. "I have never in my life met anybody like you. You have a raise, a posh job, and you're telling me not to spend money on you because you will soon leave. I can't believe it!" There was a pause. "But you gave me back my faith in humanity."

"Thank you," said Shirlè. "Now, can I have my old job back?"

"No," he said, moving some papers on his desk.

"How come... if I've been honest about it?"

"Well, now that I know you're leaving," he answered, "you won't be with me long enough to make it worthwhile for me."

Shirlè and Arne had only been together in Australia six months. Shirlè decided to wait to tell him of her leaving when he had a good job and felt strong—not when he was struggling. He was a nice guy and she didn't want to hurt him.

And the day came when Arne did have a good position working as an engineer for an electrical company, and Shirlè had the money. From working weekends at the art gallery, selling new paintings, her savings from the shoe store job, and three hundred Canadian dollars sent by her mother, she had the plane fare in Australian money and bought a ticket with a three-week departure date.

She finally confessed to him—being an artist was foremost for her, and whoever she married had to be able to support her financially so that she could paint—and Arne was not that dependable. She simply did not love him enough to give it all up.

Lost hope was written all over his face. "Yes," he said quietly, "Frank told me that I'd be with you here only six months."

"Frank told you that?!"

"I promised not to tell. Now it doesn't matter. Frank told me that in a previous life, I was a Roman soldier who arrested you and things were so bad between us that we had to meet and marry to neutralize the karma."

"Arne," she said, "remember what you said when we first met: 'There's something I have to do for you?' Well, I guess this was it. And now it's time for me to leave."

***

For a year Arne sent letters. He should find another, she answered; she wasn't coming back. There were some galleries, he wrote back, interested in the twenty-five paintings she left, and she should return.

"Sell them and send the money," was her answer.

He never did. Perhaps he badly needed cash. After Shirlè left, he lost his job, grew more negative, and Frank stopped helping him.

Shirlè and Arne drifted apart. Shirlè had a new path to follow. Arne had fulfilled his mission with Shirlè in their year-long marriage. She would never have gone to Australia without him, and it was there she learned to handle things herself and be stronger. His dependence on her became her strength.

Back in Canada—"Eight" for Eliminated Karma

Finally arriving in Vancouver, Shirlè picked up the phone and dialed the number. "Frank, I'm back!" she squealed.

"What took you so long?"

"I'm coming down to see you," she said, and hung up.

"My God," she said as she entered, "you really tested me."

"And you were aware of it," he said, grinning. "Very good."

They were alone in the shop. She brought out her sightseeing photos and in each picture, he pointed out the spaceships—little dots, hardly noticeable, in the sky. Frank had told her as she left for Australia, should a UFO be unavailable to accompany the plane, or for some reason it would be unsafe to fly or make the trip, a fog would appear to delay the flight and keep her safe. As promised, the UFO's were with her wherever she went.

"Let me see the bracelet I gave you," he said. She handed it to him. Smiling, his eyes on her, he placed paper over the bracelet's hieroglyphic symbols and rubbed over it with a pencil.

"You're an eight," he said, grinning, obviously impressed. **(See photo in book center.)**

"Well, I hope that's good," she said.

"You did great," he added. "You learned to be self-reliant."

On her departure for Australia he had also given her an intricately designed rectangular disk. On it was the likeness of the "High Priestess" on a tarot card, signifying a teacher. With a delicate instrument he broke off small parts of the design.

"It shows where you're at," he explained. "How much karma you've eliminated." He looked at her then, a broad smile on his face. "You've passed them all. We're[9] real proud of you."

Shirlè then pulled out a small plastic bag from her purse. "Guess what?" she said, eyes shining. "I found two diamond rings!"

Frank held them and smiled.

Her story unfolded, but of course Frank already knew the plot. Arriving in Montreal from Australia, she had stayed at the home of her sister Mary and brother-in-law Leonard, and they took her on a weekend camping trip. As soon as they entered the campground, Shirlè and Mary made straight for the washroom. Shirlè doesn't know why she put her fingers into the sink drain, for it was not something she would ordinarily do. Her fingers pulled out two diamond rings with the owner's name on them. She was about to go to the office to leave the rings there for the owner when Mary stopped her.

"Wait a minute," said Mary, "let's first ask at the office if anyone by that name is here. You can't give the rings to just anybody. They might just keep them."

---

10 The group of seven guides.

That made sense, so they went to the office and the manager looked at the records. "No," he said, "we don't have anybody by that name now or recently."

Shirlè thought a moment. "Maybe they were here a year ago," she said.

"No, I'm sorry," he said. "We don't keep records that long." Satisfied, they left with the rings.

Her story ended and Frank handed her back the "found" rings. "Now go to a jeweler," he said, "sell them and get some money."

The jeweler gave her $50, a fair amount in 1972. Pleased, Shirlè hurried back to the shop to report the deal.

"Good!" said Frank.

"Don't tell me you *put* them there…"

Frank was silent, a mischievous smile on his face.

"You did that for me?!"

No answer. It was his way of helping her get by. He knew how low her funds were by the time she made it back to Vancouver.

"I really need some shoes," she muttered one day, "but I can't spend a lot of money."

"Well," he said, "if you'll go to the Army and Navy store downtown, you'll get shoes."

She went there and found a whole table of her size six, all brand new, just what she needed and wanted. She left with three pairs of really beautiful shoes at only a dollar each.

A few days later, walking in a park with a woman friend, she spotted a twenty-dollar bill on the ground. She handed her friend ten dollars and kept the twenty.

The next day when she went to see Frank, he was there at the door to greet her. "We know you're a nice person," he said.

"What do you mean—a nice person? What are you talking about?"

"Well, we wanted you to have twenty dollars," he continued, "but you gave ten dollars away, didn't you? That was beautiful." He paused for a few moments. "And the chairs you left behind…"

She had two old-fashioned chairs with her father's beautiful embroidery on their covers. They were so precious to Shirlè that she brought them to Australia, but due to the cost of shipping, she was forced to leave them there. She had not told Frank of those chairs—she had no reason to, but of course he "knew."

"We know how much you miss those chairs," he went on, "so we've decided to get you two chairs exactly like them to put in your house when you 'leave here' (go to another planet). So you'll see them again."

"Now," said Frank, "you must close another chapter in your life." He explained that she was to go back to Montreal to try to recover the money her friends had swindled her out of after her husband Hymie died. Secretly, she felt it would be of no use. But Frank felt it was up to Shirlè to give him the final opportunity to do the right thing.

Shirlè made the trip. Confronted, the man gave excuses. Finally he paid a small amount and said he would try to repay the rest by a certain time. However, the money never came. She thought of suing, but didn't. Not long afterward, the man died.

Shirlè wrote his widow, her best friend, for the money.

"You loaned it to my husband," she wrote back, "not to me."

Well, Shirlè figured, she had done everything; she would just let it go. She was stupid, so maybe she deserved it. It was useless to cry about it.

She kept working for Irene in Gas Town, but only part-time because she felt she simply had to have time to paint. She still had Hymie's pension and insurance money. She would manage, somehow. HaShem (God) would look after her. She would be all right.

And now that she had passed her Australia tests and those on returning to Vancouver, she was to take on a new burden—or her next challenge—the main and most important reason Frank had come.

Chapter Five

Her Most Important Mission
"There will come a time."

"The weal or woe of the future will be decided neither by the attacks of wild animals nor the natural catastrophes nor by the danger of world-wide epidemics, but simply by the psychic changes in man."
Albert Einstein, 1957Atlantic Monthly.

"I do not know with what weapons World War III will be fought, but World War IV will be with sticks and stones." Einstein.

"The only way we can help mankind is through truth—and the truth is that life is about love, God is love. Whatever we do on Earth—the lessons we've learned, accomplished, carries on into the next lifetime."--Alien Frank.

***

They were alone in the shop. Frank studied her intently. "Now," he said, "we want you to gather people of your vibration."

"I don't understand," said Shirlè.

"People of your vibration," he answered as he sat down facing her, "are your *soul* group—those who came to Earth when you did. They would all be 'going "home'."

"How many are there?" asked Shirlè.

"About 30,000 people," he said.

Shirlè was silent, dumbfounded.

"They're like you," he continued. "Just ordinary people. Let me see the disk I gave you."

She handed it to him. He studied it—then faced her squarely. "You must gather together those of your vibration," he repeated, his voice soft and kind, "and raise their awareness."

"But how? What do you mean? I'm scared."

"Don't worry about it—your spiritual level is good, you have all the abilities, but most importantly, you have the love that is required."

"Please, Frank, don't do this to me," she begged. "I don't know enough. I'm not intellectual enough. All I've got is one little degree. I'm nothing. What about the government people?" she pressed. "What about the scientists? Why not them?"

"We've tried and we don't want them," he said. "They're all on ego trips. Besides, if we needed high intelligence we have an apparatus that makes the brain instantly brilliant."

"If that's the case why don't you put that on me?"

"We want you to be *ordinary* because you'll be talking to ordinary people, to make them aware. *It's people with heart, people who care,* that we look for, and you're one of them."

"But I..."

"Don't say another word. We've chosen you for the job and that's that."

"But do you really think I'm capable...?"

"Shirlè," he said firmly, "this is it!" So he was serious. He was quiet for a few moments before resuming. "There will come a time..." he said quietly, and again he paused.

Shirlè leaned forward, startled.

"Of course, nothing is a certainty," he reassured her. But *we[10] have to prepare for it, just in case the time comes when it's uninhabitable here."* Again he paused. *"We're going to save a segment[11] of the population."*

"You mean you're not going to save everybody?"

He shook his head. "No, we're not. We're saving[12] only a certain

---

12 The group of seven.

[12] Many years later, in a séance, she was told that leaders on other planets believe that transference of all humans to other planets would not be feasible. Only the planet Sirius would remove some children from Earth, and not on a massive scale. A few humans had

number. You'll understand later on."

He went on to explain; he had a message[13]. The Earth is heading for catastrophes—some from natural causes, others from warfare and man's destruction of the environment resulting in global warming. Although it's the destiny for planet Earth and its inhabitants going from third to fourth vibrations, the effects can be lessened if earthlings take stock and make changes.

In addition, he warned there are other aliens with their own agenda regarding humans and the Earth—and we should be discerning. But most importantly we must learn to get along with one another and work on our spiritual evolution.

"How can we know where the catastrophes will strike?" ventured Shirlè, still in shock. "Will there be any places untouched by it all?

"There would be 'safe' places," he answered, "if and when the catastrophes come—some parts of Canada, Australia, New Zealand, Colorado, Utah, Arizona, and New Mexico."

"How many might survive in those places?"

"A rough estimate could be about three million from a total of six billion in the world. However, whether or not it will happen is still only a *possibility*."

"I'm confused, said Shirlè. "If it's not *fated* to happen, and it's only a possibility—then what can make it a certainty?"

"Shirlè," he said, his face grave, "*we* have the power—we have the *free will* to *make* our future!"

Shirlè sat back, ready to hear more. "We are prepared, in any case," he continued. "One landing will be in Surrey close to the border of Canada and the US. The group I am connected with has placed various devices marking the location that can be detected from space. It's on the farm you and Arne lived on."

Yes, of course, thought Shirlè –even today there are no buildings on it. It would make a good place to land. Still, she was not sure she was hearing right. She leaned forward as Frank went on.

"There'll be a spacecraft," he said. ***"When the time is right, your job is to help bring children to the craft."***

---

already been taken. The future number would be only a small percentage of our 6,000,000,000 Earth population.

[13] Similar messages have been received by other contactees.

Dumbfounded, Shirlè got up from her chair. "Why are you telling me all this? It's not going to be in my lifetime. After all, I'm not getting any younger!"

Frank went over and faced her. His voice was soft and kind. "It *is* in your lifetime," he said. "You'll be one of the teachers. You'll be looking after children whose parents are not going to make it. You'll have help. It'll all be worked out. Just leave it to us."

Shirlè was silent, a tense look on her face.

"Don't worry," he reassured her. "You are protected in every way." He paused for a moment. "But you should be careful," he continued. "There are beings from other planets that are destructive to humanity. As a matter of fact, there's a ship coming in right this minute that could be bad for the planet."

He picked up a small gadget, spoke into it in a foreign tongue, and an unplugged TV turned on. He said he was communicating with the commander of his spacecraft which hovered overhead, invisible to Shirlè. Instantly there appeared on the screen a man who looked human, seated at what looked like a cockpit. On his head was a light yellow helmet with antennae-like projections, and on the shoulder of his steel gray uniform were strange insignias. As an artist, Shirlè particularly noted the design—a snakelike line and dot. The screen then went blank.

"I've got to go," said Frank. "I'll be back soon."

Uninvited, Shirlè felt obligated to watch the store in his absence. She had no idea where he went or what he did. Did he contact his superiors? Did they drive the other aliens away? She didn't ask.

He soon returned and picked up where he had left off. "And if anyone tries to hurt you," he said, "we'll take care of him. And by the way, if you ever think of killing yourself, 'the rope will break'."

Shirlè's mouth opened in surprise. She had never thought of it growing up. She had been "too busy being miserable" as she put it. Nor had she ever entertained the idea as an adult. But he had seen into her future, to some time after his departure. (And it so happened, some years after leaving a stressful relationship and feeling depressed by life, she *did* think of it.)

Shirlè changed the subject. She asked about a dream she had. Two porpoises came to her and gave her their two little porpoises. She brought them to her house, put them in water and looked after them. Then she brought them back to the ocean. The two porpoises thanked her and swam away.

"That's one of your jobs," said Frank, "helping people evolve *little by little, one by one.*" He paused, and looked squarely at her. "Shirlè," he said, "there's still something you have to go through…more karma."

"Oh, God, don't tell me there's more…"

"You were supposed to stay…" He didn't finish, as though he felt he had already said too much.

But Shirlè knew where it was. "Okay," she said, resignedly. Then her sense of humor kicked in. "Well, if I have to go through more stuff, how about a man in my life? And this time, please…make him Jewish…for my family's sake!"

Frank paused a moment, a dead-pan expression on his face. "We'll do our best."

"How will I know him?" laughed Shirlè.

There was no joking in response. Frank's face was serious. "He will say 'I know you'… But first there will be someone else."

Shirlè was silent. If she had to wait, she would wait. She had complete trust in Frank. But she never knew when the day would come when he would leave. He never told her how long he would stay, and she didn't ask. Each day she feared, is *this* the day, the last day—is *this* the day he will leave?

The Goodbye Gift—Eight Alien Inscribed Copper Plates (Photos in center of book)

> "My race and others are watching over Mankind trying to
> help without interfering with Man's free will."—Alien Frank.

Shirlè was all dressed up and on her way to a party one evening, when a sudden compulsion came over her. She turned the car around and went directly to Frank's shop.

"Not bad," said Frank, looking at his watch. "Fifteen minutes!"

"You mean you called me?"

"Yes, we're training you."

There was a pause. Shirlè was sure there was more he wasn't saying. Then he came out with it. "Shirlè," he said, "I must leave. I must look after someone else, up north."

So the time had finally come. She felt weak, faint, but didn't let it show.

They sat down together. "My next project," he said with a smile, "is a person even more difficult than you, Shirlè."

"Really? More difficult than me?" she said, trying to be upbeat.

"Much more. Look," he said, getting up. "We have decided you should have something."

She accompanied him to his worktable at the back of the store, which had nothing on it but a few tools. And before her very eyes, to her amazement, a very thin sheet of copper-like metal appeared on it out of nowhere. With a pen-like instrument, he marked off sections, engraved strange hieroglyphic-like letters on each one, and then with scissors, cut out the sections, making eight rectangles.

"We want you to have these," he said, handing them to her, "but for the time being, put them in a safety deposit box for safekeeping." **(See photos in center of book)**

"But what are they? What are they for?"

"They're your identification plates[14]—your driver's license, medical card, whatever you need. *It involves space ships, when the time comes. That's all you need to know.*"

Naively she accepted the explanation. Later, as she thought about it, she smiled—a driver's license and medical card? Ridiculous! And in a safety deposit box[15]? They must be really important! But at the time she was too stunned by the thought of his leaving to make sense of it.

"I'll be leaving in a few days," he said, simply.

She didn't know what to say, how to handle it. How could she express what he meant to her, all the help he had given her. She cared so much for him. He had given her confidence, strength, and a reason for being. Now, *without* him—how would her life be?

She looked at him dry-eyed. "So, I'll be seeing you before you leave," she mumbled numbly, and left.

On his last day, she found him inside the shop beside a brand new shiny motorcycle.

"Where'd you get that?" she asked. She figured it was from his boss, the owner of the shop, in exchange for working two years for no pay.

"It was given to me," he said. "But wait a minute, come with me."

Shirlè followed him. From a drawer he produced a copper bracelet[16]

---

[14] A Tibetan monk in Iceland told her the writing is that of 40,000 years ago, and tells the history of her people. Three years prior, a person who channels Saint Germaine said the same.

[15] She put them as requested, in safekeeping. Years later, under hypnosis, she was told that she was given them so that when she tells of her experience, she will be believed.

[16] She wore it day and night for about twenty years, even slept with it, and never had arthritis. Eventually she lost it in a restroom somewhere.

with insignias. "If you wear this," he said, "you won't have arthritis."

She thanked him, but there was something else on her mind. "Please, Frank, tell me more about the plates."

They sat down. "Your voice is imprinted on one of them," he said, "and it can activate a spaceship. Another is a message for other aliens."

She wanted to know more. "All I can tell you now," he said, "is that there are four others who have plates with the same inscription in a binary code."

Amazed and confused, she didn't ask to know more.

A few days later, arriving at the shop, Shirlè spotted the motorcycle outside—and she knew this was the end. Frank tried to console her. "Don't worry. The next five years are going to go well for you."

Shirlè didn't want to hear it. "What's going to happen?" she wanted to know. "Are you coming back for me?"

"Yes, I'll be back for you."

"When?"

Frank stood, a puzzled expression on his face. The concept of time was always difficult for him.

Shirlè tried to help. "Is it five years? Ten years?"

He pondered a long time. "Five years, I think."

Well, thought Shirlè, better than the ten she thought it might be.

She had long tried to picture their last goodbye. Knowing Frank and his reticence she knew that the scenario she had dreamed of could not be hoped for, so she held his shoulder as she pecked him on the cheek. She didn't know what else to do—he had never initiated a hug, nor had she. Her reverence for him prevented her. He was a higher entity, she felt, not of this world. Still, she had hoped for a like response. None came. Sadly, she walked towards the door. Then she turned around. They stood for a few moments looking at each other. Then she turned quickly away, close to tears. She walked out of the shop, and looked back once more at the man standing in the doorway who had become such a part of her. It was now at an end. She walked to her car, opened the door, sat down, and sobbed uncontrollably.

For so long she had refused to think about his leaving her. And now it felt like another death. She knew she would have to learn to let Frank go, as she had learned to let Hymie go.

***

She realizes now that Frank had to come to her in the physical. With no fear of him she would be a willing contactee. She remembered Frank telling her that some people whose contact was by physical or astral abduction with their memories intact or only partially blocked, ended up in psychiatric wards or mental institutions believing they were hallucinating, unable to distinguish illusion from reality. For supersensitive Shirlè, contact and training through abduction or channeling would have been too risky. Furthermore, it took time for Frank to help her with her karma and raise her consciousness, to ready her for her mission. He could only do this adequately face to face in the physical with continual meetings.

He came as a teacher. But was there a more personal reason? I wondered—who were Frank and Shirlè in a previous life—on Earth or on another planet? What could have been their prior relationship? Could it be why Frank came for Shirlè?

He left in September of 1973[17], ending their two-year relationship. Thirty-four years later, Shirlè still has not heard from him, still has not received any kind of contact. But he left an indelible mark on her being.

***

---

[17] Some time after Frank left, Shirlé bumped into the owner near his shop, and asked how he was doing. He lamented that business had dropped since Frank left, he was unable to keep the shop going without him, and was thinking of closing it.-

Chapter Six

Somewhat Similar Contactees Witnesses to Frank

No artifact – short contact in English (MUFON July 1997)
USA—1940 Udo Wartena, a 32-year-old Dutch immigrant miner. An extraterrestrial, looking like us, came out of a UFO about 100 feet across, offered a ride, gave technical information, used water as energy fuel. Warren Aston, UFO researcher of 20 years who interviewed Udo believes some alien races live and operate among us here on Earth undetected.

No artifacts—short contact:
ENGLAND– Policeman Tony Dodd had contact with an alien who came out of a UFO and spoke to him telepathically.

USA -Philip Krapf, LA Times journalist and author of *The Contact Has Begun* met with aliens on a mother ship for three days.

One artifact – short contact:
USA-1952 George Adamski_–Alien "Orthon" from Venus, in a cigar-shaped craft, gave him a **crystalline stone.** The craft was witnessed by six people and legally attested. Photos and plaster-of-paris shoe prints were taken. Adamski described the incident in letters to the US Congress, Eisenhower, Kennedy, and the Pope, but was later discredited.

SPAIN – 1954 Sr. Alberto Sanmartin "The Violet Tablet From Space"- Published in a Brazilian journal "Disco Voador" #2, pages 18,19,20 in Portuguese. Contact took place near a small railroad bridge near La Corona, not far from Madrid in Spain. The alien in a bell-shaped "scout-ship," told him he was not from Earth, and gave him a **flat rectangular stone 12cm x 4cm x 2cm with violet specks,** mostly bright yellow which faded to ash green.

BRAZIL –Sr. Helio Aguiar at Piate Beach near Itapoan, Bahia, Brazil. Aguiar, a 32-year-old statistician, lost consciousness while about to take a picture of a silvery metallic craft with portholes around the base of its dome. His motorcycle engine died. When he came to, he found a **paper with strange symbols.** On the other side of the paper were these words in Aguiar's own handwriting: "Put an absolute stop to all atomic tests for warlike purposes. The balance of the universe is threatened. We shall remain vigilant and ready to intervene."

USA – Donna Butts (*Star Children* by Jenny Randles P. 123—story similar to Shirlè's.)
Donna Butts' mother was told her child would have a mission, and was given a **necklace with alien writing on it.** Years later Donna Butts was contacted by a tall blond alien man who told her the earth was going through its end times, and that she had a mission regarding rescue plans.

No artifacts – long term contact in Spanish
VENEZUELA 1970-1976. Enrique Castillo Rincon, engineer, rare contactee and UFO researcher, author of ***UFOs—A Great New Dawn for Humanity*** (English translation in 1997). Three years after his four-month friendship (listening to music, going to movies etc.) with a man he met in Caracas, Venezuela, Enrique met the same man, in uniform, descending from a UFO. Then on five different occasions from 1973-1976, he was given messages and information while accompanying him in a UFO.

Many artifacts – long term contact in English:
USA- 1970 to 1972- Shirlè Klein—"Frank" from planet Sirius, working in electronics in a thrift shop in Vancouver, B.C., showed Shirlè scenes on other planets as well as his saucer-shaped earlier model UFO in a wooded area of B.C.—on an unplugged TV.
Frank told Shirlè of Earth's coming natural upheavals, warned of

planets that had self-destructed, and of people who had mutated through wars. Her mission, should earthlings head in that direction, would be help in the rescue of children. His planet, he told her, while not being allowed to interfere directly, would do what it could to help should the Earth go through natural and man-made upheaval.

While the mission and messages are not unique but rather common to contactees, what *is* unique is that none have had such a lengthy, face-to-face relationship as Shirlè Klein Carsh with an alien who had been living and working in Canada for many years, and none have received as many diverse and fascinating artifacts as:

Two disks (one lost)

The remaining disk similar to a Tarot card (in her possession)

Bracelet with Frank's inscription (copy of inscription in her possession)

One belt with special magnets (in her possession)

A two-page letter with Frank's writing (no copy)

Eight copper plates with Frank's inscriptions (in her possession)

WITNESSES TO FRANK

1) Arne Moller—a stockbroker and a believer in aliens who was introduced to Frank in 1972. He was immediately accepted by Frank, believed Frank was a real alien, and became Shirlè's second husband.

2) Patrick O'Hoolihan
He was a fellow tenant in an apartment building in Vancouver. When he was in need of a chest of drawers for his apartment Shirlè introduced him to Frank and the second hand store. Shirlè has been unable to track him down, and doubts he is still alive after thirty years.

3) The Mathematician
He was the "blind" date who entered the shop with Shirlè, witnessed Frank's equations, and conversed with him. Thirty years later, Shirlè cannot remember his real name.

4) The Owner of the Store
Shirlè cannot remember his first or last name after so many years. She believes he was aware of Frank's real identity.

5) Sharon

Shirlè's daughter, a nurse and grandmother met Frank briefly and believes her mother is telling the truth about her experience, but also says she has no way of proving that the man she saw and talked to was, in truth, an extraterrestrial.

INTERVIEW WITH ARNE

I wanted a face-to-face interview with Arne, but unable to go to Australia, I asked him to write or send something on tape about Frank, himself and Shirlè. To help him, I mailed some questions. He wrote back, answering each one by number, giving no more, no less than requested. I gathered that he is not one to talk much, especially about feelings; the answers were short and to the point—so short, I have bunched some answers together. My interview follows:

Describe Frank—your impressions, feelings.
"Frank was approximately five feet, six inches tall—an average looking fellow, friendly and easy to talk to, on many different subjects. He would tell Shirlè and me about space and the power that drives space vehicles, but he would hold back on information I could not understand anyway, like mathematics."

What else did you do or talk about?
"He sometimes let me and Shirlè listen to recorded music from space."

Did he tell you where he came from, his family?
"Frank said he came from Sirius. He never mentioned a family."

Tell me about the belt Frank gave you.
"I don't have the special belt anymore. It was in a car badly damaged in an accident. But I still have a plaque and a copper bracelet he gave me." (Shirlè never mentioned this.)

I understand you "took" to Frank immediately.
"I think it's because I wanted so much to know about our neighbors on other planets."

How, if at all, did Frank change or affect your life?— "I learned a lot about space travel."

Do you think he will return?
"As far as I know he has returned to his old home."

What was life like on the farm in B.C. and how did Shirlè handle it?
"Work on Mr. Durante's farm was very hard and not much money. Shirlè was very unhappy."

Did Frank tell you if you or he had a previous lifetime with Shirlè?
"Shirlè and I apparently met up in Roman times, but no mention of Frank in that time period."

What did the marriage to Shirlè do for you—positive and negative? Did knowing it was karma from being together in Roman times, help you in any way?
"It was an exciting marriage, while it lasted. If it was karma, it did not help me, to the best of my knowledge."

From your point of view, what went wrong with your marriage to Shirlè?
"My salary was not sufficient to keep us in the style we would like."

How is your wife Megan different from Shirlè?

"Megan is quiet, pragmatic—you might say a typical "Aussie."

Before meeting Frank, any previous alien contact or abduction?
"To the best of my knowledge—no."

After Frank have you had any UFO or metaphysical experiences?—"No."

Have you kept up with UFO interests?
"Now and then I read about UFOs, but there seems to be little interest here in Australia."

How do you like Australia?
"I feel very much at home here---good climate and friendly people."

Chapter Seven

Reactions to the "Alien" Frank

"Aliens on other planets, okay, but telling an audience there could be aliens all around them and they wouldn't know it—that's too much."
—Hymie's twin brother Morris

Reactions to Shirlè and her "ET" were varied. Daughter Sharon was supportive and curious, and went to the store with baby Lisa to see the man her mother believed was an alien. Whether she truly believed Frank to be an alien after hearing Shirlè's stories is hard to say. She does not involve herself in UFO subjects, has not had any metaphysical or UFO experiences, but backs her mother wholeheartedly in her UFO activities.

Son Ronnie was another story. He wanted his mother to be the ordinary mother, baking cookies, staying home, being a little bit subservient –all the things she isn't. It was hard for him growing up to accept a mother who was—"a little far out" as he put it, writing and lecturing on television and radio on a ridiculed subject. As a child he was not too pleased. But now as an adult, he seems to accept her in a way that seems to say, "I'll humor her, but I just can't believe in that stuff." Her daughter-in-law however, seems more open and accepting of her.

~ The Artist and the Alien ~

At first her sister Mary believed Shirlè was telling the truth as she saw it, but that Frank was pulling her leg. However, with more information, she soon accepted that Frank was what he said he was—from another planet. She accompanied Shirlè to the Iceland UFO Conference. The subject interests her, she reads about it and listens to Art Bell on the radio, but it isn't a dominant interest in her life.

Shortly before Mary's husband Leonard died in 1988, Shirlè told him of her alien experiences. She couldn't tell if he believed her or not, but a month after he died, Shirlè had a dream. In it, she entered a building, passed through double doors, and a receptionist told her to leave her purse at the desk. So she did. After some time, however, she realized that in her purse was the belt Frank had given her for her protection and she must have it. But on her way back for it, she lost her way. A woman helped her find the desk and her purse was there. She opened it, but the belt was gone. She was stunned, not knowing what to do. Then Leonard came over to her, put his hand in his pocket, pulled out the belt, and handed it to her. She believes the dream meant he was trying to tell her that he knew and understood her alien mission.

Only recently she had renewed her relationship with her sister Nancy. For many years they hadn't spoken to each other. When they *were* speaking, Nancy was a strong disbeliever of her alien connection. "Actually," says Shirlè, "it wasn't so much she, as her husband David. He thinks I'm really crazy, that it's all my imagination."

Shirlè doesn't even discuss the subject with her brother Leon. "I don't think he's open to it," she says. His attitude is—if it makes me happy, that's what counts."

Her father and husband Hymie had passed on before Frank had come into her life. Only when she was about to marry Arne did she tell her mother about her relationship with the alien, that she believed and trusted in him, and that it was he who said she should marry Arne. Her mother stared at her for a few moments, expressionless. Then she turned away without a word. "So it's hard to tell, said Shirlè, "what my mother was thinking or feeling."

Years later, in 1986, Shirlè asked her mother if she had ever seen a spacecraft.

"Yes," said her mother, "Dad and I saw one when we looked out the window of a hotel."

"You mean you saw lights?"

"No," said her mother, "we saw a big machine. We both saw it."

Shirlè didn't push for details, for her mother's expression and tone seemed to say "See, you're not the only one who sees them." Shirlè was sure her mother was sincere, that she's really not the type to fabricate it.

Hymie's twin brother Morris didn't believe any of Shirlè's stories, alien or metaphysical, until many years later when, he told her, the spirit of Hymie came and sat on his bed. Then he came to believe the metaphysical, and is amazed by it all. "He sees me in a different light now," says Shirlè, "but I've always been the same. He just wasn't ready to see it before." As for the alien part, she isn't sure he actually believes that her alien is real or just a figment of her imagination. He attended one of Shirlè's lectures in Montreal. *"Aliens on other planets—okay," he said, "but telling the same audience that there could be aliens all around them, and they wouldn't know it—that's too much."*

Alex, another brother of Hymie's, felt for a long time that Shirlè's story had no relationship with an *actual* alien, but that she herself believes it. Since then he has made an about turn.

Heidi, her granddaughter, (a mother herself now), believes Shirlè had an actual relationship with an authentic alien. Shirlè has always felt close to her from the day she was born. One day, when Heidi was three, they were taking a walk together.

"Look at that man standing there," said Heidi, pointing.

Shirlè saw no one. "What does he look like?"

"Tall, black hair, and he's smiling at me."

"Heidi," said Shirlè, "that's your grandfather Hymie."

Shirlè had anticipated a laugh from present husband Fred when she first told him. But his response was a respectful, "Really?" after which he asked to see the eight plates.

"If it were anybody else but you," he said further, "I wouldn't believe it. But because I know what kind of person you are, and I've seen the metal plates, I know you're not lying. I accept your experience, but don't feel that I have to believe in aliens and all that."

"No, it's up to you," said Shirlè. "But at least you know it's possible."

"Everything is possible," he said, "but some people I just don't believe."

"Well," she said, "that's your choice. That's okay as long as you believe me."

Recently, he asked Shirlè more about aliens, the fourth, fifth and other dimensions, and the Ashtar Command. And she told him what she knew. "It sounds possible," he said, quietly, respectfully.

"I can't believe it," said Shirlè. "He just slid into the whole scenario."

A group of five professionals, friends of Fred and members of Chabad, an Orthodox Jewish group, got together in Port Townsend, Washington, one weekend in the 1980's, for discussions on various topics. Shirlè asked if she could talk on something other than of Jewish interest. "Of course," they said, and she related her alien contact. They listened respectfully—yet the same people would not have listened in the environment of organized religion.

Outside the synagogue she found rabbis to be open and quite knowledgeable. One, from Bellingham, said that Dvorah (Debra), a priestess warrior, and Ezekiel of the Bible, were in contact with aliens. The rabbi believed her story, and borrowed her UFO books. Another said that the Tanach mentions other planets and aliens. And they had all studied the Kabbalah[18]. One rabbi would openly discuss UFOs and aliens in front of others, but not in the synagogue. "So it's not that they dispute it," said Shirlè. "They just don't want to further it in the synagogue, because it would take them away from their religious practices."

And there was a Catholic acquaintance and a born-again Christian who when told, reacted negatively—they could be demons, they said. One Jehovah Witness thought, at first, that Shirlè worshipped the aliens as Gods.

Friends? Back then, she didn't tell them. They weren't ready for it. They made fun of her just going back to school. They thought of her as an artist, a kooky artist, but a nice person, so when she'd laughingly say, "Look, there's a spacecraft out there and some weird looking aliens," they'd laugh it off as kidding. "Shirlè with her imagination," they'd say. But her artist friends were always open and willing to know more.

Recently, she told her friend Ethel about Frank. "God," she said,

---

[18] Recently, in both Jews and non-Jews there has been a resurgence of interest in the Kabbalah, ancient mystical Judaism. Shirlé took classes and one aspect that stood out for her was that a part of God the Creator enters every soul, and a part of every soul enters the body.

"what an experience! I wouldn't have been able to handle it." How Ethel really feels, she doesn't know. She seemed to accept Shirlè's experience without really being interested in the phenomena.

As for me: I've asked myself why I instantly (intuitively, I guess) believed from the very beginning that Shirlè was telling the truth about a relationship with a real alien, and have not changed regarding it. After all, I am quite grounded, having spent my life in medical laboratory technology, real estate investment, an electronic business and bookkeeping. I always seem to research and analyze anything I go into. But with Shirlè I immediately believed her, and I think it's because I've had a few paranormal experiences, including and especially, a near-death-experience, and I see a connection. To understand UFOs you need to understand and accept the metaphysical and paranormal—the non-material world of vibrating atoms, and to consider the premise that we are each a soul inhabiting a body; that there is life after death with our spirit returning to this Earth or another planet.

I was in no extreme physical or mental trauma when I had my near-death experience in 1968. But I was unhappy and enjoyed saying "Stop the world, I want to get off!" One day I plopped down on the couch, got my wish, and learned a few things.

One:—Thoughts have power. Better watch your thoughts.

As a medical technologist, I looked down on my body and wondered how it could do without me. My guide (who I felt to be male) answered my thought. "It's on the principle of the pendulum," he said. "Once you set it in motion, it will swing until you stop it."

Two:—The astral body, though connected, can be freed from the body. Also "guides" are for real, and in the astral plane communication is by telepathy.

"You mean my lungs and heart can take care of my body and I'm free to go anywhere I want?"

"That's right," he said. "It's your choice." And it was then I said something I would never say in "real" life. I said I wanted to see *other universes* (as if the subject were familiar, as if it were known in my subconscious or superconscious or higher self).

Three:—We know things on the astral plane we don't know we know in the physical.

And he replied, "Whatever you wish." In a split second, I sped past moons and stars.

Four:—"Ask and ye shall receive." Except in the astral state it happens instantly.

Suddenly I was enveloped in a love so intense, so powerful, and so deep that words simply cannot describe it fully. I was being unconditionally loved. But it was more than that. At the very same instant I *also* felt an intense love *for* all of life, in all universes—Oneness!

Five:—Love is what makes the world go around—it's what is behind it all.—the Creator?

I instinctively knew that to remain with this love, I had to go further on, and I was ready. "Fine," said my guide. "*It's your choice.* But you have reached the point of 'no return.'"

"What do you mean—point of no return?"

"There'll be a dead body on the couch," he replied matter-of-factly. Well, that certainly didn't concern me, nor did I think of my husband and two little children. I said I wanted to go on. "As you wish," he said as before. "*It's your choice.*"

Just as I was about to go, I heard "Mommie, Mommie!!" in a panicky high-pitched cry that tore at my heart, and I knew I couldn't leave my five-year-old daughter. Instantly I was back in my body. I *chose* not to leave her.

Six:—I have free will. Everything is my very own choice.

Near-death-experiences seem tailor-made for the individual. Mine, I believe, was to remind me of number six, for at the time I was into "blaming."

The lessons I received in my aborted near-death-experience, as well as other metaphysical experiences earlier in my life, prepared me to accept Shirlè's story.

***

Regarding Shirlè's friends and relatives, it seems that most do not believe that the Frank she met was a real alien, an extraterrestrial. They believe that *Shirlè believes* he was from another planet.

Frank had once told her: "If you tell people what is beyond them, you are really doing them an injustice. If they are not ready, they won't hear you, they'll be antagonistic, or they'll think you're funny. But the right person will grasp it, and will want to know more. People who don't want to know what is out there, are afraid. They are afraid it will bring them a lot of changes, and they don't like changes."

***

As for the UFO community, Warren Aston, Australian researcher of twenty years, made this statement in his study of the 1940 contactee Udo Wartena (MUFON magazine 1997).

"The rejection of early contactees has led to a situation today where many researchers and groups reject, out of hand, any report *where UFO occupants are like us in appearance and any suggestions that some aliens may therefore live among us incognito.* And sadly, this bias extends to some of the largest and most influential groups who routinely censor and ignore thousands of reports because reported aliens don't fit their narrow preconception."

PART II

Why Shirlè?

Chapter Eight

Possible Factors Contributing to or Leading up to Contact with Frank

Everyone asks "Why *Shirlè?* But why *not* Shirlè'? Who's to say? Nevertheless, in this chapter and those that follow, I put my analytical brain to work for logical reasons why Shirlè was "chosen."[19] What was it about her? Why would an extraterrestrial spend two years preparing her psychologically and spiritually for a possible future mission?

I wondered—did they know each other in a previous life? Frank had not discussed the possibility with Shirlè. But he *did* tell her she was "chosen" because she had "heart"—love, caring—for people, for humanity. I can vouch for that. She uses the talents God gave her, in her own little way, to help Earth and its inhabitants wherever and however she can. Interestingly, almost all her paintings show a combination of people, Earth and the Cosmos in semi-abstract form.

But there are countless loving, caring people who are not contacted

---

[19] Frank told her there were three others with similar missions. Other contactees have reported having similar missions.

by an alien and given a mission. There had to be more to it. Perhaps the *real reason* Frank had come for Shirlè was revealed in 1999, twenty-seven years after Frank had left. Shirlè and I had gone to see Dr. Leo Sprinkle[20] for our regressions—to be more exact, *Shirlè's* regression, for mine turned out to be an expensive nap, during which I lightly snored.

Regression in 1999, With Leo Sprinkle, PhD

> "Our real home is a place of absolute peace, total acceptance and complete love." *Destiny of Souls*, Michael Newton.

> "If we have earned it, we don't have to return to physical life, but if we wish to, we can."—Alien Frank.

It began with Shirlè finding herself between lives, her spirit reluctantly agreeing to go to Earth on a "mission." Unfortunately, the first tape (no duplicate) strangely became "lost" somewhere on the way home. Luckily, I had taken notes. It began with Dr. Sprinkle asking what Shirlè wanted to look into.

"Perhaps an incident at the last UFO conference, she answered. "Was it an abduction, and why?"

"Well," he said, "if that comes up, fine, but I'll leave it at what's best for you, what you need right now."

He proceeded to regress her to deeper and deeper levels, as I sat observing and writing, and Dr. Sprinkle worked the recorder. At level "twelve" before birth, she began to talk slowly and with much emotion. From my notes and memory, this briefly is what transpired under hypnosis:

Shirlè was immediately "home" with her friends and felt wonderful. Then suddenly she was before seven tall white-robed entities standing tightly together. (Similar entities, called Elders, have been mentioned by other contactees, and some near-death experiencers.)

She was asked to go to Earth on a mission she understood, one she had done before. She absolutely didn't want to go; she didn't want to

---

[20] R. Leo Sprinkle, PhD counseling psychology, U. Missouri, Prof. Psychology, Professor Counseling at U. No Dakota and U. of Wyoming. Now in private practice in Laramie, Wyoming. Professor Emeritus Counseling Services, University of Wyoming. Organizer of the Annual Rocky Mt. UFO Conference in Laramie since 1980. President and member of the Board of ACCET (Academy of Clinical Close Encounter Therapists.)

leave the good life of study and friends—where she could go anywhere, do anything—where everything is light and pure. She pleaded not to be sent. But the group of seven said that God wanted her to.

So, she reluctantly consented to be what we call today, a "wanderer"[21]

When the regression ended, we asked Shirlè what it was like. She gave this report:

"Difficult to describe… a place of all white light. I felt I was floating together with many people, yet I was a separate entity. My personality was intact. It was me. I felt not only the floating, but the serenity and the excitement. Whatever I wanted, whatever knowledge I wanted, I could have. I could be there forever and never be bored or restless. I felt I was home. I felt the warmth going into me and out from me. I wasn't a bystander, I was right there, experiencing this tremendous, all-encompassing emotion that filled up my entire being. There wasn't one part of me that was left out. It was all of me. I was basking in HaShem's light. What else can I say?

"Then there was a call out for me, and suddenly I was in a place with seven entities standing so close together, and I thought that was very strange. I knew there were seven, because I counted the heads. I have a habit of counting things, I don't know why. All dressed the same, long white priestly outfits with high collars. And each one had a different insignia. Being an artist and interested in fashion, I automatically noticed their attire.

"I didn't pay more attention to them, because I was wondering what they wanted from me. Suddenly a little stool appeared, and one voice asked me to sit down. And I said is it that bad that I have to sit down?

"We want you to go back. Back where? To Earth. I got up. I'm not going. I had enough the other times. I went on and on. They said nothing. When I stopped, they said 'you have to go back. We have need of you.' I said I really, really don't want to go there. 'Well,' they said, 'the Creator wants you to go there.' I thought for a few moments, and then I said, 'Well then, I guess I'll go.' Then I was in the womb, then in a crib, and the seven came to see me."

---

[21] Wanderers are souls from other than Earth who agree to incarnate on Earth in order help those who are evolving. They agree to be born of human parents and to forget their identity and powers. Their awakening "piercing the veil," comes gradually and follows a long period of loneliness and severe alienation.

In tape two she sees taller "grays" and is not afraid to shake hands with a "reptilian." She complains tearfully of being frequently poked, and they tell her it is for communication and protection; she is doing fine. She understands her job is to bring back the "light" to Earth—as a catalyst for the understanding of other dimensions.

***

When she came out of the regression, we discussed Shirlè's viewpoint. "Was she actually there?" I asked. It seemed that sometimes she was there, sometimes she was remembering.

"It depends where you *want* to be," answered Dr. Sprinkle, "age ten, or looking down from the Higher Self at age ten. You can be wherever you want to be."

"I remember being in the light," said Shirlè. "The light is like a jewel. It is full of knowledge, full of love, full of feeling, and I bring it back to people on Earth. It helps to prime one's thinking to search spiritually. This is my task."

So in the end, that which was more important, more pressing for Shirlè, (*her mission*) came up in the regression, rather than a possible abduction.

Now if we take Shirlè's regression and *pre-birth* experience as real, the following story seems to corroborate it. I now give you to consider— the "Angel Story"—a story not unique but certainly rare.

Shirlè's Birthday—"I've Something to Tell You"

> "Before we're born again, we pick the body and environment
> necessary for lessons we came to learn."—Alien Frank

In 1982, Ten Years After the Departure of Frank, Shirlè First Hears of Her "Birth Story"

It was a day Shirlè will remember always. She had invited a group of people interested in UFOs to her home in Surrey, B.C. Her mother, visiting from Montreal, was telling them about giving birth to her first child, Shirlè.

"I was in the hospital, in labor, in terrible pain. Suddenly, out of nowhere, a beautiful young woman appeared in the room. I just stared at her. She had on a long, flowing, white gown, and there was a white glow all around her.

"'I have something to tell you,'" the lady said. She handed me a glass of orange juice and said: 'Drink this, it's good for you.'

"In 1923 my English wasn't so good, but I understood. I was scared. How did she get in? The door didn't open. Was she the angel of death? Come to take me? But she had no wings! I was so frightened I couldn't speak. She watched me drink the juice and when I was finished, she said, 'The child you are giving birth to is a special child and will someday be recognized as special.'

"I was looking right at her and she simply disappeared. The door didn't open or close. I had more pains and pressed the buzzer. The nurse and then the doctor came in, and I asked who was the strange woman, and they had no idea who had given me orange juice. Finally I gave birth to Shirlè."

Shirlè was horrified. "Ma," she said, "you don't have to make up a story. These people like me *anyway*."

Her mother faced her squarely. "It's true, Shirlè."

Still not believing, Shirlè called her sister Nancy in Montreal. "Yes," said Nancy, "you weren't told?"

Shirlè called her sister Mary in Vancouver. "Yes," she answered. "Ma told us all when we were in our thirties. We just assumed she told you."

Shirlè was dumbstruck. Special! That it should be her, who thought she was nothing! To suddenly realize she was "something."

At the time she didn't delve into it with her siblings, afraid it would set her apart. And she didn't further question her mother. "Why did you treat me like you did?" she wanted to ask, but didn't.

***

When Shirlè first told me the weird "angel" story I thought—why would her mother, a woman in her late seventies, lie? Why would she make up such a story, and in front of all her friends? Somehow she seemed too grounded for that. And Shirlè herself could not have made up the story because her two sisters verified it for her and me. So I believe the angel story. It made sense to me that their mother told her sisters about it only when they were adults—but not Shirlè—not until Shirlè was over fifty, married, settled, and would not be too adversely affected.

That is, she didn't want Shirlè to become arrogant or feel superior.

I also did a little research. There had been other ET "prophesies" similar to Shirlè's, about a newborn being special and having a mission. The following are two examples:

The story of Donna Butts (a paraphrased version from *Star Children* by Jenny Randles, P.123):
Her parents were told that their second child, yet to be born, would be a girl, and would act as a missionary to spread a message to the world. As proof, a necklace with some alien writing on it was left behind. Donna was not told of this until she was married and had children and experienced a gaining time abduction together with her car. Years later a tall blond alien gave her information on space and aliens, told her the Earth was going through its end times, and that she was an important mouthpiece for their rescue plans.

There is also **the Story of Cynthia**, researched by Jenny Randles in Star Children, page 125. A paraphrased version follows:
Cynthia of Birmingham, England was twenty-seven with two young children when a tall blond man simply materialized before her and her four-year-old daughter. Telepathically he gave her information on space and time, science, and a coming cure for cancer involving vibrating atoms. He also had messages regarding Earth's ecology and the need for peace on Earth, and he showed her images which we now know as holograms. In 1958, he told her that she was pregnant, and that though her husband was the father, the child was of the race of Gharnasvarn—his origin. She was told that he was to be a great influence on mankind. A boy was born in 1958. (Jenny Randles was unable to trace him.)

***

After some time Shirle began to give the "angel" story more thought. Was the woman an angel or an alien? Frank had once told her that they sometimes work with the spiritual world. How can you tell the difference? she wondered. But perhaps it doesn't really matter.

Then it hit her. "My God HaShem," she said aloud, "you want something from me!" Then she wept, realizing that the "something" was to do and be and become, and maybe she wouldn't be able to fulfill what she was supposed to do. Whatever it entailed, she wasn't sure she had what it took. She hated the word "chosen."

She had other thoughts, a jumble of them. Was that why she, the child Sara was given piano lessons at the age of five? That maybe she would become a famous concert pianist? And was that why she was treated so strangely by her siblings and parents? If only she had known from the beginning; she would have known she wasn't crazy. She would have known she felt different for a reason. She would have been able to take the ridicule, the disappointments. She would not have argued, fought so much... So she reasoned.

But perhaps, if she had known, she may have argued more, made things worse. Perhaps it was to make her more humble. To become a spoiled brat would not have been to her advantage. She had to grow up. Perhaps the real reason she wasn't told was so that she would have a "normal" life—not feel "different."

But she *was* different. It seemed she was an Indigo, a "Wanderer", a "Star Child"

Indigos, Wanderers, Star Children

Indigos, Wanderers, or Star Children—all are super-sensitive and feel chaos, dysfunction, and the lack of nurturing love a great deal more than other children."—Lee Carroll and Jan Tober.

Was Shirlè contacted and given a mission because she was a Star Child? In the Preface and Introduction, I mentioned Shirlè could possibly be a precursor to Indigo children, as well as be a "Wanderer." I then compared those traits with people sometimes called "Star" children—and they were very similar.

What is a "star child"? Is it an alien soul in a human body, or one whose genes have been manipulated in various ways by aliens—or both? It seems logical that the aliens, technologically far more advanced than we are, would have been doing various experiments in genetics long before the early seventies when Shirlè met the alien Frank. Today, we know it is possible that not only a soul from another planet may enter the embryo, fetus or newborn—but various manipulations could be done genetically, as our scientists are doing on Earth today, with test tube babies, artificial insemination, host mothers, and cloning. The egg could be fertilized by sperm outside the body, and the tiny embryo placed in an unaware host mother, her memory of it blocked out. Also various combinations could be made with human or alien egg, human or alien sperm, by tampering with the DNA of any of them, or by manipulating DNA in the embryo or fetus.

Throughout Shirlè's life she held the strong feeling that she didn't belong on Earth, or with her parents. This feeling is also a common one of so-called "star children." They are emotional, difficult to handle, have above-average intelligence, and question authority. They have great interest in space, the cosmos, mystical New Age studies, ecology, or peace work. They read and talk at an early age, and enter the helping fields. They have the ability to remember very early life, even before or during birth. They may have psychic, OBE[22], floating or flying dreams, cause poltergeist effects, and have creative talents in art or poetry.

Dr. Michael Newton writes in *Destiny of Souls*, copyright (2000) by Llewellyn Worldwide, on page 155:

> One thing I have learned is that those who tell me they don't belong on Earth, need to be taken seriously. They may even be potential suicide cases. In my practice, these clients fall into one of three spiritual classifications:
>
> 1. Young, highly sensitive souls who began their incarnations on Earth, but have spent little time here, have great difficulty adjusting to the human body. They feel their very existence to be threatened because life is so cruel.
>
> 2. Both young and older souls who incarnated on another planet before coming to Earth: these souls lived on worlds less harsh than Earth. They may be overcome by the primitive emotions and high density of the human body. They may be hybrid souls. Essentially they feel they are in an alien body.
>
> 3. Souls who have been incarnating on Earth since their creation, but are not merging well with their current body. These souls accepted a life contract with a host body whose physical ego mind is radically different from their immortal soul. They cannot seem to find themselves in this particular lifetime.

***

Indigos, Wanderers, or Star Children—all are super-sensitive, feeling lack of nurturing love much more than other children. Shirlè was about eleven; and her mother was about to go on a trip. "What shall I bring you?" asked her mother. "Bring me the book *Nobody Loves Me*," answered Shirlè. Once, when her mother had returned from a trip, Shirlè ran up to kiss her, and was rebuffed with "Don't, you'll ruin my lipstick." Supersensitive, she cannot forget it.

And she felt the vibrations in the world of nature. One day she and her sister Mary were out walking. Just as they were about to cross a

---

17/Out of body experience.

stretch of lawn, Shirlè put her hand out and stopped her sister. Mary stood there puzzled and waited for her sister to explain her action.

"Mary," said Shirlè, "don't walk on the grass."

"Why not?" countered her sister.

"Because it hurts; it feels it."

"Don't say that," said Mary. "People will think you're crazy."

And yet, although Mary admonished her sister, she had experienced strange, paranormal events in her life as well. It was not something that could be talked about, they felt, and it was not until the girls were older that they shared and discussed those happenings. Both, they discovered, could hear voices that no one else could hear, and both shared the ability to catch glimpses into other dimensions.

But more importantly, from a very early age Shirlè truly believed her parents were somehow not her parents, and told them so. When she first told them-at the age of five they naturally paid no attention. But when she repeated it at fifteen, they were stunned. Her father looked at her, eyes wide, "*Taka bist mishuga* (You really *are* crazy,)" he said and stormed out of the room. Her mother, however, shocked and disgusted, slapped her across the face. But this made her feel even more misunderstood, more unloved. She wanted them to say they loved her whether she thought they were her parents or not.

At the same time, Shirlè, on another level, knew she had crossed the line, knew she had hurt her parents deeply. But she couldn't help herself. When she was already married and in her twenties, she said it again, so strong and deep was her conviction. (It wasn't until I read *From Elsewhere* by Scott Mandelker, *Star Children* by Jenny Randles, and *Visitors From Within* by Royal and Priest that I understood and appreciated that conviction.)

When she repeated it in her thirties, and stubbornly refused to apologize, her parents didn't talk to her for six months. When finally some relatives intervened, Shirlè relented and apologized.

Ironically, had Shirlè's parents indulged her, perhaps she would not have become strong and determined. Perhaps she would have been too spoiled, too weak to persevere as an artist. All in all, it seems it was her upbringing pitted against her temperament that made her strong. And it was this strength, coupled with an open, spiritually searching mind—the Indigo, Wanderer, Star-Child mind—that the aliens sought to work with.

A Searching Mind, Other Dimensions

"People will hear and see only what they are ready to hear and see. The aliens contact artists, writers, and other creative people who are open enough to embrace new ideas."—Alien Frank.

Still, why Shirlè? Frank had said that he had wanted to contact her earlier, but she wasn't "ready". She was "sitting on the fence". Only when she was ready did he "draw" her to him.

So what does "ready" mean? I think it means there were stages that mentally prepared her for her meeting with Frank—each stage evolving from the one before. Her adult belief in intelligent life on other planets had evolved from her intuition as a teenager that God's creations were *vast*—which in turn had evolved from an experience at age eight.

An Experience of Oneness:

The little girl climbed onto a chair to get a better look in the bathroom mirror. Suddenly a strange and wonderful feeling swept over her. She was enveloped in love. At the same time, she was filled to overflowing, with a loving embrace of *all of creation*. "I feel strong," she said out loud, "I can do anything. If someone hurts me, he hurts God."

She knew then that God was in her, as He is in each of us. He was part of her, and she was part of the Creator. It was the ecstasy of Oneness[23]. At the tender age of eight, Shirlè felt God's presence.

Seeking as a Young Adult:

Years later, meditating, she would ask, "Why is it, *HaShem*,[24] all the books say we yearn for You? And we do, without even realizing it. Why? Because I think the longing is built in[25]."

She was seeking, but hadn't found anyone to ask. Mentors were scarce and hard to find. She was looking for something, a missing piece of the puzzle, so she read the Old Testament, the New Testament, and books on Buddhism, until her mind was saturated.

---

[23] Resembling a NDE, a near -death experience.

[24] She always used one of the Hebrew words for God.

[25] "There is now scientific physiological verification, by various authors, that the right temporal lobe makes the connection to spirituality when stimulated"- *Where God Lives* by Melvin Morse, M.D.)

Later, as an artist, she would look at her canvas and ask herself "So what's next?" She always wanted something new, different. And *HaShem,* who can do anything, of course He would want other worlds. How could Earth be the center of the universe? God must have made other universes, other inhabited planets. So her thoughts went. But when she would *tell* people these ideas, she knew they had privately labeled her "crazy."

One day she asked the rabbi for his view. "We were made to be on this planet," he responded simply. "We cannot live on the moon or other planets."

But the thoughts wouldn't leave her. What if we humans fail, she pondered. Earth can't be enough. There must be life on other planets. Perhaps not in the same form, but life.

The Metaphysical Connection: Voices, Other Dimensions

She heard "voices." Where did they come from? They had always been with her; it was just natural. "I hate to admit it," Shirlè told a friend, "but I only got through school because a voice inside me would tell me what to study. I'd hear 'flip the pages' and I'd be shown what questions would be on the exam. I studied only what I was 'told' to study."

Often, instead of the voice, she would get a strong feeling or intuition. If she didn't obey it, she would then get the "voice"—its unemotional tone neither male nor female.

Was it her guardian angel, an alien, a spirit from the dead, or her own higher self (the God within)? No matter. One day it protected her from danger. She was on her way to some friends when suddenly the voice, calm and low-pitched said, "Shirlè, go back home." She heeded it. Later she learned that had she gone, she could have been in the exact time and place of an accident.

Seeing into other Dimensions, Seeing and Interacting with the Dead

After hearing voices, she began seeing things. One day, she was looking out her bedroom window, which faced a bare brick wall. Suddenly before her were bushes and brilliantly colored flowers. It was her first experience of seeing into another dimension, a dimension that exists in our same space, a parallel space, and which she could somehow access.

From her twenties to forties, she was seeing the "dead" in solid, as well as astral form: her sister-in-law, mother-in-law, husband, and a strange woman. They had somehow entered her space. She could see them, hear them, and converse with them verbally and telepathically.

Entering the Past

Then one evening, she felt it was *she* who had actively entered another dimension, the past. She had just gone to bed when a strong vibration coursed through her body. For a Seefew moments, fearful, she tensed and it stopped. She then understood she was about to be shown something. "It's okay, *HaShem,*" she said, "I want to experience it."

The vibrations started again. She asked for His protection, and relaxed. Instantly she felt she was "one" with everything and everything was possible. It was like a window in her mind had opened up. She watched people dressed in the style of the 1920s conversing, dancing to a nickelodeon. She was there as an onlooker; the experience felt natural, real—unlike viewing a screen.

Was this a glimpse into time travel? Physicists tell us of black holes into which one can enter the past, white holes which can pull one into the future, and wormholes that can speed one through vast distances. Perhaps the mind can always do what spaceships theoretically can do.

Experiencing Another's Experience

After her father's death, Shirlè's mother lived alone in Montreal. There was a baker's strike in the city and bread was unobtainable. Her mother told Shirlè (as if it were natural and normal) that she had a vision (not a dream) of Shirlè's father bringing her loaves of bread.

Hearing about someone's vision is one thing. Experiencing someone else's vision is something else, but that is what happened next. Shirlè's mother often spoke of the many visitors she had. No one believed it; her old friends had died and it was difficult for her to make new ones. The family figured she was lonely and simply made up the "visitors" story.

One day when Shirlè had returned from her art exhibit in Paris, she decided to stay in her mother's place overnight. She slept in the bed next to her mother's. Suddenly she awoke and sat upright. There in the room, milling about, were people dressed in the style of long ago, women in long dresses, men with beards. One carried a book and one wore a *yarmulke*, a skull-cap. They looked absolutely real, not at all transparent. They were just like normal people, except they made no sound when they walked, and when they reached a wall they disappeared. Two women, wearing wraparound aprons, looked closely at Shirlè and smiled, acknowledging her presence.

All the while her mother slept soundly. Shirlè let her sleep, her story verified. In the morning her mother was pleased to hear that Shirlè had also seen her mother's old departed friends.

Perhaps they had come exactly when Shirlè would be there (synchronicity?) so that she would believe her mother's experience. As for Shirlè, how she was able to, or was made to, for some reason, suddenly enter the past or another dimension, she does not know.

An interesting explanation of the overlap of dimensions is given by a regressed subject under hypnosis in Delores Cannon's *The Convoluted Universe*. A paraphrased version follows:

Our "five senses" are attuned to the frequencies on *our* level of existence. Beings on other levels of existence are tuned to *their own* particular frequency. If, for some reason, these levels of awareness were to *overlap* or share the same frequency, then the beings on each plane would be aware of each other and interact.

Experiencing Telekinesis[26]

Shirlè and her husband had been so very close it was not surprising that after his passing, she would feel that he or another spirit was taking care of her. On one particular day, she was having an exhibition of her artwork. With no help available, she had to carry a heavy stack of paintings from one hall to the other. She lost her balance and was about to drop the load, when suddenly, she felt the burden being lifted from her arms. Incredibly she could carry the load of paintings on just one finger! Somehow she knew it was not an angel or an E.T. She just knew it was Hymie.

Telekinesis or Teleportation?

Not long after Hymie's passing, when a winter snowfall had left icy patches on a Montreal road, Shirlè's car skidded into a snowbank. It was firmly stuck. She waited what seemed like forever, but no cars came by to give help. Panic gave way to tears. All of a sudden the car, seemingly by itself, lifted up, turned around, and put itself down again on the road. (There have been similar reports of cars moving without the driver's touch, even lifting up and turning around.)

---

[26] The process of moving things without touching them and without using ordinary physical means.

The Demon Story

While Shirlè was still a widow, a fellow tenant in her apartment building, a single man, asked her out. They had a nice dinner together, and when he brought her to her door, he lingered. She sensed he wanted to come in, but she didn't want him to. As he left to go to his own apartment, she went in, locked the door, prepared for the night, and got into bed.

Suddenly a small entity, like a gnome, appeared out of nowhere, jumped onto her bed, took a pillow and held it over her head as if to smother her. Strangely, she didn't panic.

"God," she said, "if that's what you want, it's okay with me." And with total trust she completely surrendered. Instantly, the demon simply vanished. It had dematerialized.

Shirlè felt it was to test the strength of her faith. But could it also be that her unconscious fear of her date attracted (materialized) the "demon," and her subsequent lack of fear had dematerialized it? According to Jane Roberts' book *The Seth Material*, "The evil that is projected outward does not exist, but because you *believe* it does, you form the materialization from your fears. To fear them is to put yourself in their reality; then you are forced to fight on their terms."

Awareness of Synchronicities

For years Shirlè had been aware of synchronicities and the part they play in nudging us on our path. I became intrigued with the subject and got Deepak Chopra's *Synchrodestiny* tapes that explain how being aware of "coincidences" can lead us to where we should be. I thought of one particular synchronicity that led Shirlè in the right direction for that particular time:

While still living in Montreal, Shirlè and her sister Mary were waiting for the Metro. A lady walked over to them. "Is this the train to go to Eatons Store?" she asked.

"Yes," said Shirlè. "We're going there as well."

The lady went back to where she had been standing. A moment later she returned to Shirlè and Mary. "Does it also go to Hudson's Bay?" she asked.

"Yes it does," replied Shirlè, studying the lady more closely. This is important, she mused. Twice. It must have a meaning. "Where are you from?" she added.

"Vancouver," the lady responded. "I've just come back from Guatemala."

They got on the train together, sat together. "Are you alone here?" asked Shirlè.

"Yes," she replied.

"So why don't you call me," said Shirlè. "Maybe we can get together."

They didn't have a pencil or pen, so the lady used her eyebrow pencil and wrote Shirlè's phone number on her wrist before they parted.

"How could you talk to a complete stranger?" warned Mary when they were alone. "You don't know who she is. It's dangerous."

"Don't worry," replied Shirlè. "I know it's okay."

Sure enough, the lady (whose name was Irene) called and invited her to her rooming house, and they spent an enjoyable time discussing various subjects. She was leaving the next day and promised to write. They corresponded back and forth. When Shirlè wrote some time later that she was going to leave Montreal to live in Vancouver where her daughter lived, Irene offered her a job in her boutique in "arty" Gas Town. It was just what she needed, art-wise, socially, and especially financially—before meeting the alien Frank, as well as afterwards.

So perhaps her experiences of other dimensions and synchronicities were a factor in being "chosen" by Frank.

Chapter Nine

The Art Factor—Passion and Focus
Paintings, Exhibits

"Among French artists only the surrealists focused on evolving
consciousness."—*The Spiritual in Art,* by Maurice Tuchman

"The painter is concerned not with his own feelings or with the mystery of his
own personality, but with the penetration into the world mystery. His
imagination is therefore attempting to dig into metaphysical secrets. It is a
religious art which through symbols will catch the basic truth of life."
--Newman.

Shirlè had a burning desire to be whoever she is supposed to be, not
just what is expected of her. She seemed to know she was
supposed to be an artist. *So perhaps "focus" was also a factor in her
being contacted.* The following story comes to mind:

The children were grown. Hymie had decided to give up his business
due to partnership problems, and he now had a franchise in an
encyclopedia company. Shirlè worked as receptionist and saleslady in his
office. Not only was she a paid employee of the company, but a great
help to him in his work.

One day, complaining she didn't have enough time to paint, Hymie
suggested she bring in her canvas, and paint during slow times. She tried
it for awhile, but didn't get much done. Finally, she told Hymie she
wanted to quit. The head office begged her to stay, with an offer of

career advancement, but she refused. Hymie continued on without her special help and added finances. Eventually his income dwindled and he left the company for another.

Shirlè knew instinctively, had she stayed, she would have lost her focus in life. She had to paint. She had to be an artist. The drive was so strong, she couldn't live without it. Only later did she learn (from Frank) that not only was she an artist in another life, but that painting was part of her mission in this life.

***

In the 50s being feminine was letting the husband completely support the family; to ask the wife's help was a blow to his ego. So when they married, Hymie made up his mind he would sacrifice his desire to be a physician and make his goal the financial stability for his wife and children. However, he was unique in that he also encouraged and supported his wife's artistic endeavors and future—definitely not the custom in Canada at that time.

But I wonder—what woman today would not work to help a husband make ends meet, even if she believed it was the husband's role to support a wife? I know I would help such a husband and put my own needs on hold. In fact that's what I did. However, I think Shirlè's case was different. I think she was so determined to be an artist that it had to come first.

And now the ambivalence… If the reason we are here on Earth is for a purpose, and the purpose is felt by us, and we know that it is to express our talents and contribute to the world in our own unique way, we must be *true* to ourselves. And when we are true to ourselves and do the work we are meant to do, there will appear those who will assist, if need be. And isn't this the case with Shirlè? Didn't Hymie appear to be exactly what she needed? Didn't the teachers support her desire and then did not Frank encourage and help her? Didn't Fred appear on the scene, the right mate at the right time? So perhaps when we have our *purpose* we are guided. When we hold to our purpose we are taken care of.

But I still feel ambivalent with that scenario. Who then will take care of the sick mother, or child, for example, and give up his or her own needs and desires? *Unless, of course, our real purpose is to do exactly that!* I think there's a fine line to tread. What's needed is balance— balance in everything.

Shirlè claims the following writing by Venita Ramirez mirrors her thoughts and feelings so closely, I am including it for better understanding of an artist like Shirlè.

CONTINUAL MOTION TOWARDS GOD
–by Venita Ramirez

I can't go back and I can't remain as I am, no matter who or what stands in my way. I can't even get in my own way for long. Believe me I try. Sometimes I wish I could stop this wild pace, but the wish is a fleeting one, interrupted by the excitement of new inspiration, new vision, new hope of God, growth, Divine Union.

Sometimes the struggle between growing and clinging becomes so strong that to escape it, I choose someone outside of me to become the "bad guy." They are putting me in this prison. They are the ones who are trying to control me. "Let me be me," I want to scream. "Let me be the God that I am!" But deep down I know that I am screaming this plea to myself. No-one can control me but me.

Painful, painful. Because in order to free myself from my own bondage I must keep letting go of people and things I cling to so desperately. I must let go of my expectations of them, and learn to disregard their expectations of me. I must risk losing them, so that I may be free to choose moment by moment what is truly important to me, give them all up for literally God knows what. At these times I forget why I'm on this path, except that the pull towards God is so strong.

Many times I just want to throw in the sponge, and feel "what am I doing here?" How difficult this life is. And I know that as I go towards the Light I get stronger within myself, less needy of the people I love, less tolerant of my destructive ways of being, less tolerant of their destructive ways of being with me.

And so I simply have to let go of them, and allow them to continue to fight their own battles without my help--while I take a brand new set of my own.

Yes, I'm holding on for dear life, but slowly my attachments to people and things are slipping from my desperate grasp--soon to be merely memories, refuse of an illusory past, as I live more and more consciously in the moment. Nothing can stop the continual motion towards God--nothing, as I soar ever higher into the Light of Consciousness.

And always, after the pain comes the quiet. As I awaken I step cautiously into newness. I look around curiously, and wonder, "Where did I end up this time? Nobody looks familiar. Who am I now?"

There is such an emptiness, but for awhile the darkness has left. Now the emptiness is lighter, provoking me to fill it with color, swirling color, and music, the music of the soul, the music the Heart. "Be you," it says, "whatever you are. And in that being you'll discover that being you is enough. It is more than enough. It is Blissful.

Then you discover that pain gives your music depth, the pain made your artwork a masterpiece. And in your pain you were living vibrantly and openly the life of God. Go ahead, paint your way. You are free... at least for awhile...

Until you try to figure out which color to put there, until you start comparing your masterpiece with someone else's--until you start judging one better than another. Then the pain comes again, and the darkness, and the clinging...

Until once again you let go and slip into an opening, even bigger than this one, with even more room to Be You. And the Light streams even brighter, and fills you with an energy so strong that it moves you even faster into the next opening, until soon you are moving so fast that any form of attachment drops from your hands. God wants you now. There is no time to reconsider. God wants you now."

And so, beckoned by the emptiness and the hunger for the Light, I paint. I paint with laughter, tears, passion and rage. I paint with loneliness, pain, compassion and love. I paint with wisdom, honesty, joy and faith. I paint with everything I know, pouring out my heart and soul. And the more I paint, the more I learn that I can paint anything, because I am free. And the freer I feel, the more I let myself Be Me. The joy escalates, the pain softens, and somewhere nearby I sense God. I can't go back. I'm here now, I'm here.

Shirlè has kept her passion, her *focus*, to this day.

Some Paintings by Shirlè Klein—from 1986 to1997

COSMIC FAMILY: 41 paintings, 1986. The manifestation of spirit in an organized universe, and man's awareness of it

"After eleven years of painting, I had come into my own being, and was hit with an idea--people's names. By meditating, I could delve into their lives, their vibrations, paint their lives--and "Cosmic Family" was born. Each is individualistic, personal. I feel a kin to every name. Though we're not related by birth, we're all one, all connected."

UNITY: 9 paintings, 1987--inspired by a dream. Very strange people "in space" seen by astral projection.

"I was on an island, in a house, in a large room with my contact Frank, a woman and a baby. The woman was showing me her paintings. I told her they were good, and suggested the woman write children's stories to go with them. Then I went over to Frank seated in a corner of the room, and showed him my own paintings, quietly, so no-one else could see them. The water was muddy and high, and I was about to leave. Frank's interpretation: 'We are going into the unknown, leaving everything except the paintings behind.' The dream inspired me to do the UNITY series."

MAGICAL LANDSCAPES: A series of 7 paintings, 1987.

~ The Artist and the Alien ~

"I don't usually do landscapes; I'm more involved with people."

MIRRORED IMAGES: 7 paintings, 20 by 24in., 1987 They represent the positive and negative, the duality of male and female, and how we have to learn to work together.

CITY BY THOUGHT --4 paintings, 1988. Projections of actual places, or creations of a fertile mind

FLASHES, FACES, & IN THE MIDST OF TIME came out of CITY OF THOUGHT

THREE MURALS—In 1990 some paintings were in the Total Contemporary Art Gallery in Toronto. The owner Theo Kwack, requested three murals 4x8 ft— to be completed in two months, for Russia. The subject: Ancient thought on aliens from distant planets.

"I hadn't the foggiest idea what to make. Then a voice in my head said: 'Go to your sketches.' I did, and found a note there: 'for future murals.' The note provided the theme. One of the murals was later copied, made into a tapestry and exhibited in Israel. Theo Kwack notified me that someone wanted to buy them. However, when I went to his gallery in Toronto, I found his place closed, and lost all three."

THE PLANET EARTH (#1) An attractive Earth woman, and an alien that looks kind of strange.

"It was inspired by Genesis: 'The sons of God came down and found the Earth women fair.'"

THE CONCRETE CITY (#2) A view from a spaceship. Two Earthlings have come back and are viewing this gigantic city from the spacecraft.

FUTURE TRAVEL IN SPACE BUBBLES (3) Everyone floating around in space bubbles, the outskirts of a city in the background.

NAISSANTE COSMIQUE #1 –(48 x 62) Cosmic birth. Nine human faces, each in a circle. The first of two additional paintings for Theo Kwack.
NAISSANTE COSMIQUE #2 (48 by 62) Numbers in circles, a 5 and a 3 and a 1 between the 5 and 3, making nine. (Nine in numerology is the completion of Man) Two faces—one side male, other side female.
THE MAGIC OF LINE SERIES 4 landscapes, one each for east, west, north, and south.

"Only when they were completed did I realize they were seemingly viewed from the sky. Rotated, the scene would completely change.

COMPLETION MASK ONE & COMPLETION MASK TWO, 1990: 2 miniature paintings (30 x 30 cm).

"They were strange but delightful—like layers on the background. One I gave to my son and daughter-in-law. The other won a prize of $200.00, of which $100.00 went to the gallery.

TWO LETTER WORDS: 9 paintings.

"Strange-looking canvasses, with words "is, an, so, be, we, us, me, no, do. I haven't sold any of them, but I sure had fun doing them."

THE UNIVERSAL CODE--11 paintings --A conglomerate of various parts of the human being, brought together.

We are like a quilt, all one, but made up of pieces put together. A copy of one was made into a tapestry and shown in Israel.

"The exhibit in Toronto didn't make much money, but I have to be an artist, because that's what it's all about for me. When I see things, I see them in design form, and I say to myself: 'My God, this would be fantastic for a painting.' It just comes natural for me."

THE ASCENDED GATEWAYS Series of 8. A musical gateway into another dimension. The scale Abra, Fah, Soh, and Allal (another name for God), as well as ABC and 111(in numerology adding up to God)

THE CRYSTAL CITY OF ATLANTIS on a large round Mexican canvas. Three people in a spacecraft are viewing the city before them in all its detail.

"I had never worked with iridescent paint before and at first I was very nervous, so I did only a little at a time. I think it's one of my best works." With the painting is a poem by Rebecca Panzan.

THE FLOATING CITY OF SIRIUS -A poem by Rebecca Panzan accompanies it.

"I visited (in astral form) the planet Sirius B, and experienced the "water" surrounding "The Floating City" to be so buoyant you could float on it. You could put your hand in it, pull it out, and it would be dry.

THE STEPS OF ADROMEDA and the "GOLDEN CITY OF RETICULA"

"It looks like gold, but I know it's not. Strange houses with a protecting belt around the buildings—why I don't know. Commander Zella has a net over her face. I didn't meet anyone else- only her."

THE COMPLETION OF MAN 1992--9 paintings (9 stands for Man)--a series of huge faces

"One, which sold well, represented people from the planet Condor in a beautiful city with a diamond in the center, as a port-hole to another dimension, another world.

THE CELTS–11 paintings, (each with a poem by Frank Morton)
"The result of my fascination with the Celts after reading 'The Ancient Celts' by Barry Cunliff They were searching for the universal creator, the one God, at a time when most people could not even conceive of it. I feel I was a Celt in a previous life."

EONS 1993—4 paintings on small circular canvasses of people with no mouths (aliens who take nourishment through the skin and communicate telepathically)

MALE AND FEMALE, 1994--2 paintings, each done on huge round canvasses 36" in diameter.
"She is gigantic because the twentieth century female is a power-house, a dynamo. On one side she has the male energy; on the other—an emerging sense of caring for the future, disturbing as it is. She has to know, and not just through others. She has to find out for herself. And yet, she must forever be the clown; otherwise no-one would accept her, want her--she is too powerful.
"The male is a strange species—ruler, hunter--always autonomous. He has two faces--a sarong, and a business suit. And his super-ego--we, as females, allowed it all along. His sensitivity, seen until now as weakness, is only now creeping out.
"Now, the female and male energies, the clown and the little boy, must work together."

PLANETARY LIFE FORMS, 1996—series of four
On one planet, huge flowers give birth to spores that evolve to fully grown human beings. On this planet, it is their only means of reproduction. On another planet, an entity listens through a thin book, attached to the ear. On another, "rubber" people--you touched them, and suddenly an arm would appear. The fourth--people who look like bears with bear-like ears.
"I was wondering where I was getting these ideas. It was towards twilight, and suddenly I was shown to add a particular object {which I had apparently left out} around the neck of one of the entities I was painting. When I astro-project, I don't always remember every detail. The aliens want me to put down what I see in my own style, but not leave out anything important."

FLOATING GIGANTIC PODS --4 paintings. Pluto, and the seeds of Saturn, Uranus, and Neptune.

THE OLMEC--4 paintings of the pre-Columbian time--The Dancers, The Musicians, The Man With Spear, and The Lovers. Inspired by the Olmecs who pursued a religious or philosophical goal to find the means to transport enormous blocks of stone over vast distances
"As another artist, I could see they were seeking something. That is how matter evolves. If we do not, we stagnate or go backwards. Motion is, and

motion will always be. This planet is not still, never will be, and we move ahead at all times, for the positive or the negative. But motion is."

THE CHILDREN OF LIGHT, 1997—People with knowledge who hold the Light—spiritual beings.

***

INTERNATIONAL ART EXHIBITS by SHIRLÈ KLEIN

1965   Montreal, Que. Juried exhibit of Quebec Women Painters, sponsored by Quebec.

1970   Sherbrooke, Que. Invitational exhibit at Bishop University.
Montreal, Que. One woman exhibit, Liewellon and Packard Gallery.
Montreal, Que. Invitational group exhibit of Quebec artists, Place Bonaventure opening.

1971   Vancouver, B.C. Group exhibit, Mary Frazee Gallery.

1972 &1973   Australia. Exhibits at four galleries.

1975   Vancouver, B.C. One woman exhibit, Arts Club,
Vancouver, B. C. Group exhibit, Imago Gallery.

1976   Vancouver, B.C. One woman exhibit, Danish Art Gallery.
New York City, N.Y. Galerie Internationale
Paris, France. Joint exhibit, Galerie Mouffe
Biarriyz, France. Group exhibit, Galerie Vallombreuse

1977   Vancouver, B.C. One woman exhibit, The Canvas Company

1978   Solvang, Calif. One woman exhibit, Copenhagen Galleri
New York City, N.Y. Group exhibit, Womenart Galleries

1982   Vancouver, B.C., Eaton's of Canada. Group exhibit of B.C. artists
North Vancouver, B.C. One woman exhibit, Art Cellar Gallery

1983   Paris, France. Invited exhibits of international artists,
International d'Art Contemporaire de Paris

1985   Surrey, B.C. One woman exhibit, Surrey Art Gallery

1986   Surrey, B.C. Group exhibit, Surrey Art Gallery

1988   Fort Langley, B.C. Group exhibit, Langley Centennial Museum.

1989   Gabrovo, Bulgaria. Group exhibit, 9th International Biennial of Humor & Satire in the Arts

1990   Moscow and Riga, Russia. Three murals in a group exhibit
Paris, France. Group exhibit, Modern Art Gallery, Paris

1991   Toronto, Ontario. First prize at the Annual Award International Exhibition
French Riviera. Exhibit at Caszou Picture Gallery, Chateau of the Villeneau

1992   Toronto, Ontario. One woman exhibit,
Theodore Museum of Contemporary Art Gallery
Seattle, WA. Group exhibit, Kirsten Gallery

1994   Sechelt, B.C. One woman exhibit, Sunshine Coast

1995   Seattle, WA. Group exhibit, Kirsten Gallery

1997   Toronto, Ontario. Miniatures—11th Annual International Exhibition & Sale of Miniatures

2001   Brazilia, Brazil. Showing and sale, Brazilia Gallery

2003   Delta, B.C. Group exhibit, North Delta Rec. Center

Chapter Ten

The Personality and Character Factor
Shirlè, Family, Soul-mate Hymie

"Man must know himself; otherwise how can he deal with anyone else?"
–Alien Frank

"You must be who you really are, then do what you need to do,
in order to have what you want." – Margaret Young

What about Shirlè's personality and family background? Were they also factors in being "chosen" for a mission? Her personality and character… Was Frank seeking a passive subject he could control, or the opposite—a spunky character who had strength and self-sufficiency?

Struggling for her Identity

Shirlè's given name was Sarah. In second grade, four or five girls in her class would answer to Sarah, a common name in a Jewish neighborhood. It caused confusion every time. To alleviate the situation, the teacher asked all Sarahs to choose (for the classroom only), another name starting with "S."

Shirlè went home. "I don't want to be just another Sarah," she announced at dinner. "I hate the name. I want to change it to Shirlèy."

Her mother was aghast. "You were named after Grandma," she said, her voice rising. "You want to remove her memory? How could you think such a thing!?"

Shirlè stubbornly insisted, and after a few months they gave in. Years later, at age forty-seven, she decided to give it a French flair. She dropped the "y," put the accent on the last syllable, and became the Shirlè of today.

Her brother, who was fourteen years younger, was doted upon and spoiled by her parents—as were all Jewish boys in those days. He saw life as a big joke, while her two younger sisters sought peace, accepting the status quo. Shirlè, however, was plagued by a yearning: to know more, learn more. Ten-year-old boys could attend Hebrew School; ten-year-old girls could not.

It was a little *shul*, and she would go there every Sunday, sit in the back and listen to the Hebrew teacher, hoping he wouldn't notice, or wouldn't care. One day he

"What are you doing here?" he asked kindly. "Why do you come here?"

"Please, rabbi," she said. "let me stay. I won't do anything. I'll lie on the floor and no one will see me."

"You really want to know what I'm teaching?"

"I have no one to talk to, no one to ask questions. I want to learn."

He let her stay. One day, a question was asked of the boys regarding Moses or Abraham and they couldn't answer.

"Sarah, what do you say?"

Her mature answer stunned the boys and astounded the rabbi. He could tell from the way she spoke that she possessed an intuitive knowledge of God. After that he allowed her to sit closer. However, she refrained from asking questions. As a non-paying student, she felt she was imposing. When her father heard she was studying with the boys he laughed and admired her gumption. Her mother, however, was livid.

"You're a *schlok*, always making trouble!"

"Ma," countered Shirlè, "can I still go to Hebrew school, even though I'm a rotten kid?" Her mother firmly refused, so she read children's bible stories in the library instead.

Her search for knowledge disturbed her mother. "Shirlèy[27]," she

---

[27] Shirlé was still being called "Shirléy" at this time.

warned, "you'd better watch it if you want to get married. You're getting too smart. Men won't look at you twice."

But Shirlè wanted to make her own destiny. At ten she wanted to be a scientist who searched for answers to the mysteries of the universe. Or perhaps she would be an artist; at school the teacher said her drawings were very good.

"Ma," she said one day, "I want to be an artist."

"An artist? Artists are whores," her mother sneered.

Soon, an elementary school teacher sent her home with a note to this effect:

"Dear Mr. and Mrs. Edelstein, your daughter Shirlèy shows great artistic talent. She should be taking art lessons to develop it further. I would be happy to help her take courses in our school or outside. I would give her every support. Please call me so we can talk about this further. Sincerely...."

"Never!" shouted her mother, tearing up the note. "Artists starve. Better you should take commercial courses, so you can support yourself!"

Ironically, or understandably, her mother had married an artistic type who turned his embroidery talent into a viable business. She knew the pitfalls, the financial instability of it. Going to her father didn't help. "What Ma says is right," he said. "I can't fight the both of you." He loved her and admired her spunk, but his wife was his world, and life revolved around her. He tried not to interfere with Shirlè's relationship with her mother.

When Shirlè returned to school and reported her parents had refused, her teacher sighed and shook her head. At home in her bed at night, Shirlè cried herself to sleep.

She went to Commercial School, albeit unwillingly. And her mother was right. It proved to be of great help later on, when she supported herself as a bookkeeper. At the time, however, her thoughts were filled with resentment and sadness. Nobody understood her. She wasn't allowed to be herself. She didn't belong here. What was she doing here? She felt so out of place, never really a part of anything, always searching.

The combative mother-daughter conflict was exacerbated not only by the difference in generations, but also by culture. To her parents, Bella and Meyer Edelstein, physical survival superseded attaining psychological health, considered a luxury in those times. They had immigrated to Montreal during the late 1800s to escape Jewish persecution in Poland.

They were well liked in the community. Many a time her parents offered a helping hand to individuals in need, donated funds to a Jewish hospital, and helped to set up an interest-free loan fund for the needy. The family attended an Orthodox, then a conservative synagogue, where her father's embroidered scrolls revealed his considerable artistic talent.

In the home, her parents' medley of Jewish, Polish, and beginner's English vied with the children's Canadian English. Her parents loved each other. Arguments between them were scarce, and together they formed a united front when it came to conflicts within the family. Every Friday night her mother put out the "good" dishes for the Sabbath meal. Then she solemnly made the blessing over tall candles. Like Shirlè, her parents believed strongly in God the Creator. Instinctively Shirlè understood the meaning of their heritage, and was proud of being a Jew.

Though her parents were not rich in the formal sense—there was always food on the table—they never lacked for material comforts. Shirlè had everything.

But all Shirlè wanted—the bubbly, talkative, talented, questioning, joyful child that was "Shirley"—all she wanted was to be truly appreciated. All she really wanted was to be loved (with hugs and kisses), and her talents and goodness recognized. Some children could do with less attention. Not Shirlè. Her strong need for love could not always be satisfied, and with her clear goal-oriented mind, she was terribly hurt and frustrated by her mother opposing a career as an artist.

***

Strangely, or not so strangely, my background is similar to Shirlè's. My Jewish parents and grandparents came from the same area as Shirlè's—at times Poland, at other times the Ukraine or Russia. My parents too, were relatively poor, with little education, and left to escape the "pogroms" (killings of Jews by their Christian neighbors). They too, worked hard in America to have a better life for their children. What's more, I discovered that both Shirlè and I had married survivors of the Holocaust; had lived in Montreal at the same time, had gone to the same evening college, and had a common friend living there. However, our paths had never crossed; I was a medical technologist and she an artist.

I understand Shirlè's upbringing—the absence of hugging and kissing, and especially the superstition (also in other cultures) of never complimenting one's own for fear of bringing bad luck. We both experienced the resultant low self-esteem and the feeling of being unloved. And just as Shirlè's mother refused to help her study art, my mother refused to help me get into nursing school because she objected to the profession.

Of course Shirlè's parents loved her and cared for her, especially her father, but not in the way Shirlè desired or needed at the time. She felt unloved until Hymie her soulmate, appeared on the scene.

Soul-mate Hymie *"That's the girl I'm going to marry"*

"People are attracted to people of the same vibration. People of lower vibration will reject you or punish you. People of higher vibration will have understanding."—Alien Frank

Was Hymie "chosen" for the part he was to play? Without him, would Shirlè have been ready for Frank?

It intrigues me, fascinates me—the idea of a soul-mate and how it works. Is it our own spirit that somehow (on an unconscious level) reaches out and connects with the soul-mate, or do outside forces bring it together with synchronicity? Shirlè did not recognize Hymie as the one, was not attracted to him at first. But Hymie psychically "knew" just as he "knew" that his life would be cut short.

That Hymie had come as the answer to her prayers, she realized only later. He just happened to be in a certain place at a certain time, not only to fulfill her destiny, but his. The place was Sainte Agathe in the Laurentian Mountains—the time was a beautiful day in June. Shirlè was taking a walk along a grassy slope that led towards a lake. There, in a rowboat, sat Hymie Klein and his twin brother Morris. Synchronicity[28] was at work.

"See that girl coming down to the shore?" said Hymie, eyes riveted on her. *"That's the girl I'm going to marry."*

"Are you nuts?" laughed his brother. "You haven't even spoken to her."

Shirlè was not attracted at first. He had to pursue her, and the more he pursued, the more she resisted. If anything, she was more attracted to his twin, the boisterous one. But this changed one day as the three of them walked in the woods.

"What's the matter, Morris?" asked Shirlè. "Why are you so quiet?"

"Will you please tell 'Little Boy Blue' to get lost?" he answered.

---

[28] Synchoniciity is the awareness and recognition of the usefulness for your benefit of a person or object that directs you on your path.

Hymie, stung by the remark, immediately turned away and walked on ahead.

"That wasn't very nice," admonished Shirlè. Morris simply shrugged his shoulders, and Shirlè ran to catch up with Hymie. They spent the rest of the day together, laughing and sharing. From that day, a bond was formed that neither time nor space, life or death could break. Had it not been for Morris's timely remark she may not have married Hymie, attracted as she was then, to the flamboyant type.

Hymie, quiet, subdued, only two years older than Shirlè, was wise beyond his years. There were other worlds, he told her, and other life forms, and other places where people were not as brutal as here. He taught her all he knew about the world, and she loved to listen. At seventeen, sheltered Shirlè really knew nothing about sex. Patiently, Hymie answered questions, explained things, never taking advantage of her. As time went on, she could tell him her deepest feelings, everything. She began to appreciate his kindness, his caring. He bolstered her when she was down, helped to lessen her insecurities, gave her confidence in life. Then she knew. He was her soulmate.

"How long have you known her," a friend asked at their engagement a year later.

"All my life and beyond," he answered.

Told that they looked like sister and brother, Hymie responded, "Well, I've known her before."

"What do you mean *before*?"

"Before time and space," he answered.

Shirlè, not finding a job after graduating from high school, helped her father in his business. By September 1940, Canada had already been in the war a year. Both brothers had enlisted. Hymie's twin was sent overseas, while Hymie ended up in a training camp in Quebec Province, where Shirlè visited him each week by bus.

When, after the war, she finally heard about the Holocaust, she was horrified and then depressed. Any kind of injustice was painful to her. Many would say there is no God after Auschwitz, but Shirlè was unwavering in her belief in God, in her love for the Creator.

They were taking a walk one day, discussing mundane matters. They found a bench and sat down. Then he turned to her, took her hand in his and looked into her eyes. "I want you to know now, before we marry," he said quietly without emotion, "I'm going to die young. I'm going to have a short life. I won't be with you long."

"How do you know?" was all Shirlè could muster.

"I just know," he said.

She put it out of her mind, figuring he just wanted to be dramatic.

After the wedding, her father gave them a start in a business designing and making handbags. Shirlè came up with ideas for hats and bags. Her father, as an embroiderer and designer, appreciated and complimented her artistic endeavors, but strangely, not directly, only to others.

As for her painting—it all really began when she married Hymie at eighteen. With her husband completely devoted to her, her life turned around. Feeling loved, she became less defensive, gained some confidence and self-esteem, and was able to concentrate not only on painting but preparing for motherhood.

Visits From In-Laws, Alive and Dead

"Our birth is but a sleep and a forgetting: The soul that rises with us, our life's star, Hath had elsewhere its setting, And cometh from afar. But trailing clouds of glory do we come From God, who is our home. Heaven lies about us in our infancy. Shades of the prison-house begin to close Upon the growing boy."
—William Wordsworth (1770-1850)."Ode: Intimations of Immortality From Recollections of Early Childhood" (1803-1806)

Shirlè never seemed to be frightened by any of her metaphysical experiences *(a trait of hybrids[29]and wanderers);* she seemed comfortable, at ease with it. *And since psychic happenings are often connected to previous visitations from aliens—could this have been a factor in being "chosen?"*

There were metaphysical incidents during her two pregnancies. It is interesting that not only Shirlè's family, but also Hymie's, experienced the paranormal, and when her in-laws' spirits came to visit, Shirlè interacted with them.

A Sister-in-Law's Precognition

At twenty-two, while eight months pregnant with her first child, Shirlè had a visit from Hymie's youngest sister, ten-year-old Libbila. She was blond, unlike her dark-haired siblings, and serious, like an old soul.

---

[29] A cross between a human and an alien.

She stood, quietly observing Shirlè, and then sat down across from her. "Let me feel your belly," she said as she leaned forward.

Shirlè obliged. Libbila beamed, thrilled with the idea of the life within. Then she leaned back in her chair and her face became serious. "I have something to tell you," she said. "You're going to have a beautiful little girl. And I'm glad you married Hymie. He's the best of my brothers, my favorite."

Shirlè was speechless. A ten-year-old talking like that?

"And you're going to know something others don't know," she continued. "You will have wonderful and incredible experiences in the future and learn many things," she said, "but don't tell your in-laws about them."

Confused, Shirlè tried to dismiss her, not knowing what to think, but Libbila went on. "You have to watch yourself," she said, "because you don't always see the bad in people who could hurt you. I'm telling you all this," she said, "because I'm going to die. Nobody knows it, but I have a lump in my stomach."

Doctors could find nothing wrong with Libbila. She finally told them to look in her stomach, and it was discovered she had a cancerous growth that had spread. She died a few months later.

Libbila's forecast about Shirlè's in-laws[30] seemed to come true not long afterwards. One sister-in-law would mock her for driving a car, another for going back to school. What followed was Shirlè's first audible message from "beyond."

Hearing Precognitive Messages from Libbila on the "Other Side"

Thank goodness the terrible nausea she had suffered throughout the pregnancy was over. But she was scared—it was time for delivery. If only Hymie could be there for support…

Suddenly Shirlè heard her name being called. It was her dead sister-in-law Libbila[31]: "Shirlè," she said, "you are going to have two severe pains, and then you will deliver."

Sure enough, after two very painful contractions, she gave birth to her daughter Sharon[32]. She was surprised at the depth of feeling coming over her, overwhelming her with awe and love.

---

[30] Over the years the attitude of her in-laws changed, as they learned more of metaphysics and were more accepting of her.
[31] Her first communication from the dead.

Libbila's spirit came to her again a few months into her second pregnancy. "Shirlè," she said clearly, "we're[33] going to take Ma. Promise me to look after Pa for us, because he's going to be very helpless without her."

She promised, though she and Hymie would be moving from their basement apartment to a far-away section of town. A week later her mother-in-law, Rosa, died suddenly. If she was ill she never told anyone. As promised, Hymie's father came to live with them.

The Departed Soul of Rosa in Solid Form

Close to her due date, Shirlè had her third visit from the "other side," this time in the physical. Shirlè was in bed with Hymie when all of a sudden, Hymie's dead mother, Rosa, appeared by her side. Shirlè loved and admired her mother-in-law and they were happy to see each other. Rosa was clearly a solid body, dressed in a light green blouse and large white apron with an embroidered pocket. She began caressing Shirlè's huge belly.

"Wake up, Hymie," said Shirlè, "your mother's here."

"That's good," he said, without looking, and fell back asleep. Rosa gave Shirlè a strong hug and kiss—then her solid body became invisible.

Hearing voices was one thing. Now her dead mother-in-law was doing one better than Libbila—visiting her in the physical. Luckily, Shirlè did not fear the dead in solid form. Neither did she think she was going crazy (unlike the boy in the movie *Sixth Sense*). But what was happening here? Was it her own ability as a receiver or the ability of the sender, or a combination of both that made it possible? And where did it come from?

At the time she paid little attention to it, for to her, it seemed normal. If family members are contacted as well, which is usually the case, they too, may have such experiences. Perhaps the talent is hereditary.

Family Paranormal Experiences:

Shirlè's sister Mary also had peeks into other dimensions such as visits from dead people. Like Shirlè, she kept it to herself growing up, never telling her parents or siblings. Not until many years later did Shirlè and Mary confide in each other, yet they still withheld it from their

---

[33] God and his helpers.

parents. There was the fear of revealing the paranormal, the fear of being labeled crazy.

Attachment to the Physical Realm

"Now my friend has departed from this strange world a little ahead of me. That signifies nothing. For us believing physicists, the distinction between past, present and future is only an illusion, however persistent."—Albert Einstein.

"The soul lies where thoughts come from, where interpretations and meanings are given, where action is generated. It is not in the brain in a physical or chemical form; the soul merely uses the body to express itself"
—Deepak Chopra.

Lessening one's attachment to the physical... Was this another requisite for contact and a mission? Frank had told Arne when he was getting ready for Australia, that if Shirlè didn't lessen her attachment to her belongings, "they" were going to "take" her.

Shirlè's story is a reminder we all must let go of attachment not only to physical belongings, but to people we love. And Shirlè was quite attached; she struggled with it; it wasn't easy for her. She hated to give up things she loved. Worse, she had to face losing the man she loved, then her father.

***

Years passed and Hymie and Shirlè moved to another house in Montreal. Only their son Ronny, just finishing high school, was still at home. Their married daughter Sharon[34] lived close by. One day they bought the most beautiful new diningroom set she had ever seen— bleached wood, Spanish style, and very elegant. How she loved that set, and with drapes her father made, the house was their little palace. It "spoke" to her. It became part of them. In it she felt surrounded by love. For her son's bar-mitzvah she joyfully made a mural of Montreal on a basement wall.

So she was surprised, when, five years later, Hymie wanted to sell the house. How could he ask her to give it up?

Only when he finally told her his dream, did it all make sense. He

---

[34] Sharon, married with two grown children today, works as a nurse and is now a grandmother. "I'm the luckiest mother to have a daughter like her," said Shirlè. She's more than a daughter--she's my friend, my confidante, my everything. And so wise. I'm so proud of her."

dreamt he was told to put his house in order, because "they" (God and his helpers) were going to take him. At forty-six, he was ill with serious heart trouble. He hid the severity of it from Shirlè, not wanting her to worry. He was preparing her for the inevitable, wrapping up finances, taking care of everything. But she was in denial; she didn't want to hear it.

He tried to teach her acceptance. "I learned one thing on this planet," he said, as he took her in his arms, "and that is to accept what life has given me and make the most of that, and not wish for things that are impossible to obtain."

But she didn't really understand it, wasn't ready for it.

***

They moved into a simple one-bedroom apartment, in anticipation of Shirlè living alone. Her favorite piece of furniture was too big for the apartment and had to be sold. The dining room set she had always loved, she was now forced to give up. In a bittersweet way she learned that you can't have things for too long—otherwise the things you think you possess, possess you.

Shortly thereafter, Shirlè held an art exhibit. A man by the name of Fred Herscovitch bought one of her paintings from the exhibit manager. Two weeks later he phoned.

"You are searching for the truth," he said in a matter-of-fact tone. Shirlè was silent, taken by surprise. "I'd like to talk to you," he continued. "When can I see you?"

Hymie had to go to the bank, and said goodbye, he'd see her soon. Shirlè, in turn, said she was seeing Herscovitch and would return shortly.

They shook hands as he invited her in. He was a young man in his twenties, unshaven, with long hair, unusual in Montreal in those days. Known as a budding artist, he also played the piano, and wrote poetry. He showed her where he had hung the painting. "I couldn't afford it," he said, "but I just had to have it. It was a present from my father."

Suddenly, she had a gnawing pensive feeling that she couldn't quite pin down. She knew it had nothing to do with Hershcovitz, but at home. Still, she squashed the feeling. She wanted to hear what the young man had to say.

He went to the piano, played some classical, and Shirlè relaxed a bit. Then he got up and took a chair facing Shirlè. "You're searching for the truth," he said once more.

"How do you know?"

"Look," he said, "I'm an artist. Look at the painting, look how you left holes in there. You didn't see it as complete, because, for you, it isn't. You are searching for the 'whole' and I sense this." He got up, picked up a book from the shelf and returned.

"Read this," he said, handing her "Cosmic Consciousness" by Raymond Bucke. "You'll get some answers."

It was Ronny who found Hymie at home, sitting in a chair. "He's not dead!" screamed Shirlè hysterically as the medics took him to the hospital. He was pronounced dead on arrival.

Grieving was enough to go through, but more shocks to her psyche were to follow.

Losing Financial Security

A few months after Hymie passed on, Shirlè's best friend's husband asked if she would loan them her inheritance from her husband. And she lost it all. She didn't sue. She felt that *HaShem*, God would look after her somehow. Fortunately, she still had Hymie's pension. She kept working at Irene's boutique, but only part-time. She *had* to have time to paint. It helped her in her grief.

A few days after Hymie's death, she called Fred Herscovitch. He tried to comfort her, but what do you say to one who has lost a soul-mate? He recommended she attend the Agni Yoga Group. She never did see the guru who led the group. Each time she tried, something prevented it. Later, she understood that help from the guru would have prevented her from learning to be on her own.

A Consoling Apparition—Then a Life-Changing Vision

"There are no justified resentments. Send blame out of your life. You are here because of the choices you've made."—Dr. Dwayne Dyer.

It seems there was another pre-requisite for meeting Frank— working towards being more compassionate and forgiving. How could she carry out her mission with friction in her personal life? More broadly, how can we expect to have peace in the world when there's resentment and little compassion in our own private world?

Shirlè had made a lot of progress in her relationship with her mother.

She was beginning to see her mother from a parent's point of view. Still, she would sometimes revert to her old ways. There was still conflict. Her super-sensitivity, stubbornness, and inability to get along with her mother caused her suffering well into her thirties and forties. What Shirlè had to learn is that it's not what happens to you or how you are treated that's important, but your reactions to it. At the time, however, it was difficult for her. She had to learn that she couldn't change her mother—only herself. It was her choice.

But first she needed to be comforted, assured that she was loved—and a woman materialized in her room.

The Apparition

The only time Shirlè could paint was in the middle of the night while the family slept. Still, it was difficult to find time for everything—the housework, the meals, the laundry, the kids and their needs. Hymie played "mother" and "father" (as their daughter called it), when she could not be there for them, but it was still difficult—attending college classes and studying at night, especially with her mother voicing disapproval.

One night, instead of studying for upcoming exams, she was lying in bed upset because her mother had just criticized her lifestyle. "You're neglecting your duties with your *ambitions*," she chastised. "What do you need a degree for? And art! Better you should quit school and take care of your husband and children, like a normal wife and mother."

A grown woman—and her mother was still trying to control her! She felt angry, then deeply despondent. She didn't care anymore. School, the children, the home, no time to paint… It was all too much.

Suddenly a woman appeared close to her bed. She reminded Shirlè of a teacher she once had: forty-five or so, nondescript facial features except for very large dark eyes, hair in a bun, an open long black coat over a long skirt and white blouse. Shirlè stared apathetically.

"Get up," said the woman in a determined voice.

When Shirlè still did not move, the woman climbed into bed with her and cradled her. Her arms were soft and warm and comforting. But Shirlè could hear the children in the background. "You'd better get out of here," she warned the spirit. "You'll frighten the kids."

The woman smiled, kissed her lightly on the cheek and became invisible. One of God's helpers, she figured, had come to give her hope.

It was Shirlè's first experience of an entity other than a known deceased family member, materializing and then dematerializing.

Vision of The Chastising Teacher: (alien, spirit guide or angel?)
She had always been sheltered. Without Hymie, she wondered, how strong, how weak would she be? Though Hymie had built up her confidence, she really wasn't that strong, she realized, if things her mother would say could still hurt her.

Again, she was lying in bed, feeling depressed and unloved by her mother. She got up, went to the livingroom, and spread out on the carpet. She stared in amazement as the ceiling above her disappeared, revealing the sky. It was the most beautiful blue she had ever seen—a blue she could not describe. And against it was the huge figure of a man standing behind a lectern wearing a black graduation type cap and gown. She watched as he unrolled a white scroll revealing large black Hebrew letters. Somehow it reminded her of Daniel in the Bible and the "handwriting on the wall."

"I know," he said, "you don't understand Hebrew, but *if you don't change your life and learn to get along with your mother, we're going to take you.*"

And she understood that "taking her" meant she would die. The vision changed her attitude. From then on she wasn't so sensitive to remarks from her mother, so defensive, so always on guard, ready to react. She decided not to talk back or argue like she used to. She would try to be kinder to her mother, more loving, no matter how she was treated by her. She would accept what her mother would tell her. Let it be, she told herself.

She finally changed her way of thinking, and incidents that once made her very defensive, didn't bother her as much. She was learning to be more compassionate with her mother, more forgiving. She was on the way to being "ready" for Frank.

***

As I see it, Frank "chose" Shirlè for definite reasons. Firstly, for her art mission she had to have a *strong purpose* and she did; her conscious focus on art. She also had an *unconscious purpose* for her main and important mission—her personality as a "wanderer" or "star child". There was also the story of her birth, and Dr. Sprinkle's regression of her in which she agreed to go to Earth with a mission, Frank made it clear that for these missions Shirlè needed to be strong, self-sufficient, unattached to the material, and compassionate. Hymie had already given her love and support, building up her confidence and self-esteem. But she still needed to be readied for the missions, so Frank guided her with tests and lessons. With the loss of Hymie, her father, and money, she learned to lessen attachments; in Australia she learned to be self-sufficient, and the friction with her parents helped her to grow spiritually—to be strong and more compassionate.

She already had, before Frank, two other traits that were possible factors in being "chosen"—awareness of synchronicities and an understanding of the metaphysics/alien connection.

Whether her paranormal experiences were the *cause* or the *result* of alien contact—or *both*—apparently she had the right "vibrations"—a deep love for the Creative Force—and a deep desire for spiritual learning. Not that she has achieved super-spirituality; like all of us, she struggles with the shadow side. And like all of us, she fumbles and falls every so often, as she did (in Part III) sometime after Frank left.

Photos Pertaining to the Story

To view photos in color, go to the artist's website

www.nsartists.ca/shirlekleincarsh

The Embryos
See page 26

Newfounland Painting
See page 26

Austrailian Gallery
See page 39

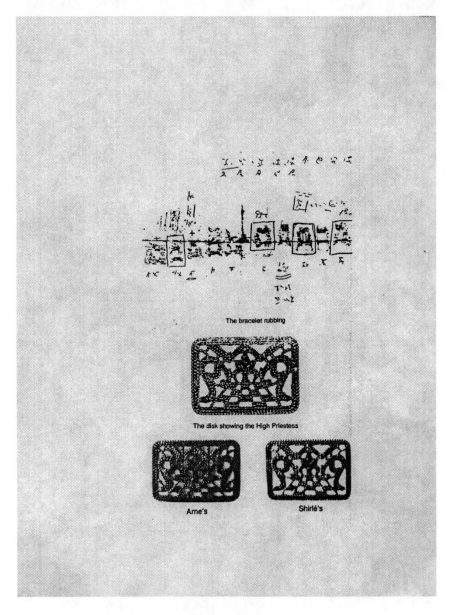

The bracelet rubbing

The disk showing the High Priestess

Arne's

Shirlé's

Frank's Alien Writing, With Bracelet and Disks
(see page 42)

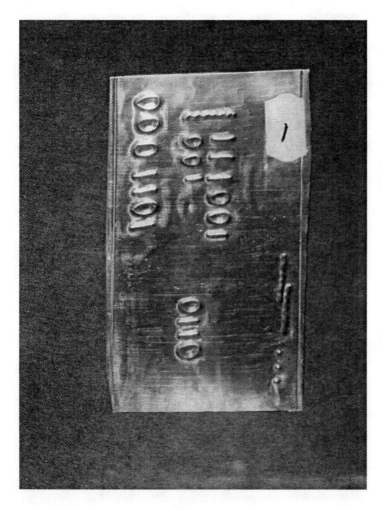

Plate 1
See page 50

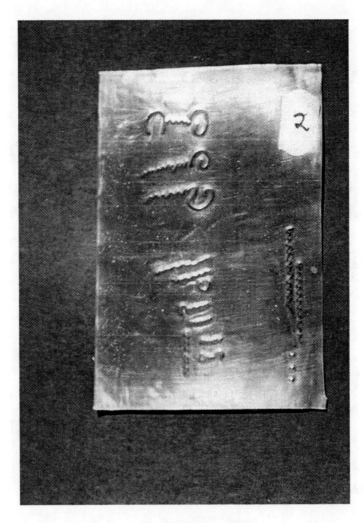

Plate 2
See page 50

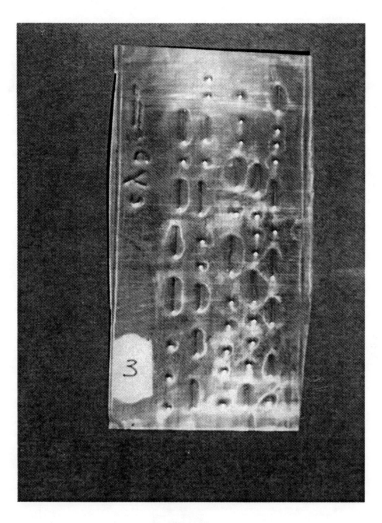

Plate 3
See page 50

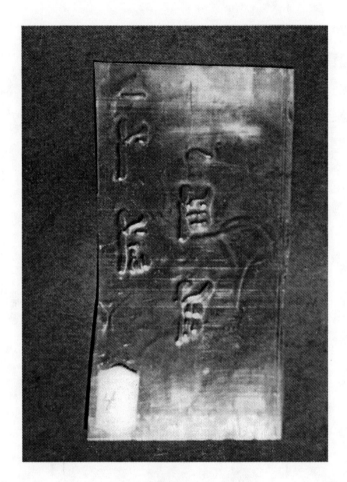

Plate 4
See page 50

Plate 6 (Plate 5 missing)
See page 50

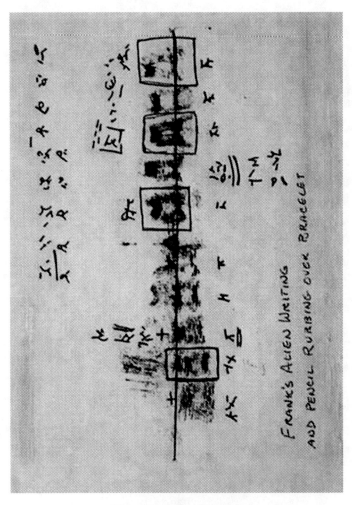

Frank's Alien Writing

Shirlè at Art Gallery

Black Woman Pottery
See page 134

Alien with Spokes
See page 158

Reno and Vegas from Air
See page 166

Shirlè at Holiday Inn AZ

Iceland Posts
See page 170

Skirt Stamp
See page 170

Shirlè at Home

Visiting other planets and other dimensions

To view photos in color go to the artist's website:
www.nsartists.ca/shirlekleincarsh

3 Girls 2 Suns

Children of Light

City of Thought

Concrete City

Figures Dancing

Floating City of Sirius

Gigantic Figure

Group of Children

Pods of Pluto

Three and a Pet

Yin and Yang

Sons of God and Earth Women

PART III

Life After Frank

Chapter Eleven

Yannish
"So which planet are you from?"

"Everything in the universe has its appropriate place—
every event its appropriate hour."—Alien Frank.

It was now three years since Frank had left, six years since Hymie and her father had died—and Shirlè was lonely. Frank had told her that before she would remarry, there would be someone she would live with. And there was. It was Yannish. She wondered at first, if somehow it had been a mistake, because living with him was so difficult.

But there are no mistakes. She realized it was in the two years with Yonnish that she further developed her art and began a new way of painting, of expressing herself, as Frank had foretold. It was with Yannish that she had to face squarely that there were people who looked upon the whole subject of metaphysics and UFOs as evil. It was with Yannish that it was brought home to her that there is a price for everything as she struggled with her conscience on how to leave him. And it was with Yannish that she experienced bilocation where a person is in two places at once..

***

Shirlè opened the door of the ceramic store and stepped inside. The owner turned from his glazes and powders, leaned against the wall and stared at her.

She looked him over. The man was young, rather short, with brown hair, and unremarkable, nondescript features... She was not too impressed.

"So which planet are you from?" he said with a slight smile.

Were those the key words to make her take notice? She was dressed simply in slacks and blouse, not in any strange artist's attire, so she knew he wasn't making fun of her appearance.

"Which planet do you *think* I come from?" she countered.

"A strange planet," he said, cocking his head, as if he knew something she didn't know.

"Well, I'd like to get to know you better," said Shirlè, intrigued. She figured he knew something of UFOs and aliens and wanted to talk about those things. However, she soon found out his interest in her was in another area. (Years later she asked Yannish why he had made those remarks. He answered that he had no idea why.)

***

They had met in a roundabout way, with the town of White Rock, B.C. playing its part. When she had lived there with Arne, she had attended a portrait painting class. There she met Irene, a fellow artist, and the two became friends—but not close enough that Shirlè would confide her alien experiences. One had to be careful—it took time to trust another.

Deciding one day to visit Irene, Shirlè drove from her apartment in Vancouver to White Rock. Irene happened to be all out of material she needed for her art project. "Could you do me a favor," she said. "Could you get it for me at the ceramic store?"

And so Shirlè met Yannish and they dated. One day he mentioned that White Rock would be a good place to live. It was small, on the sound, and attracted artists. Besides, his shop was there.

Shirlè then remembered what Frank had said years earlier, "You haven't stayed long enough..." He had paused, reluctant to say exactly *where*. But she knew it was White Rock and understood Frank wasn't allowed to say it. Now she realized that Yannish was playing his part in getting her back to White Rock. She was fulfilling her karma, though she had no idea what it was all about.

So Shirlè found a house close to where she and Arne had lived in White Rock. It was old, and ready to be condemned, but the porch facing the ocean made up for it. On it stood her easel, and from it she spotted a few UFOs. Soon Yannish moved in with her.

The house was cozy. Taking the place of a heater were a huge antique oil stove and hot plate. At odd times, artist friends, writers, or musicians milled about. Heated discussions emanated from the rooms on religion, politics, paranormals or UFOs. Sometimes, returning from teaching an art class, she would find friends sitting on the doorstep, waiting to show and discuss their work.

Yannish introduced her to the outdoors—gold-panning, something she would never have done. And he was a caring person, driving a long distance to get her sister's medicine. But most importantly, he gave her a much needed job, that of helping him run the store. He taught her a good deal about art—how to use the spray gun, how to experiment with clay, how to do background a certain way with a brush, how to get certain effects. He made and paid for a newspaper advertisement for her art show at the Arts Club, helped her in the exhibition and worked hard making her frames. He did much to help her. Inspired, and with his encouragement, she produced two large murals and a huge painting of an African woman with clay pots. **(See photo middle of book.)**

It was during this time she discovered "a new way of painting" as Frank had foretold, a new style—one eye, one foot—to communicate the idea of "oneness," and an appreciation and reverence for the Creator. It opened up for her a whole new way of seeing things.

"Where shall I go from here?" she mused one day. "The world's my oyster. I'm a creator—a co-creator with the Creator." She was on a "high," expressing her feelings more freely now on canvas. She wondered if she could have done it without Yannish's help.

Frank's second prophecy, that there would be someone before she would eventually marry would also come true, for in time she knew she did not want to marry Yonnish. Another side to him had become evident, and she knew she would not be happy.

She had brought with her to White Rock her spiritual and alien books—books she had had for many years. Placed openly on a shelf, Yannish had made no remark on them. However, one day, when she returned from an errand, they were all gone.

"Where are my books?" she said, calmly, thinking he had a better place for them.

"I threw them into the ocean," he replied matter-of-factly.

"How could you?!" she screamed.

"They're of the devil," he said. "Those books are turning your head."

When they had first met, she told him she believed in aliens, and he had said he did too. She thought they had aliens and art in common. Later, realizing she was serious, he told her he had thought she was just kidding, and because he wanted to be with her, he had played along.

Now he was telling her that her "alien" experiences were the work of the devil—she was most likely possessed by demons—and he was saving her by throwing out the books.

Worse, he was obsessed with Shirlè, and was jealous of her friends. In the two-and-a-half years they lived together, he watched her constantly, attentive to the point of smothering. He had to know what she was doing every moment.

And she couldn't talk about metaphysical things, as she had hoped. She tried. "You know," she said one day, "when you sleep you can travel to different places."

He looked at her, his eyes wide. "I thought you were nuts before," he said, "and now I know for sure."

He came home one evening as she sat at her easel. "I thought I told you," he said, "that blue goes there."

"Too bad," she said, "I don't feel that color."

Angry and hurt, he didn't speak to her for a week. His silence was hard to bear, and she didn't laugh the way she used to, as little by little she was being made to submit.

She had another worry. She had bought more UFO and spiritual books to replace the ones he threw out—would he find their hiding place? She couldn't relax.

"What's the matter with you," said her sister in a worried tone. "You're not the same person anymore!" And when someone remarked that her usual joyfulness had gone, she knew she should leave him.

But how? He was so attached to her—leaving him, she felt, would hurt his male ego. He was already supersensitive from past hurts. His previous wife had left him and Shirlè didn't want to hurt him even more and incur more karma for herself. At the same time she was thankful for his help. She felt she needed the security of the job, the money it brought, and his half of the house rent. If she left him and the house, she would lose her job, and have to once more find work and a place to live. Yes, she appreciated his help, but she just didn't want to live with him anymore. She was in conflict.

"Please, dear God," she prayed, "show me the way to say goodbye to him." And not long afterwards, a "voice" told her what to do. She was to play a game for a compromise solution.

At the time, she had an art exhibit scheduled in France, so before leaving for Paris, she put all her newly collected UFO and metaphysical books in a place one would likely hide things, knowing he would look for and find them. When she returned, he picked her up from the airport, and proceeded to drive her home.

"How's everything?" asked Shirlè.

"So-so," he said. So she figured he had found the books and was upset. She acted as if nothing was the matter, chatting about Paris, but he remained subdued. In answer to simple questions he gave only a "yes" or "no".

When they arrived home, Shirlè saw that her books were missing.

"Where are my books?" she cried, pretending to be surprised. "They're gone!"

"I threw them out, like the others," he said. "They're the work of the devil."

"No, they're not!"

"They're evil!" he shouted.

He took down his suitcase and began to pack. "What are you doing?" she asked in feigned innocence. Then, pretending she realized he was leaving, she wept. It was the best performance of her life. The more she cried, the quicker he packed. "Don't go. Please don't go," she begged. "I can't sleep alone."

But he had had enough. He was ending the relationship. He closed the suitcase, said goodbye and left in his truck.

She could have kissed the floor in gratitude. "God, I thank you," she said.

He didn't call the next day, Sunday, or Monday. Wednesday was her scheduled day to work for him. Tuesday the phone rang. "I've decided to raise your wages because you have to pay the full rent now."

"You mean I'm still working for you?"

"One thing has nothing to do with the other," he said. "I need you at work."

She went to work and he was cordial, and asked her to go to dinner with him when work was over. She had dinner with him, then he went to his place and she went to her house. On Friday it was the same. Nothing but small talk passed between them. Saturday came and the phone rang.

"How come you haven't asked me to come back?"

"Because I'm doing very well on my own," she replied.

By leaving the books where he would find them, she felt she had left the decision up to him, and he had chosen to leave. Thus, she found a compromise—she saved his male ego and she didn't lose her job.

The Bilocation of Yannish

Bilocation is imagining with intense focusing. The unconscious mind sends a double by astral projection which is viewed by someone in another location while the sender's conscious mind is usually unaware.

There is probably also the component of telepathy between the two minds. Edmund Gurney, one of the pioneers of the Society for Psychical Research included in his book *Phantasms of the Living* the result of experiments done by S. H. Beard in 1881, where "apparitions of the living" or bi-locations, were solid enough to interact with people and move objects—and be taken for normal living persons.

It was January 30, 1976. With Yannish gone, Shirlè was having the usual trouble sleeping alone, but finally she slept. At 3 a.m. she awoke with a start. She felt someone was in the room looking at her, though the door and windows were locked. Then she saw the form. As it came closer, she realized it was not from the spirit world, as she first thought, but of a living person of this world—for it was Yannish. His astral body was porous, not completely solid, but his facial features, shirt and pants, were clearly recognizable.

After a moment of shock she collected herself. "It's okay, God," she whispered. "He wants to see me so badly, let him come." He got into bed with her, and she felt his warmth as he tenderly held her. Then he vanished.

Considering how attached he was to her, Shirlè wasn't entirely surprised to see him. She knew that desire is a force in itself, and can move mountains.

But "senders" do not always get "receivers" like Shirlè. Apparently her vibratory rate not only could receive while out of body or in dreams, but as in this case, physically, while wide awake. Yannish, the sender, apparently went out of body. He then became solid enough to react with Shirlè, while his physical body remained in his bed.

Yet ironically, he believed that metaphysical phenomena were of the devil. At first she was afraid to question him about it. Months later, however, she did ask him, and he strongly denied that he could have been in her room. So she figured he was either conscious of it, denying having willed it, or was completely unconscious of it, which was more likely the case. It was her first and only experience of bilocation—she had viewed a living person being in two places at once.

***

Yannish had been kind enough to raise her pay after he left, knowing she had to pay the full rent, but she felt he'd done it in hopes of getting back with her. He was so obsessed with her, he even hired an artist to paint a picture of her which he hung over his bed. He took her out regularly, and was good to her. She kept seeing him because she didn't want to hurt him. Perhaps it was also because she didn't want to be alone. One way or another, she realized, there were prices to pay, and depression was one of them.

After Yonnish, Shirlè went on with her life, worked, taught art, and had a social life. On the surface she appeared busy, cheerful and content. Inside, however, was another story.

Chapter Twelve

The Dark Night of the Soul
and the Power of Gratitude

"The mind is its own place, and in itself can make heaven of hell, a hell of heaven."—Milton in *Paradise Lost*

"What do I mean by loving ourselves properly? I mean, first of all, desiring to live, accepting life as a very great gift and a great good, not because of what it gives us, but because of what it enables us to give others."- Thomas Merton

"If the only prayer you say your entire life, is 'Thank you,' it is enough."
-- Meister Eckhart.

Nothing and no one could give her a sense of belonging. Yannish had been gone for over a year and she felt relieved, but she didn't have anyone else who interested her. She didn't want for dates. Men kept calling but she refused to go out with them. They would soon want to sleep with her and she didn't want the whole scene. She returned to Montreal and looked up two male friends but nothing seemed to work. She was waiting for the *one*—the one who would say the magic words.

"At least he should be interested in UFOs!" she told a friend. "Once I went with a guy I liked, and I started talking about aliens, and he said 'I'm going to tell you right now, I like you a lot, but I don't like you *that* much!'"

She missed Hymie and resented that he had been "taken". She hated to be alone. If she was talking to someone's husband, the wife would see her as a threat. She functioned better in a marriage, having the protection of a man.

But there was more to it, of course. When five years had passed and Frank had not returned as promised, she grew anxious and depressed. She missed him terribly. Would he ever come back? She remembered how Frank had wanted to take on her karma, and his superiors had said "no," she had to go through it herself, experience things first hand, so that she would have empathy. Well, she was alone now, struggling to support herself, struggling to be an artist. She was learning empathy.

All the while, the idea of her mission weighed heavily on her mind. She wondered if she could live up to what was required. She knew that she had to change, but she was afraid of that change. Yet if she were to do her mission, she had to. It meant not relying on others for everything, as she was used to. She would have to stand on her own two feet, and that frightened her. Hymie, Frank, others, had always helped her. If things got a little difficult living alone after Yonnish left, she was ready to give up. She was very insecure. She had a low image of herself, although she tried desperately to hide it. She was good at everything she did, yet she still felt inadequate.

At her hairdresser's one day, she proudly showed some photos of her artwork.

"I don't know anyone who would buy your work," said one woman. "I think it's terrible."

"Well, you don't have to buy it," retorted Shirlè in anger, "others will!" But at home she broke down. "Maybe it's really no good," she cried into her pillow. "Maybe they're right!"

More than once, in despair, she had wanted to destroy all her paintings. But then she'd think of Frank and how he insisted she leave all but four paintings when she went to Australia.

"Why?" she had asked.

"Because your paintings are important," he had said. "There are messages in each one."

Bravely, but fruitlessly, she would send out her work to different galleries. One day, however, in a Vancouver gallery, she heard the familiar "I'm sorry we can't use your work" once too many times. At home, she threw herself on the bed and wept. "I'm already forty-seven. I've given my life to this, and for what?!" In a way she was like the children of Israel waiting for Moses to come back, and she had lost faith.

She felt abandoned by HaShem—and yes, abandoned by Frank.

And one day, she was *really* depressed, "at the end of her rope." She hadn't confided her feelings to anyone, not even to her daughter Sharon, with whom she was so close. She felt unsuccessful as an artist, and fearful of confiding her alien experience to friends. Who would believe her? She felt so alone.

She worked herself up and began to fantasize. What was she waiting for? She should end it all. She simply didn't care anymore. She would take poison. But then she'd be in such agony and pain by the time they would come to pump it out—so what was the point?

One evening while returning home from visiting Sharon in Vancouver, she was driving her car through the Dees Tunnel. She knew what she would do, she said to herself; she would bang the car against the wall of the tunnel. But cars were behind her and she would involve them. So she left the tunnel and entered the regular freeway, and figured she would stop the car suddenly and let someone bang into *her*. But that wasn't good—she didn't want to hurt that person either, and it would be her luck that the car would be totaled and all she would get would be a broken leg. So, what's the use?

She went back to her house, stood on her balcony and looked out at the ocean. As she watched, the surf was dragging in debris from the beach, then moments later throwing it all out onto the sand. All the while, the rolling waves were throwing a log towards the shore, little by little. Then and there she came to the realization—she had to eliminate her negative thoughts, throw them out, little by little, just as the sea tossed the debris onto the shore.

On Gratitude

She regained her faith in God. God had always been there for her. She had always listened to the little voice inside her—to love everyone, be of service to mankind, to think not only of oneself.

And she realized she had been thinking only of herself. Like a child, she wanted certain things and wasn't getting them, wasn't being fulfilled, and she was angry. And then it hit her... "If I cared for HaShem," she asked herself, "how could I even think of it? Instead of being grateful for what I *do* have... I had forgotten God, forgotten family and friends. I was self-absorbed. All I could think of was me, me, me!"

She realized her ego had taken over. She walked onto the beach, sat on a log and wept. "I could sink that low," she mumbled between tears—

"after all I had, all HaShem had given me. I should have been thankful, happy—I was growing, developing. I was getting to know my real self."

She wandered further along the sandy beach and came to a rocky prominence. And there, on top of it, was a lone flower, miraculously surviving. "My God HaShem," she cried, "You are incredible!"

It was then she remembered what Frank had said: "If you ever think of suicide, the rope will break." And it reminded her of her mission. She was here for a purpose.

***

Then she met artists who complimented her work. She started to believe more in herself and be more patient. Didn't Frank say that she was a futurist, that her work may not be accepted in her lifetime, but that nevertheless she had to continue?

She began to paint. Immediately she was in another dimension and the sadness evaporated. Suicide, anger, misery did not exist. She was in total bliss, in total connection with HaShem. Suddenly a great idea for a painting popped into her head. "My God, HaShem," she said, "how do you come up with this stuff? *I* couldn't think of it. But you planted it in me and I thank you so much for that. I don't care if nobody likes it. *I* do. You didn't give me this gift for nothing. I will wait for Your time, and I will do the best I can, and I will keep on painting, because everything has a time, and maybe the time is now."

Chapter Thirteen

Fred –"I Know You"
And Strange Incidents

"Synchronicity is the awareness of the usefulness for your benefit
of a person or object that directs you on your path."—Deepak Chopra

Meeting Fred

Painting helped, but she was still lonely. She longed for a mate. And when she no longer pined, it happened. Synchronicity was operating once more; she was being guided, slowly, one step leading to another. And the first step came, eight months after Yannish left—in the form of a call from a psychic friend in White Rock.

***

She was sitting in the kitchen nursing a cup of tea when the phone rang. "I had a dream," said her psychic friend, "telling me you should move to North Vancouver."

"Well, it will have to wait, Maureen," replied Shirlè "I'm not ready to move. I love this place."

But Shirlè had a phobia about mice, and when one appeared in her home one day, and again the next day, she took it as a sign and finally decided to leave. She gave up the house she loved in White Rock and as her psychic friend advised, found an apartment in North Vancouver. Thankfully, Morton, one of her art friends, got his buddies to move her. She didn't have much furniture, just a lot of paintings, books, and plants.

Shirlè not only talked to animals, but trees and plants. One in particular, a cactus, is in her home to this day. She had cared for it from a tiny plant and became attached to it. In its first four to five years it had grown very tall and straight. She spoke to it, cried to it, confessed her desires and needs to it, and she felt it "understood[35]. While moving Shirlè's plants from one place to another, the tall cactus broke in half. Shirlè cried, apologized to the plant, and tried taping it together. When it didn't work she gave the broken-off piece to Morton. Was she really so strange, she wondered, that everyone there laughed at her?

***

The move to North Vancouver turned out to be a turning point in Shirlè's life. She knows now that she was guided. If she hadn't moved there, she might not have met her next husband, Fred. But at the time, she had to be pulled and nudged to where she would meet him, so synchronicity could do its job.

It was November 1978, and Amyra, the daughter of Shirlè's friend Shirlèy, was having a baby shower. Shirlèy begged Shirlè to accompany her, but not knowing any of the others, Shirlè was reluctant. Finally she agreed.

There she was introduced to Fred Carsh, the father of the mother-to-be. When it was time to leave, he asked her if she needed a ride home. She thanked him and told him she had already asked his daughter, Ilana, for a ride. She was afraid to accept; she had already met his ex-wife months before and had heard only very derogatory remarks about him.

Also, during this time, she had written to a rabbi in New Jersey and mentioned she had promised her mother she would marry a Jewish man. He replied there may be a man for her there. As he requested, she sent a photo of herself and a little of her background, omitting, however, her

---

[35] Peter Tomkins author of *The Secret Life of Plants* relates how a Hindu scientist Jagdish Chandra Bose in 1920 studied plant reaction to stimuli. In 1966, an American researcher, Cleve Backster, did similar experiments on a polygraph. In one, the plant reacted to fire even before the cigarette lighter came close. He concluded, after two years, that plants are telepathic, they sense and react to harm directed towards them or any other living being.

UFO experience. He replied that someone was interested in her. Could she arrange to come to New Jersey to meet the man? She decided she would. She was not interested in Fred, and was preparing to go to New Jersey.

A week later her singles group was sponsoring a dance, and she loved to dance. Fred had never gone to one, but there he was. As they danced a few numbers, he talked with interest on various subjects and books. How, she wondered, could an intelligent man like him do the terrible things his ex-wife had claimed he had done? She would have to find out more about him herself.

That weekend, both had been invited to a singles house party, and she let him take her home. On the freeway they passed a seafood truck. "What if I buy some shrimp," he said, "and you make a salad, and we'll have dinner."

As they dined, he filled her in on his background. He had a happy, loving childhood and youth in Germany, and felt close to his family. His parents had been well off, owning a block-long department store. They were Orthodox Jews, respected in the community. In 1938, at the age of fifteen, Fred and a couple of Jewish boys were attacked by a group of Hitler Youth. When the Jewish boys used their Judo training to beat the Hitler Youth, their lives were in danger and the family had to escape or hide. His father died after "kristalnacht[36]". His sister survived a concentration camp, and his mother survived by hiding in a convent.

Through a Jewish underground organization that rescued children, Fred made it to what was then Palestine, despite a British blockade preventing the entry of Jewish refugees. He then fought with the British in North Africa in the Jewish[37] Brigade. Eventually he had the satisfaction of arriving in Germany with the Brigade just before the end of the war.

He and Rita, a fellow schoolmate and survivor, had been in separate illegal refugee ships[38]. He found her in Haifa, had three children, became

---

[36] The night of "broken glass" when the Nazis smashed, robbed, and burned Jewish businesses and synagogues. He cut himself on the broken glass of his smashed store and didn't survive the infection that resulted.

37 Jews in Palestine who wanted to fight Hitler were not allowed as part of the British forces; he had to wait until, after long negotiation, Jews were allowed to fight as a special unit alongside the British in North Africa.

[38] Hers had been caught by the British. The 2000 refugees in it, rather than be returned to Germany, blew up the ship, and the survivors were smuggled into Palestine. Fred's ship managed to escape the blockade.

an electrical engineer, and in time moved with his family to Vancouver, B.C. However, after many years of marital tension, he and Rita divorced.

The following Wednesday, as she sat in her living room, the phone rang. It was Fred.

"I want to marry you," he said simply.

"You're absolutely crazy," she said, annoyed and bewildered. "We met only two weeks ago. I don't even know you."

"But I know *you*."

Shivers went through her. Those were the words—the key words Frank had said the man she would marry would say!

If Fred had not spoken the magic words, she probably would not have bothered with him, and would have gone to New Jersey. She had only been waiting for the right words and was surprised they came from Fred.

And they came just in time, synchronically stopping her from going in the wrong direction. She took her time however, and little by little, came to really care for him. They were married in 1979 and are still married... after twenty-eight years.

Soon after the marriage Shirlè's mother, visiting, turned to Fred. "With this one," she said, with a tilt of her head, "I wouldn't start up with."

"That's what I like about her," Fred retorted. "She's got spunk, courage, and she says what she thinks, and I admire that."

Two years earlier, Frank had wisely said "You need a special man, Shirlè—a strong man."

"Cause I'd make mincemeat of him?"

"You're right!" he said.

***

Unlike Hymie, Fred gets her to do things on her own. "What if I'm not here?" he would say. So he forces her to do things she would not ordinarily do, like work on the computer—or he reads and explains the directions, and then she's on her own.

"So I've grown up and he treats me like a grown-up," says Shirlè.

He lets her be herself, yet he's his own person—a challenging combination of two strong-minded personalities. She appreciates not only his ability to make a good living as an electrical engineer, but his sensitivity, thoughtfulness, and his many talents and interests—world affairs, gardening, reading, fixing things, model train collecting, cooking, and (a new world for her) camping.

At the same time, he understands her and appreciates her art and spiritual yearnings. If she is painting or her mind is on otherworldly things, he takes care of the down-to-earth necessities. He's a "grounding" for her—a left brain for her right brain—balancing her spiritual and metaphysical interests with his more concrete and earthy view, but with a mind that is always open.

And Shirlè can talk openly with Fred on UFOs and aliens. She can meet others who have had odd experiences, attend lectures, and join groups.

UFO Groups Plus More Strange Incidents

> "Spacemen are guides, not gods, and are not to
> be worshipped or made into a religion."—Alien Frank

Besides attending JORPAH[39], Shirlè was a member of UFO Contact Center International. In 1983, its founders, contactees Eileen and Dan Edwards, were trying to get support groups started nationally, and asked her if she would start one in Vancouver. She easily obtained speakers, became associate director of the group, and the meetings were highly successful for nine years, when she left and others took over.

For the first two years of her UFO group, she was wary of sharing her own "alien" story with the larger UFO community. By 1985, however, she felt it was time so she attended a UFO meeting, and during the intermission, approached the lecturer, Graham Conway. She showed him a copy of Frank's writing she had kept. He was excited, wanting to know more.

She invited him to her home. With him was a UFO investigator from South Africa, David Powell. Her story and the artifacts Frank had given her, the discs, the bracelet, and most fascinating of all—the eight inscribed thin copper plates—impressed them. But it seemed to go no further. Apparently Shirlè wasn't truly believed.

In 1986 she received an invitation to speak before a large community at Prince George in northern B.C. It was her first paid lecture ($50.00 plus airfare and quarters). Today people are more open to the possibilities of aliens here on Earth, but in 1986, the subject was still rather new. The reaction was mixed. Some believed, some were skeptical, most did not know what to make of it. But she was treated with respect.

---

[39] A "gathering" (from Greta Woodrew's book *A Slide of Light*)

Next were lectures here and there, in person and on the radio. She had just finished an art exhibit in Nelson, B.C., and was to give a UFO lecture that evening at the university. Her talk would be broadcast live on local TV. Instead, the station ran a video in that time slot. The station manager was called and was asked why her talk was not televised.

"Something went wrong," the manager explained. "The machine wouldn't work." However, as soon as Shirlè finished her speech, it was all right. Was the station afraid of what she had to say, she wondered, and prevented it? (The area was known as the Bible belt.) Or did the aliens themselves stop it for some reason? Did an overhead invisible UFO cause it—or was it all a mere coincidence? Shirlè wasn't sure what to think.

At each lecture, she learned to stand up more to criticism in public. Once, her lecture centered on the subject of public response. The media, she told the audience, was airing the subject of UFOs more and more, and people could feel the truth behind the cover-ups. In the question and answer period, one woman screamed that Shirlè was dealing with the devil.

"I wouldn't be here if I thought this was evil," replied Shirlè with absolute calm.

"But you could be an ignorant party!"

"No," said Shirlè, "I'm not ignorant in this area."

Today researchers concur that some alien races, though certainly not "from the devil," are not as benevolent as others, their motives questionable, at least in their behavior in abductions and genetic manipulations.

***

Shirlè could understand the disbelief of individuals, but the disbelief of the educated UFO community was what she had to learn to live with. Because of their skepticism of her claimed two-year relationship with an extraterrestrial living on Earth, they seemed to also discount her story of the "scuba divers," the missing times, the possible abductions at ages three and five, the voices, the appearances of the dead in solid and astral form—all her metaphysical experiences—without wondering if they were relevant to UFO and alien activity.

After Frank's departure the strange incidents continued. The following are just a few:

Invisible Marks on Her Body (seen only under black light UV)

At a UFO Contactee Conference in 1978, headed by Dr. Leo Sprinkle in Laramie, Colorado, Shirlè participated in an experiment with a black light UV on the bodies of contactees and abductees. Of those tested, some had the odd one or two marks. But Shirlè's back was covered with them. When she came to the next conference a year later, they greeted her with "Oh, you're the lady with all the marks. Could we show people your back?" She obliged the crowd. Some were fading, but some were fresh.

Ghosts in Solid Form

Up to now, only family spirits with strong emotional ties had come to Shirlè in solid form. Now a little boy, a spirit unknown to her appeared to her in a hotel room, just as in the movie *Sixth Sense* about a child who sees departed *strangers* not as ghostly forms, but as solid bodies.

"Time Slips", Other Dimensions

In an instant, while wide awake and without warning, Shirlè entered the *past*—surprised to find herself an onlooker, viewing people dressed in the late 1890s or early 1900s dancing to the music of a nickelodeon.

Another time the scene before her suddenly changed to running horses of various breeds and colors. And once, the ocean view before her completely disappeared and a strange vase appeared in the windowsill in place of what was actually there—a display of rocks. In each case, moments later, the scene reverted to the "real" world.

An Implant

It was not a dream. Early one morning in 1987, Shirlè awoke to see a long needle being drawn from the back of her head. Intuitively she felt it was not for a sample of something, but was an implant of some kind.

"Another implant[40]?!" she yelled angrily. "Without my permission?! You have no right! I don't care what it's for. Tell me first!"

She was aware of this implant on a *conscious* level. Recently,

---

[40] The spot is still painful to touch.

however, through muscle testing (kinesiology) [41], she became aware of having received an implant at age three and one at five. Also through this procedure, she discovered she may have had, over the years, many implants, put in or removed at different times by the aliens. However, she does not wish to have them removed. She feels they were put in for *her* benefit, as well as theirs.

***

With so many paranormal happenings before, during, and after her relationship with Frank, it was no wonder that supersensitive Shirlè, while appearing happy on the outside, was crying on the inside, never feeling accepted—always feeling different.

And if Shirlè felt different then what came next made her feel *really* different.

Initiations for Those Who Feel "Different" And More Happenings

"An initiation takes one outside society. We don't know if they are aliens or angels or both. But as we receive the contact, and as we learn more about ourselves, we say hey, it's OK that I'm different. Then we step back into society and don't need initiation anymore. Now we help other people go through their initiation."—Dr. Leo Sprinkle.

Wide awake she had a vision. She gazed in wonder as a wreath of white feathers slowly floated down towards her head, then blinked out. Later, she was told by a psychic that this was a hologram of feathers representing air—one of the four elements (air, water, fire and earth) and her first initiation.

Some time later, she was with a Seattle UFO group, in a circle, meditating outdoors. It was raining, and she wore a heavy plastic raincoat. With her eyes closed, she had a vision. She saw a group of Sasquatch[42], standing and observing. Their faces, kind and loving, looked human, though their bodies were very hairy. One who she sensed was male, came over and caressed her forehead and face. She wondered why his hand was dry in the rain so she felt herself. She was not wet, yet she felt rain running down her body. Was this self-hypnosis? She had been in another state of reality where she felt dry when she was actually wet—

---

[41] Through muscle testing (kinesiology) answers to yes or no questions are given by the unconscious using the arm muscles to go up or down.

[42] Another woman sensed the presence of a Sasquatch, but did not visualize it.

the opposite to our reality.

She asked "upstairs" the meaning of all this. And the answer came into her mind, as intuition, that since she accepted all forms of life, the Sasquatch wanted to be the ones to initiate her into the next spiritual step—water.

A year later she experienced another water "initiation." Shirlè had invited a well-known contactee at the time, Gabriel Green, as well as a few friends, to her home for a kind of meditation. Green asked everyone to sit with eyes closed. "I'm going to send someone into orbit," he said. Then after a pause, "It's you, Shirlè."

She envisioned herself floating down through a glass tube into a large UFO. A sliding glass door opened and she entered a hallway where she came upon a few aliens working at computers. She greeted them, and then continued on to a pool of water, understanding she was to go in and swim. "With all my clothes?" she questioned. When she came out, her clothes were dry. (Water which isn't really water has been noted by others as present on other planets.)

Shirlè was by then quite blasé about her "happenings"—as more incidents followed:

Huge Light Diving Into Ocean

In November 1986, Shirlè and her present husband Fred were sightseeing by camper in Australia. They arrived at a small island on the Barrier Reef and obtained cabin quarters. At 3 a.m. Shirlè awoke and went out on the balcony. Suddenly, out of nowhere, a huge light[43] much larger than a full moon, shone above her. At first she thought it was from the lighthouse, but realized it couldn't be, because the lighthouse was on the other side of the island, out of sight. The ball of light hovered for a while, and then suddenly dove cleanly into the ocean. Was it a hologram, she wondered, or was it a real UFO entering an alien underwater base?

Hebrew Writing

On May 12, 1989, Shirlè awoke with a jolt. Black letters of the Hebrew alphabet were on the palm of her right hand, a Star of David on her right wrist. Who or what made it and how? And what did it mean?

---

[43] UFOs can be solid, immaterial and invisible, or appear as lights—depending on their vibration, which they can control.

Fred who spoke Hebrew, having lived in Israel, had just left for work. Unfortunately, it faded within minutes as she sought a translator.

It was the second time Hebrew writing was presented to her. Years earlier she had a vision in which the huge figure of a bearded man unrolled a scroll of Hebrew writing and reprimanded her for not getting along with her mother. Were they both messages from aliens in another dimension, or from the spiritual realm? Or are they one and the same?

Smells—indicating the presence of an entity

Recently Shirlè and I were hiking on a trail in the woods, talking about the book, when a strong smell of corned beef assailed her nostrils, stayed for a minute, then stopped. I, however, smelled nothing. Later, a psychic, knowing nothing of the incident, asked her if she knew anybody who had a butcher shop who had passed on. This departed soul, she said, wants her to know he is sorry he said nasty things about her art; he understands her work now and wants to help her from the other side. While in Australia Shirlè knew a man named Zellinger who later died. He had liked her scenes and portraits but couldn't stand her avant-garde painting and had told her so in no uncertain terms. He had a butcher shop with delicatessen meats.

The next "hello" I believe, came not from a departed soul but from an alien. Shirlè and I were in a motel in Roswell, New Mexico before interviewing a former military man who claimed to be a Roswell witness. As we stood talking of aliens and Roswell a bleeding cut appeared on my finger and a strong smell of cinnamon or some sort of cooking filled the room. The motel had no kitchens and no one was cooking on a hotplate on either side of us when we checked.

Materialization?—The Quill Story

Shirlè was at a psychic fair in Vancouver, B.C., and was standing alone before a glass counter in a booth of American Indian and Metis[44] artifacts attended by Dale, a man who had bought one of her paintings. As he and his girlfriend (also Dale) conversed behind the counter, Shirlè felt a tickle on her thigh but ignored it. Then she received a sharp jab. She looked down and pulled out a porcupine quill sticking through her pants.

---

[44] Half-breed Native American.

"Look at this!" she exclaimed.

"My God!" shouted Dale. "It's been missing for months. I thought I'd never see it again." He gingerly took the quill and opened up the glass counter. "Shirlè," he said, as he placed the quill with the others lying on a velvet pillow, "this is your gift to us. And what a gift! Aliens, spirits, angels, whatever they are—they certainly act in mysterious ways."

But why, she wondered, was she the carrier? Does she have a connection with the Metis? Were Dale and Dale meant to come into her life? Was this a synchronicity she was not yet aware of?

An aside on materialization versus technology: I can't help thinking if thought alone can result in materialization, why bother with machines? In our evolution, the use of thought alone came *before* machines. If the ability were subsequently lost, technology would take its place. Could it be that some alien cultures have already gone through a stage of very high technological achievement—only to find that everything they get their machines to accomplish can be attained with pure thought—thus coming full circle?

Chapter Fourteen

Animals, Departed Souls, Aliens Communicating with Humans and vice versa

"Telepathic communication throughout the universe comes from one cosmic mind. No distance can stop it."—Alien Frank

An Animal Spirit Communicating in a Dream

The Dog Named Blue:

B lue was a dog owned by Shirlè's long-time friend Irene, also an artist. When Shirlè would spend the night at Irene's home in the next town, she would bring the mixed shepherd some left-over meat and bones. He was a rather homely dog, Shirlè thought, but a good soul, devotedly watching over Irene and her house. Finally he passed away.

On one particular visit after Blue's death, Shirlè found herself extremely sensitive to Irene's criticisms—her art needed improvement; she should do it this way or that; why was she always traveling so much—why was she always running?... Shirlè was quiet and polite in response, but inside she was hurting. That night, crying softly, she fell asleep. She dreamt that Blue came to her, his chest open and bleeding, and she felt he understood. His heart was bleeding for her.

"He was a very special dog," Shirlè said as she related the story to me. "Somehow I feel he will evolve to a human." Just then, she stopped speaking and stared. "Hi!" she exclaimed "I just saw a *blue globe*. There's an *entity* by the door!"

At that very moment a strange thing happened. As I sat watching the tape recorder, blood gushed out of the top of my right middle finger. I went to get tissue paper. As I wiped away the blood, a thin laser-like cut was apparent. It was not the first time I had experienced cuts oozing blood *while thinking or talking about aliens*. But I wondered—was the blue globe an alien trying to communicate its presence to us both, or was it the spirit of Blue come to show his love for Shirlè?

It was her first experience of **an animal being used to announce the presence of UFOs, her first participation with people contacting aliens, and it was her first witness of the aliens' reciprocal action.**

Shirlè was at a facility bordering on woods, where people from all over had come for an annual weekend get-together of JORPAH (a UFO group). Early in the evening, two or three people had been meditating, asking to see and communicate with a spacecraft. Then, about midnight, as Shirlè and her friends stood outside conversing, a young fox came up to them.

"We were stroking the fox," said Shirlè, "and I knew then that something big was going to happen." They looked up, and in the sky were six medium-sized white lights lined up forming what appeared to be letters—first "I" followed by a pause. Then it continued, forming "L". After another pause it went on to make the letter "U". The sixty people watching were unanimous in what it meant. Telepathically they felt they had received it as "I love you." They all danced around with excitement. Shirlè yelled for others to come out and see six UFOs in a special formation, but to no avail.

A Semi-corporeal Departed Soul

One night Hymie came to Shirlè in the astral, enveloped in a dim golden light. He stayed in bed with her, hugging her, and she felt his warmth. He caressed her hair, telepathically telling her he had to go. She begged him not to, but he left. Only much later she understood that her constant yearning for him kept bringing him back, preventing his soul from progressing.

The Alien? "Healer"

Some time later, alone and in pain, desperate for help, Shirlè sought contact with aliens. After two years of back pain, some X-rays and a CAT scan showed a slipped disc and arthritis in two vertebrae. Strangely, with all her experiences, Shirlè kept only a dream journal. Nevertheless she scribbled: "1:30 a.m. I can't sleep. God, aliens, anyone… I'm in agony. Help me… please. I promise… And I'll do whatever you ask, whether you help me or not, no matter how much pain."

She fell asleep. A sneeze awakened her just as dawn was breaking. A strange man stood by her bed, head bent over her covered legs. Her first thought was one of relief. Thank goodness they sent someone to help, or at least to reassure her. Was he from another dimension or another planet, she wondered. He reminded her of Danny Kaye, or an elf of normal size, with his curly, light brown hair and artist's smock. His brown pants, she noted, were most unusual—the material filled with loops. And the sneeze—he seemed to want her to be fully aware of him before he vanished.

But she was worse off than before. She cried, exasperated, unable to get out of bed. The pain continued for two weeks before gradually subsiding. When her doctor then re-examined her back, she had no pain on heavy pressure, yet before the "Danny Kaye" incident, the doctor had recommended surgery. "You're okay," he said, looking at the new X-rays. "You don't need surgery." She never again had such severe back pain.

Aliens[45]--and their Reciprocation:

While in Safford, Arizona, Shirlè was visiting her friend Dorothy Braatten[46], whose home is in a vortex (an area of such high vibration that its energy field can allow access to another dimension.) On one particular day both Dorothy and Shirlè could actually see what appeared to be a metallic saucer-shaped UFO in the sky. They initiated communication by

---

[45] "Alien" does not necessarily mean from another planet. It could mean from a parallel reality, some interpenetrating dimension, our past, or our own future.

[46] Dorothy, who had often been contacted by aliens and claimed to have been cured of cancer by them, would sometimes suddenly get a feeling that a UFO was outside. She would get her camera, see nothing, point it somewhere and take a shot. When developed, however, a UFO would be in the picture, (similar to Uri Geller's story in Andrija Puharich's book).

blinking a flashlight toward it, and the UFO responded with a blinking light[47].

My Own Alien Communication Story:

One day as I was working with Shirlè on her experiences, I jokingly blurted out: "I'm jealous, you have all these fantastic experiences and I haven't even seen a measly UFO!"

Shirlè looked at me, her face serious. "Dena, all you have to do is *ask*."

"What do you mean, ask?"

"Just say you want to see one," she said simply.

Well, it so happened that the next day I had to travel two hours away to my ex-husband's home to go over some important papers. I got in the car and said out loud, "Okay you guys. Do you hear me? I want to see a UFO! *Please* show me a UFO!"

I put on the radio, listened to my favorite music, and with my thoughts on my important papers, forgot completely about UFOs. About an hour into going over our papers—suddenly, for no particular reason, I got up, walked over to the window and looked up. And there against a clear pure blue sky—rare for Seattle—was a rectangular pure white object with a black undercarriage moving slower than an airplane. Its edges were clear; it had no tail or wings. I'd seen videos and pictures of "cigar-shaped mother-ships" but none with a clear black underbelly.

"Tom," I said, "look, there's a UFO!"

He came over. "It's an airplane," he said quickly and walked away, disgusted and repulsed that his ex-wife entertained such ideas.

Meanwhile, I kept my eyes on the object. "Okay," I said silently in my head, "if you're really a UFO, *do* something to convince me!" Suddenly it dropped down from the level it was on and then continued on. A moment or so later it simply vanished.

A few weeks later I attended a UFO conference in Nevada, and on the last day a film was shown of various UFOs and there among them was my UFO—exactly as I had seen it!

Aliens Communicating with Humans by Means of Implants and

---

[47] The organization CSETI, in group meditation and chanting, have obtained similar results—the appearance of UFOs in physical or light form, followed by communication in some form.

Telepathy:

A buzzing in the ear (from implants) could convey[48] to Shirlè a nearby alien presence. The aliens could also communicate with Shirlè by telepathy (or hypnosis?). Shirlè would be drawn inexplicably to a certain place for a particular reason, as she had with Frank.

Alien Communicating With a Human in Person

Early one morning Shirlè awoke and had a vision. An entity was standing at the foot of her bed. He was pointing to needle-like protrusions in his neck area. She immediately understood she had left them out of the painting she had made of the alien the day before. She thanked him, promising to put them in. (Apparition, hallucination, hologram, or real? **See painting in center of book**)

Aliens Initiating Contact With Humans by Means of a Hologram

There was an interesting woman next door to Shirlè's hairdresser-- Charlene, who did psychometry[49]. Shirlè paid her a visit. Charlene asked for an object owned for a long time. Shirlè handed her Frank's disk on a key ring. On it was a symbol that Frank had told her was her space name. Not looking closely, she took it, closed her eyes and exclaimed "You're connected with space!"

She meditated again, eyes closed. "Your departed husband is sitting beside me." Though she had never met Hymie, she claimed she could see him clairvoyantly. Shirlè asked that Hymie give his pet name for her. She received *tuchas*, Jewish for "behind"—her nickname known only to family.

Charlene broke the silence. "You have no idea who is right here," she said, her eyes wide."Jesus, Buddha, and they're here listening to us. *Space people are here too*." She was then quiet for a few moments. Then suddenly she stood up. "There's a *spacecraft* outside," she said, matter-of-factly.

They went outside. By now it was twilight and the street was deserted. They looked up into the still light sky. There, to their amazement, was the gigantic figure of a man in a brightly-colored shirt.

---

[48]Another purpose of these biological implants could be to gain knowledge of humans by monitoring their health, or to obtain what the aliens may be missing—important neuro-chemicals received via nose or ear implants in humans.

[49]The ability to tell about a person from an object by merely holding it.

He had a head, two arms, trunk, but no legs. His face was definitely male and middle-aged, with distinct features—rosy cheeks and light brown hair to the level of his ears.

"The Man in the Sky" Hologram

They were amazed, not knowing what to make of it. No one else ever mentioned seeing it, yet it was huge. Today, it would be called a hologram (a three-dimensional projected picture). But who or what made the hologram? Aliens?—just to let them know they were around?

It was her first color hologram of a man, inspiring her to convey in her painting called "Motion" the idea of movement and change—thoughts travel, creating form, design—in other words, the physical comes out of the non-physical spirit.

However, rather than show what she actually saw—details, in color, she painted a nebulous figure of a man surrounded by swirling designs.

Shirlè kept busy. While not painting, she loved to entertain friends at home with parties or sit-down dinners. She went with Fred to the synagogue, to miniature train shows, and was a good sport on camping trips. She made the usual visits to her two children and three grandchildren. Trips to Montreal to see her mother and sister Nancy were less often, but when she did go, it was for a week or two so that she could be of help to them.

In 1987, Shirlè's eighty-seven-year-old mother flew to Vancouver and while staying with her sister Mary she visited Shirlè. They hadn't seen each other for some time.

Mother Passes Over

"You leave the physical, become the creator again and prepare the environment in which you will journey."—Alien Frank

"Life is mostly froth and bubble, but two things stand like stone: kindness in another's trouble, courage in our own."-Adam Lindsay Gordon, Australian poet.

I found the above "froth and bubble" saying on a scrap of paper on a schoolroom floor while revisiting my high school (after thirty years). I thought it sums it all up. I put the saying on a rock that sits on my desk. It helped me to deal with my own "mother issues" so similar to Shirlè's. I had to learn that forgiveness follows easily and naturally only when one has genuine compassion.

***

Shirlè watched her, standing in the kitchen, a shrunken little old lady. The "mother issue" was still there, she realized, still "eating" her despite the vision years earlier of the old man with the Hebrew scroll warning her that if she didn't stop resenting her mother she could be "recalled." However, she had made a lot of progress. She had more compassion now, more understanding. Now, as the two silently put dishes away she sensed it would be her mother's last visit and her heart went out to her.

"Ma," she said, "I must have been pretty hard to live with."

"Yes," said her mother, with a slight nod.

"Ma, I didn't really understand you, and you didn't understand me."

Both were silent for a few moments. Shirlè drew closer to her mother. "Ma, you know I love you. Did you ever love me?"

"But Pa did, he loved you a lot."

At the time it hurt deeply, and still does. But as she looks back to 1987, she realizes she was just as much to blame. "We were both strong personalities and wouldn't give in. We just kept doing 'tit for tat.'"

The next year her mother's heart trouble had changed for the worse and she returned to Montreal for a pacemaker. She hadn't burdened her children with her illness which she must have had for some time. Shirlè's sister Nancy, at her bedside, phoned Shirlè and described her mother's last minutes.

"Isn't Dad beautiful?" her mother had said, smiling.

"Men are not beautiful," Nancy had replied, "they're handsome." She had seen no one else in the room, and didn't grasp that her mother was having a "visitation."

Her mother then took Nancy's hand. "Nancy," she said, "will you please go out of the room for a few minutes?"

Puzzled, Nancy complied, and it was then that she died. Shirlè surmises that her father had come for her mother from the beyond, and her mother wanted to be alone with him as he guided her to the other side.

***

Shirlè hurriedly made the air travel arrangements. On the plane, childhood memories flooded in. Why were they mostly of sadness, bitterness, anger? Her parents, especially her mother, never knew how badly she felt. She never let them see her cry. They never knew how vulnerable she felt. They would only see her sassy, contrary, or courageous side. She thought of the times when she was about ten and misbehaving and her mother would threaten to "call over the river"—a Polish expression meaning someone will come and take you away. Her sisters would freeze in fear, but it didn't faze Shirlè. "Ma," she said, "here is the phone, go call 'over the river'." She got smacked, but her mother never threatened her with it again.

But there were also warm good times. How she loved those moments with her mother. She was six or seven. She wanted the answer to things. Her mother knew a lot; she would ask her. And she would ask about the stars, about life after death, what was in heaven. Her mother would tell her things. She was enthralled. She felt close to her then.

And just recently, she finally heard words of praise. On her mother's first visit to Shirlè's studio, her eyes moved quickly from painting to painting. "You *have* something, she said. "I don't know what it is, but *something*."

***

At the funeral home she looked at her mother lying in the coffin. "Ma," she whispered, "you're in a better place now—and you're with Dad."

At the family gathering in Nancy's home, Nancy related once more how their mother had died, and quoted one of her last remarks: "I think Shirlè is such a nice person, a really good person."

So, at least, Shirlè had lived to hear her say that, albeit second-hand, and she was greatly moved by it. Recently Shirlè was helping a friend do a garage sale and went into the kitchen. While there, Gale Redford, a channeler whom she had met once at a psychic fair, entered and approached her.

"There's a woman standing beside you," she said. "An older woman, and I think it's your mother. She's crying, and asking for your forgiveness so she can go on."

"I forgive you with all my heart," said Shirlè. "And please forgive me for all the hurt I've caused you."

"Now your mother has left," said Gale.

Shirlè regrets she hadn't gotten to really know her mother. She thought of the time her mother having mastered the English language enough to read and write, ran to Shirlè like an excited little girl.

"See, Shirlè, I've read this book... and this book."

"Ma," said Shirlè, "that's wonderful. I'm really proud of you." And her mother's eyes lit up. Why didn't she do that more often, she asked herself. Perhaps if she had, her mother might have reciprocated—given her more love. But what did she know then, she mused. All a child knows is that when you don't get the love you need, you hit back. She was always being defensive, she realized. What a waste!

As she looked back she realized she had come a long way; she was more understanding of her mother, more compassionate. And more understanding of herself.

***

A year later in 1988, Shirlè had decided to have herself regressed. She wanted to know more about the "scuba divers" incident, and wondered if the regression would clear up something regarding her relationship with her mother.

1988 Regression With Ellie Arnold, hypnotist, regressionist, Vancouver, B.C.

Why can't we remember our past lives? Michael Newton in *Destiny of Souls* says in effect, that human beings have been made to forget so that they will not have preconditioned responses to their karma. But as a result some people, without this knowledge, see their lives as having no purpose or meaning, and try to escape from reality.

Shirlè's Regression (abbreviated to its main points)

Scene 1. Shirlè is instantly on a planet with a crystal dome. People like us, blond. They communicate by telepathy and use a signal greeting of hand over heart, two fingers up. They know her, welcome her, but tell her she has to return.

Scene 2. 1962. She's in the house she used to live in, in Montreal. She's lying in bed, but with her head at the foot of it. Two space people are present, and as she looks at them, they disappear. They take her to another planet (scene 3)

Scene 3. A past lifetime on this planet Blue grass and blue flowers— A quiet life alone, looking after and communicating with animals

Scene 4. First implant at five years She left her bed, went downstairs, saw a stranger but was not afraid. He "touched" the back of her neck. "Don't worry," he said. "You will remember nothing."

Scene 5. Another implant (recently)—body asleep on a table— needle inserted. She's angry. She asks why? They say she has things to do, and it is time to do them; they're awakening her subconscious.

Scene 6. Two people take her hands and float with her slowly up to a spacecraft. Body checked with instruments. The regressionist asks her higher conscious the purpose of the implants and needle. She answers that it is for receiving messages, and for her protection. It ends with Shirlè seeing her many guides.

The regression, Shirlè felt, confirmed the "scuba divers" incident, showed her a past life on another planet where she really felt at home, and it added to the feeling of security she already had from the aliens.

Though happy and secure with Fred, Shirlè still yearned for Hymie. Soon after the regression in 1988, he came to her in a vivid dream, dressed in a light tan suit, looking very young and handsome. Suddenly he turned into Fred, and she realized he was trying to say, "Please let me go. Don't think of me so much, asking for my help. Lean on Fred."

And Fred *was* giving her a stable normal life, emotionally and financially. Her artwork was coming along. She was a grandmother; she could relax and enjoy. So in 1990, they planned a Nevada trip. But a simple trip to Reno and Las Vegas turned out to be quite mysterious, quite confusing. Had she and Fred and the car been abducted, if that's what it was? Three times? And why?

Chapter Fifteen

"Missing Time" in Nevada
Trips to Iceland, Stonehenge, New Mexico

"The intelligence on some planets may not be human in your sense, but they are far ahead of earthlings in understanding and spirituality."---Alien Frank

Missing Time in Nevada

Shirlè and Fred were in the living room, planning their leisurely camper trip, when the phone rang. Shirlè took the call.

It was Ephrom, their psychic friend. "Shirlè," he said in a worried tone, "I'm sorry to tell you, but you're going to be in an accident."

"Why do you say that?"

"Well," he said, "I channeled it and I also checked with tarot cards and you're going to be in an accident."

"Well, if it has to be, it has to be," said Shirlè.

On hearing of Ephrom's pronouncement, Fred, (down-to-earth electrical engineer), was flatly unmoved. "I'm not listening to that," he snorted, "we're going!"

The first stop on Friday was Reno, Nevada, for relaxation and a little gambling. Everything was fine. In a few hours they had broken even and went to bed. Early next morning, Saturday, they paid their bill and were ready for their destination Las Vegas. They left the hotel and drove about a hundred miles to a stop for breakfast. Leaving the restaurant, they got in their car and Fred turned on the engine. The new van was "dead[50]." Luckily, they were able to get a mechanic to come and jump-start it. It was the starter, they were told, and they drove off. After two hours, they stopped for gas, and again the car wouldn't start. Together they pushed the van over a small incline, and as it started, jumped in.

Fred had been driving for some time when Shirlè felt strange. "Fred," she said, "that's the same tree, and isn't that the same ranch we saw before?"

"That's right," said Fred. "It's weird."

They drove on, observing more of the same scenery. Again a gas station stop, and again the van wouldn't start. Again, with no mechanic available, they pushed the car, and as it started, jumped in. On they went, and hours later, in the early evening, they arrived safely at their hotel in Las Vegas. At the desk they showed their reservation. The clerk looked in his book.

"Sorry," he said, "we gave your room away."

"What do you mean?"

"You weren't here yesterday."

"What do you mean... yesterday? Our reservation is for today, Saturday."

"No, today is Sunday!"

Fred and Shirlè stared at each other. "We left from Reno this morning," said Fred, "and it's Saturday."

The clerk was getting annoyed. "Hotels are all booked up," he said, "but you can probably get a room in the motel down the street."

The motel had Sunday's newspaper in the stand, Saturday's paper was sold out, and everyone verified it was Sunday. They were dumbfounded; they had no memory of a total of twenty-four hours. It was their first joint experience of "missing time."

Could it be possible aliens can take a person out of his "time frame," keep him for a length of time, then reinsert him into his "time frame" without his being aware of being away?

On their way home, they had no trouble whatsoever with the car, and went to see their friend Itzhak. Now in his sixties, he had been having

---

[50] Oftentimes caused by a UFO nearby

ongoing contacts with aliens since childhood. He lives with his wife and children in a remote, secluded area where a spacecraft could land unseen, and asked that his name and location be withheld for fear of being watched by government agents. Apart from his piercing eyes, he looks rather ordinary. His personality, however, had radically changed after his first alien contact at the age of thirteen (which he can recall consciously). He believes he is a "walk-in."

In Delores Cannon's book *Between Death and Life* page 223, a client under hypnosis gives a lengthy explanation of a "walk-in." The following is a paraphrased, abridged version:

There are more souls waiting to incarnate than there are bodies to accommodate them. Sometimes there comes a time in an individual's life when he finds that he truly no longer wishes to be in the physical. And so he is given the option to pass over to the other side. Then an individual on the spirit side may inhabit the body. There is a mutual exchange of places, beneficial to both. The original soul is released to his true home and the individual on the spirit side has a vehicle on which to work on his karma. But before he can do that, he must work through the karma of the former occupant.

"Come in, come in," said Itzhak as he hugged them both. "And how are your backs?"

Shirlè and Fred looked at each other. "Our backs? Why do you ask?"

"Well," he said, grinning, "they must hurt from all that car pushing."

Shirlè and Fred were astounded. How did he know? They had not told him, nor had they contacted their other UFO friends. They related how they had driven by the same scenery and had lost a day.

"They had to do it," said Itzhak. He then explained. Sensing psychically that something wasn't quite right with Fred and Shirlè, he had checked with the aliens. Fred was falling asleep at the wheel, he was told, and the aliens decided to take them up—car and all, to keep them safe. Interestingly, on returning home, Shirlè felt compelled to paint four paintings, and only after completing them did she realize that they all appear to be seen from the air. **(See painting in center of book.)**

"So you lost the day in a spacecraft," he said smiling.

"Fine thing," said Shirlè. "Now I'll have to have myself regressed."

"No need to," said Itzhak. "They didn't block out the memory, they *erased* it."

They were reminded of an earlier incident where it appeared Shirlè and Fred had been kept safe from harm. Frank had told Shirlè that a fog would appear to stop or delay the flight of an airline if, for any reason, it was dangerous to fly. Shirlè and Fred were at the Seattle Airport with tickets to Israel and a sight-seeing stopover in Turkey. The flight was delayed because of fog, and they were put into a motel by the airline. The next day, the fog still present, they waited another day in the motel. Finally they were told the flight was cancelled. They went home, but without their luggage, which had somehow been sent to Turkey. Only then, after two days in the motel, did they hear about the huge earthquake in Turkey and the murder of a diplomat.

1991 Tucson UFO Conference and the Alien Message

"All have the same Creator. People need to rise above greed
and desire, and work on their spirituality."—Alien Frank

In Part II, I went into length for reasons Shirlè was "chosen." But that is not what really concerned Shirlè nor what is important to the reader. *It may be interesting, but not important. What is—is the purpose of the mission and the story behind the purpose.* The aliens are aware that the overall free will of the world's population (in action or inaction) is pointing in the direction of disaster, and are trying to make us aware enough to do what needs to be done, in time. The story behind the purpose is that the changes befalling Earth and its inhabitants are inevitable. It has happened before, in 26,000 year cycles, with pole and subsequent climate changes in the history of Earth.

Frank had told Shirlè that she was to "gather the people"—make them aware. All along, people and coincidences were helping her in her personal life, art development, and UFO education. Shirlè figured it was time. And in 1999, Wendelle Stevens, an internationally known UFO researcher, arranged for Shirlè to speak at the first International UFO Conference in Tucson, Arizona, where speakers from various countries gave presentations.

At first she was nervous—it was her first speech before a crowd so large—about three hundred. But she relaxed, the anxiety disappeared and she related her two-year contact with Frank.

She told the audience that there are many races of aliens on many planets on many universes with various agendas, as well as intelligent life in various dimensions. She explained her mission: Because of natural and man-made catastrophes likely to happen on Earth, his race (Sirius) would try to save some children, and Shirlè would play a part. According to Frank she had consented before birth to her future role—others had similar or different roles to play. At the right time, she would be given direction to guide the children to spacecrafts, and the eight plates he gave her inscribed with his writing would be understood at that time.

She concluded with Frank's message, in brief: Firstly, that we must remember that we are more than physical beings. Secondly, the answer to Man's inhumanity to Man is to have compassion. The ecology of Earth is endangered in many ways, including the development of nuclear fission without neutralizing enormous nuclear waste; in time Earth will be unable to adequately support life. While new technology will help support food production, some aliens, fearful of Earth's future, gather specimens from plant, animal and humans. Eventually some humans will be removed from Earth.

There will be many physical upheavals to the planet from earthquakes and floods. But there will be some places of relative safety in North America—some parts of Arizona, New Mexico, Colorado, and Canada. To lessen the impact of the changes—positive energy and love is needed.

She was kindly received, but it was hard to say whether she was really believed. Shirlè painted, went about her daily life, and patiently waited—for the return of Frank, for a message. Then one day, three years later, a strong telepathic "pull"[51] came over her to attend the November 1993 UFO Conference in Iceland. She figured there had to be a reason.

UFO Trips to Iceland, Hologram at Stonehenge
Recent Experiences of Losing and Gaining Time

"There is one light of consciousness in every human being, and that light is divine. It is capable of making a whole and harmonious man."—Alien Frank

This part of the book is about the power of synchronicity in keeping one on one's path, and the strange experience of invisible aliens (?) leaving marks on clothing to show their presence. There is also, and I don't understand it really, not only a witness *of,* but an interaction *with* a hologram of a person.

---

[51] This same "pull" was experienced by Tony Dodds in his book *Alien Investigator.*

Iceland

Husband Fred agreed that Shirlè should go to the UFO Iceland conference, if she felt so strongly, but she didn't want to go alone. She was sitting under the dryer getting her hair done when she heard loud and clear, "Why don't you ask your sister?" She often heard voices telling her things, but she resisted the idea. Mary, sitting under the next dryer, wasn't that interested in UFOs, and Shirlè would never have thought of asking her. But the voice repeated "Ask her!" So she heeded it.

"But it's expensive..." said Mary.

"You have free mileage, right?"

"Yes, but I can't find my 'points.'"

"When you go home, look for them," said Shirlè, "and we'll go to the travel agent."

They went to their respective homes. Soon Shirlè picked up the ringing phone.

"Guess what?" said Mary excitedly. "I found them on the diningroom table. I could swear they weren't there before."

"The moment I stepped off the plane," said Shirlè, "I had an eerie feeling, like kinship, like I belonged there."

They checked into the Saga, one of the newest hotels in Riekejevik, boasting a movie theater and a complex of meeting rooms. There she met Michael Dillon, who had planned the conference.

"Why did you pick Iceland?" she asked.

"Well," he said, "I asked three psychics where the aliens would come down. Each made a drawing of a mountainous area. All, more or less, said the terrain and surrounding area looked like Iceland."

After the smorgasbord lunch, they met all the so-called "big shots": Wendelle Stevens, Virgil Armstrong, and Celia and Bob Dean from the US, Michael Hessemann from Germany, and Tony Dodds from England.

The following day, the UFO group bussed over to Snaefellsnes, an area known as a vortex. Here the aliens were expected to land. The mountain and surrounding flat area was arid, eerily beautiful, and freezing cold. Shirlè and Mary sat with others on the ground, glad they had brought their fur coats. They ate their box lunches, talked and joked and waited... All the while planes flew back and forth. According to an Icelander, the US has a base in Iceland and there is frequent air traffic.

Soon it was twilight and nothing had happened. And nothing is *going* to happen, thought Shirlè. The CNN, the BBC, the *Icelandic News* and all the other reporters… It was ridiculous. Michael Dillon had called the press and they had nothing to report.

When it was almost dark, the aurora borealis began flashing vertically, white against the black sky. All of a sudden it parted enough to reveal the shape of a typical saucer-shaped UFO.

"Michael, look," said Shirlè. But he saw nothing. Was it because as an artist she noticed such things? Or was it a hologram, meant only for her eyes, to assure her that they were there without revealing themselves to the American planes?

"Let's hold hands," someone called out as a group of Icelanders arrived to join them. Shirlè felt like a shrimp next to them, they were so tall.

One collective "Ohm" reverberated in the valley. Then all were silent in meditation. Still nothing happened. Everyone went back to the hotel, had a bite to eat, and went to sleep.

In the morning Shirlè dressed and faced the full-length mirror in the black pants and black tunic she had worn the day before—which was unusual, for she was a person who never wore the same clothes for two days. She was surprised to see what looked like a white mark on her black tunic. She showed it to Mary wondering what she had leaned against and was about to clean it.

"Stop, don't do that," said Mary, excitedly. She pointed to the markings. "Can't you see that's where we stood? These are the posts we were standing near, and this is a UFO."

"My God, you're right." said Shirlè. She laid the tunic over a chair, got her camera, and took a picture. When did it happen? she wondered—while they slept, or the day before, outside?

She thought of the synchronicity. Mary's actions prevented Shirlè from destroying the "mark" that gave the sign of the aliens' presence. Without Mary's being there it could have been wiped off. But why didn't the aliens openly show themselves? Could it be that it was not for the eyes of the US military on the Icelandic base?

At the conference downstairs, they approached UFO researcher Wendelle Stevens.

"Look what I have," said Shirlè. "It looks like a stamp."**(See photo of stamp in book center.)**

"So what did you lean on?" he asked flippantly.**(See photos of posts in book center.)**

"What could she have leaned on?" demanded Mary. "She was wearing a full length fur coat. See the spacecraft? And that's the posts where we were standing last night!"

Wendelle looked at Mary, looked at Shirlè, shrugged his shoulders, and walked away. Apparently he related the incident to the other speakers, for all avoided Shirlè. Only Virgil Armstrong approached her. "Shirlè," he said, "this is quite interesting. I think you should look into it."

During her twenty days in Iceland, an evening of UFO lectures was set up with Shirlè as a speaker. The event drew a large audience and led to lecturing on television. When the conference ended and it was time to leave, she sadly said her goodbyes; she had made so many friends. At home, she had the film developed, and what looked like part of a figure could be seen in the stamp.

Interestingly, when Shirlè returned to Iceland two years later in 1996, she learned that while none of the UFO group had received the "stamp", three or four Icelanders who were there had, but in different colors. (Since Shirlè was wearing black, the stamp had to be white to be seen against it.)

On her third trip to Iceland in 1998, her good friend Magnus arranged for her to be in the newspapers and television, while he and his friends made sure she was taken care of and shown around. She stayed at the home of the mother of a friend she made on the previous trip. Like so many Icelanders, the woman was a psychic.

"Unfortunately," she said, "like your previous trips, you're not going to see the aliens—but they will be there just the same."

Hologram[52]? At Stonehenge

On the way back home, Shirlè and some of her group made a sightseeing stopover in England. Michael Dillon picked up Amadreus, a friend of his, and they drove one hundred miles from London to Stonehenge, arriving about two in the morning. But they couldn't get close—a fence surrounded it to prevent people from chipping off souvenir pieces. While Shirlè stood staring at Stonehenge, the others went across the road to the brightly lit street, close to the caretaker's little house. They were hoping to see a spacecraft, but only Amadreus saw

---

[52] A hologram is made by two beams of laser light that form a three-dimensional figure that looks quite solid, but which turns out to be a mere projection of light, like an image on a cinema screen.

one, or thought he saw one.

It was quiet. No other cars or people could be seen. All of a sudden a girl appeared on the road. Shirlè crossed over to see her. Michael and Amadreus asked her where she had come from. She told them she had walked from a town five miles away.

"At this time of the night?" asked Michael.

"Well," she said, "I'm going to Salisbury."

"Salisbury? And how far do you think that is? It's *twenty-five* miles!" exclaimed Michael.

The bright street light revealed a young blond girl, wearing a necklace on a long dress under a long open brown coat. Modern yet old-fashioned, thought Shirlè. Suddenly her face turned into that of her granddaughter. Shirlè knew, of course, that the girl wasn't Heidi, but she wanted to hug her, feeling somehow sorry for her. But at that very moment she heard clearly, in her head "Don't touch her." The voice was calm, yet firm.

All of a sudden a car appeared, driven by two Americans. "Where can we find a place to sleep?" asked one.

"There isn't any place here," said Michael. "You have to go to a place farther down."

"Wait, could you give the girl a lift," interjected Shirlè, "to find a phone there?"

But the girl didn't want to go; she just stood there. Shirlè explained that there was not enough room in their tiny car and it would be better if she went with them. Very reluctantly she went into the American's car.

Shirlè and her friends stood and watched a puzzling scene. The car drove a very short way, stopped, backed up, stopped again and then went on. Shirlè could see the two men in the front but there was no one in the rear, and no one beside the car or on the road as the car finally left. (There have been reports of similar happenings with pick-ups.)

Arriving home, Shirlè asked a psychic for an explanation. "What took place is a message," he said. "You shouldn't believe everything you hear, and the woman turning into your granddaughter means the message is for *you*."

So, was she a hologram—especially with the warning not to touch her? Or had the girl come from another dimension?

One year later, in 1999, Shirlè and I made an interesting trip to Brazil, and then attended a UFO conference at Laughlin, Nevada, where we both had strange experiences.

Chapter Sixteen

Brazil Exhibit, Nevada Abduction
Losing and Gaining Time
Synchronicities

"It is possible that UFO activity is part of an educational program for
'cosmic consciousness training' and for assisting humankind to learn more
about the merger of 'science' and 'spirituality.'"—Dr. Leo Sprinkle.

Brazil Trip

Life went on. Shirlè continued painting. Over the years she had
held exhibits in New York, Paris, Moscow (three murals), Riga,
Bulgaria, Montreal, Seattle, Vancouver, and recently Brazil. I attended
the latter with Shirlè. Our friend and generous hostess Maria Thome was
kind enough to arrange and advertise, with the help of her family and
friends, a private exhibit of Shirlè's art in the city of Brasilia. It was
beautifully done and well received.

While in Brasilia I noticed that many people wore a Star of David—
and I wondered how many Jews were in that city out of a total population
of one million. I discovered that there were so few Brasilia Jews that they
met on Sabbaths and holidays in a room above a restaurant, though a
synagogue was being planned for the future. I was told that in Brazil, the
Star of David does not mean "Jew" as it does in most of the world today,
but is regarded as the ancient spiritual symbol it is. Maria, a non-Jew,

always wears one.

In our travels around the country, we also noted that Brazilians are very open to discussing UFO and aliens, personally and otherwise. At a residential school in the country, a teacher invited us on a tour and told of his UFO experiences and sightings in the area, as commonplace and natural. There doesn't seem to be the fear of being labeled "crazy" as in the United States.

On another sightseeing trip, we visited a place or complex called The Valley of the Dawn whose members have a faith that includes *all* faiths and peoples, *including extraterrestrials*. And there the Star of David, prominently displayed throughout, actually *does* refer to the Jewish people and their religion. On special days, members, men and women, wore cloaks with the symbols of each religion on them.

Aliens and the Valley of the Dawn

In the complex were not only symbols of Christianity (a *huge* statue of Jesus next to a cross draped with a Jewish prayer shawl), but Muslim (the crescent), Egyptian (a pyramid), and four large similar statues of a female (East Indian Hindu or the feminine principle?) with a six-pointed Star of David in the center of her forehead. On her flowing gown was a symbol that could be either the sun with seven rays or the Jewish candelabra (Menorah).

Also in the complex were signs representing Judaism (numerous *huge* Stars of David and *menorahs*). Against one of the menorahs was a face, we were told, that represented or symbolized *extraterrestrials*—and in front of another menorah stood a *huge* double staircase.

They believe that the giant "winged ones" (Nefilim in the Bible) came to Earth 32,000 years ago, that they created the human race, and will *one day return and descend the steps*. They also told us that their ancestors were Jews who had fled to Brazil from the Spanish Inquisition in Spain around the year 1492. But when the Inquisition had reached Brazil and they had to convert to Christianity or be killed, they converted. Though outwardly Christian, they were actually secret Jews, often called *Marranos*. They secluded themselves inland to the area now known as the Valley of the Dawn, and the group's message evolved to include not only all of humanity but extraterrestrials.

* * *

UFO Conference in Laughlin, Nevada:

On the last night of the UFO Conference, a group of "lights" were seen in the late night sky of Laughlin, Nevada. Many stared in awe, but it bored Shirlè and me; we had seen enough "lights" in conference videos. Tired, we went up to the hotel room we shared, and to bed.

I awoke hearing a distinct loud electronic beep and wondered what it was. At the same time I was seized by strong chest pains. Thinking it could be angina (but which had never been diagnosed as such, only as heartburn) I worried that my return by plane that morning might have to be delayed. Suddenly I heard another beep like the one before and the chest pain immediately stopped. I felt alright, and had no further pain. (However, the incident motivated me to see a *new* heart specialist back home, who diagnosed blocked arteries.)

Interestingly, Shirlè, already awake, did not hear either loud beep. She got up from her bed to go to the bathroom, and came back very disturbed. "How *dare* they!" she yelled. She had pushed back the long sleeves of her nightgown, and on each arm, just above the wrist, was a flaming red band, about two inches in width. Strangely, it did not feel hot or inflamed. Within an hour it disappeared.

Had she been abducted while I had remained, I wondered—or had I been abducted between the two beeps? It had not occurred to me to look at the clock for missing time.

When Shirlè returned home, she e-mailed an account of the incident to Linda Maupin, a friend of hers who channels an alien. I know nothing about Linda. I can verify nothing, but her e-mail is interesting.

Wednesday April 7, 1999, 8:32 a.m.
You were put in a kind of pressure chamber on the spaceship. As for the red bands, there was something at the wrist but not primarily to restrain you. We are studying the human body in evolution. You humans do not know you are going through physical changes as we speak—very basic subatomic changes at the cellular level. Humans on planet earth are a bit off, out of sync—enough to cause discomfort and illness. It can be very painful and could get worse, unless we can tie in the old vibrational pattern with the new accelerating one approaching. We are trying to help. Some things are painful for her and she should not have to remember it. Memory gets wiped out, but this is the price.
We are Shirlè's dear friends, in love and light

***

The following is an interesting (condensed) excerpt from p.79 and 80 of *"UFOs--Key to Earth's Destiny"* by Winfield Brownell. Aleuti Francesca is channeling the alien Orlon from the Solar Tribunal and the Galactic Tribunals governing Earth's section of space, regarding density level transition. Again, I cannot vouch for the authenticity of the Francesca-Orlon channeling, or for that matter, any channeling—but in it, is an interesting explanation of vibrational or frequency change:

The frequency change[53] may take place abruptly, due to cataclysmic events of nature, not only on the Earth but in the solar system. The Earth is at the end of a great cycle of approximately 26,000 years. Several times in the past the earth has changed its axis. A quarter-turn flip may happen again. Since the ice is melting at the North Pole and building up at the South Pole, an unbalanced condition already exists.

Comets and the stepped up vibrations of the Central Sun Vela emitting ultraviolet rays can disrupt the force field surrounding Earth, causing a change in the electrical force-field. Your Earth and the people in it, have to undergo structural changes, and changes in consciousness in tune with the Earth changes. The energy of an individual will then emit such a high frequency as to raise the molecular structure of the cells to a point whereby the body will then vibrate in the fourth etheric level. Transition of matter into a finer more etherialized matter will take place. Your sense perceptions, rather than being eliminated, will become heightened and an awareness of all that which is of beauty, love and eternal nature will become as one with you.

***

I went over Shirlè's life for other examples of possible abductions not mentioned. I found that during the next two years she had a recurrence of possible abductions—one with a combination of "missing" and "gaining" time that in a way involved *me*.

Recent Experiences of Losing and Gaining Time

"Matter is not primary, consciousness is; we ourselves are transcendent beings who only temporarily inhabit material bodies which we then mistake for our essence."—Timothy Conway, PhD.

---

[53] Earth scientists are in agreement, but they think it will be a very slow progression, not an abrupt one.

Missing and Gaining Time in One Day

It began with "missing time." Shirlè and I were at a UFO conference in Laughlin, Nevada. I had been in the Arizona hospital, just over the Nevada border, fifteen minutes away. I had been suddenly and completely incapacitated by what turned out to be an extreme inner ear disturbance.

She visited me twice that day. Taking into consideration the one-hour difference in Arizona and Nevada time, there was a loss of an hour-and-a-half on the first trip, followed by a gain of about three hours on the second trip, making a total gain of about one-and-a-half hours in the one day. Thusly she attended lectures that would have already ended.

There are many other cases on record of missing time, and a few of gaining time. Two examples follow:

Missing Time for Ten Days

Alec Newald, of New Zealand, author of *"Co-evolution"* claims he and his car were abducted for ten days. The aliens gave him detailed information and two crystals before returning him. His life was then threatened by men claiming to be scientists. His flat was broken into. The only things taken were one of the crystals (the other was not in the flat) and papers on which he himself had made hieroglyphic-like marks and doodles.

Gaining Time-One Hour

There is the case of Donna Butts told by Dr. Scott Corder, a Kansas GP physician, in *"Star Children"* by Jenny Randles. In 1980 while traveling with her mother-in-law and two children, a beam of light came down from a UFO and the truck ahead of them vanished. They then arrived at their destination an hour ahead of time; the aliens having put the car down ahead of where they would have been on their route, had they not been abducted.

"Missing Time" at Home

Fred and Shirlè had gone to bed about 10 p.m. Shirlè usually had insomnia, but she apparently fell fast asleep. Strangely, they both woke up at the same time and looked at the clock. It read eleven, yet they both felt they had slept for hours! Shirlè walked around the house, noting the time on each clock. They all read eleven or very close. However, as she stared at the last clock, it suddenly showed *three* o'clock. She ran upstairs to tell Fred. Fred looked at the bedside clock, and it, too, now read three o'clock, yet it seemed that only five minutes had passed.

How easy it is to dismiss an experience like this and just forget about it. But Shirlè and Fred wonder if their conscious memory of the hours between eleven and three had been wiped out, and instead it seemed that one moment it was eleven, then it was three. They wondered, had they both been abducted, or could one of them have been abducted and the other made to wait, unconscious of it? This latter appears quite often in UFO literature.

***

All the while, synchronicities continued in Shirlè's life. Her attention to coincidences were playing a part in keeping her on her path—the path to doing what she had come here to do and be—making her life run smoother.

Synchronicities—After Frank's Departure

"The way we know we are in contact with higher forces, is through coincidences. They do it through signs and symbols—the more coincidences, the better the contact." – Leo Sprinkle, PhD

As I have heard synchronicity defined, it is when the inner thought is meaningful to the outer event and vice versa, surpassing the probability of chance. Also playing a part is the relationship of time and space. There is a force bringing together another force. When you come down to this planet, your road is set. There are people you are going to meet in the play you are going to perform. You need players for your act. The people you meet give you the lines for you to follow. Synchronicity is a force that brings it about. One action brings a counteraction, and one step brings another step, which leads you to people you would not otherwise meet. By not being aware of synchronicities—or by fearing them—you miss out. By being aware you go faster and farther on your path. If you take the opportunity, you gain; if you don't, you stay in the same place. Everyone has choice.

But who or what are responsible –aliens, angels, God, our Higher Self? The following experiences contain more synchronicities.

Celeste, a Channeler

A man Shirlè knew as a shaman (and who wishes to be anonymous) called one day, saying she needed "tonings" and should see a certain woman.

Shirlè made the call. "Celeste Crowley? The 'space brothers' told me to see you for my heart."

There was a pause on the other line. Then, "Come right over."

They sat in the livingroom. It was Celeste, however, who needed to unburden herself. So perhaps this synchronistic meeting was more for her than Shirlè.

"Since I've started channeling," she said in a worried tone, "aliens have been coming through. They want me to help people get tones for healing. I was frightened at first."

"They must think a lot of you," said Shirlè. "They sent me to you."

Reassured, Celeste meditated, and then began a ritual using a rose quartz crystal on Shirlè's chakras. "Pick a tone," she said, finally.

"Ahhh…" said Shirlè. Without realizing it, she had chosen the note of G, for the heart. She was then able to relax and go into alpha meditation. Two days later, Shirlè received a birthday present from Celeste: the rose quartz, which, she was told, enhances one's intuitive powers, as its tone puts one into the alpha state for meditation.

Selling the House

One day, back in 1990, Shirlè was looking out a window, when she heard a voice in her head loud and clear "It's time to move."

"Okay," she said to herself, "the very next person who comes to the door and is a realtor…"

Ten minutes later, synchronicity was at work. There was a knock on the door and a woman handed her a real estate broker's calendar.

"Happy New Year," she said.

"Happy New Year to you," said Shirlè. "Come back in a few days, and we'll be selling our house. Then she realized she hadn't even asked Fred. When he came home, she told him.

"Good," he said.

The number 117,000 came out of her mouth spontaneously. Within a few days of putting up the sign, the house sold, and they moved to another house—in Surrey, B.C.

The Tucson Lecture Story

One place Shirlè and I visited on our New Mexico trip was Roswell. There we visited Christopher Stone, who was recounting his experiences with the government cover-up on the Roswell incident, and was writing a book about it. On our way back to Phoenix we stopped for gas in Tucson, and Shirlè happened to discover that a UFO meeting with a speaker was to be held that evening. Unfortunately, at the last minute, the speaker could not make it. Of course, synchronicity was at work and Shirlè gave a brilliant impromptu speech to a good sized crowd, keeping her "cool" while being challenged by a forceful skeptic after her talk.

The Thai Restaurant Story

Shirlè and I were working on the book and it was lunchtime. I asked her if she liked Thai food.

"Yes," she said.

"So it's Thai," I said.

I found out later, that she really felt like Chinese, but found herself saying Thai was fine. I also wanted to go for Chinese, but I thought she preferred Thai, and there was a new one in town, so I'd take her there. We didn't know then that it was part of a synchronicity unfolding.

It was early and a young man came in and took a table. He was the only other diner. Shirlè was seated facing him. As he asked the waiter about Thai words in the menu, Shirlè struck up a conversation about it. He said he was not familiar with Thai food. He was from out of town and was going to go to another restaurant but impulsively went to this one. In the midst of the mundane conversation that followed, he threw in that he was clairvoyant, saying he heard us mentioning it. We looked at each other. Shirlè and I had absolutely not said anything relating to paranormal or about the book. We understood that "clairvoyant" was the key word to us that he needed to talk.

He went on. He said he could sometimes tell what would happen to people, and it scared them, as well as him. We explained we understood how he felt, and also that he needed to have more knowledge and know where to go for it, since it was obvious he was talking about precognition, and gave him some leads.

At this point I suddenly felt terribly nauseous and ran to the bathroom to vomit. While I was there, Shirlè, becoming concerned, got up to see how I was and had to pass his table. As she did, she touched his shoulder and said: "You are not alone. We are here." He knew then he could talk freely.

I had eaten in this restaurant before and loved the food, so it was strange for me to react to the food like that. But without my getting up, it would have been awkward for Shirlè to just go over to him. It was apparently my part in the synchronicity.

When I returned to our table I was weak from vomiting. Ordinarily we would have left after eating, but I wanted to rest. By now the restaurant was full and noisy, and conversations could not be overheard. We invited him to our table. In the ensuing conversation he threw in that he had been contemplating suicide. Shirlè very deftly gave him empathy and understanding, and as he left, his eyes shone with hope.

It was a perfect example of synchronicity. All parties gained from coming together. The young man got what he badly needed, Shirlè had confirmation that she was doing what she came here for, and I... well I guess I was saved from gaining weight. I was just the supporting actor in the play. However, I don't remember asking for the part!

Not long afterwards I became a supporting actor again—this time in a synchronicity play with a UFO theme:

Synchronicity on the Airporter Bus

When I fly to California for only a week or so, I do not take the Airporter; I leave my car at the airport. I love to drive, and like the freedom of having my car anytime I want. But on this particular trip, I strangely decided I should save a little money and not worry about driving on a holiday weekend.

Getting on the Airporter were a few seniors on their way to Thanksgiving get-togethers. I took a seat about mid-way in the bus. A young man of about thirty-five or forty came straight to me and asked if he could sit next to me, though there were empty seats where he could sit alone. I said "Sure."

He sat down—and I listened to a one and a half hour monologue, broken only by the rare, very short, interview type question from me. All the while he looked straight ahead, not at me—and he bared his soul.

He began by saying that he needed to talk, and that if I wasn't there, it would look like he was talking to himself. He said he needed to put it all out, hear himself talk—sort out his thoughts.

It was all about his sense of mission—the world does not realize the danger we are in—catastrophes are coming, and the children should be saved. He had been told (voices in his head?) that his mission is to teach people to learn to love one another—warn them of ecological disasters and possible nuclear holocaust—and save the children—if the world continues on the same path it's on. He went on about spiritual truths—we are all one; being religious is not important, being spiritual is. He was brought up as a Catholic; one sister is a fundamentalist and believes Earth is the center of the universe.

It doesn't make sense to him, he told me. Scientists know there are millions of galaxies, millions of universes—God made it all, so it stands to reason there would be people on other planets. And there can't be only One Way (Jesus); there are many ways to the experience of God. And he doesn't believe that Jesus is God Himself, but a son of God, a child of God, as is every one of us. But his family believes there is a heaven and hell; there is only one chance at life here, and if you don't believe in Jesus you go to hell.

Reincarnation makes more sense to him. And his mission, he told me, is to advance a certain technological device that would help mankind be more "in tune." It has to do with spiral electromagnetic energy.

He described its workings, the theory of it, but my mind couldn't quite grasp it. He impressed me as having the talent for figuring things out for himself, whether spiritual or mechanical, like the mind of an inventor, but though he did not actually say so, he seemed to imply that the technological knowledge was "given" to him.

I asked him what work he did, and he said he wasn't working now. At fifty-eight (he looked so much younger), he still hadn't found his niche. I told him that as a certified graphoanalyst, I do career counseling through handwriting, and he gave me a sample.

The dominant was that he had a feeling for people. There were no obvious signs of mental disturbance. I wanted to study it more later and add it to my collection, so I carefully put the writing with his signature in a special zipped up part of my handbag. (Strangely, when I arrived at my destination, it was gone from my purse! And I didn't ever find it.)

We did not have a real discussion on anything. My role, as I saw it, was to be a listener. I was to be a "stranger" on whom he could bounce off his ideas and get a reaction. He didn't seem to want to know anything about me; didn't ask me any personal questions. But here I was, writing a book about a woman who had similar experiences—even to the mission to save children, and she sometimes had doubted her sanity after some strange metaphysical experiences. So I wondered if his "voices" telling of a mission and prophesies were possibly telepathic messages from aliens—extraterrestrials. I mentioned this casually, and he took it casually, saying he believed extraterrestrials come here to Earth. He left it at that, as if leaving it to me to figure out.

"Look," I said, "I just happen to be someone who understands and is familiar with all you are talking about, and believes in your philosophy. Not everyone does. If I were you I'd be careful who you tell these things to."

"I am," he said. "I knew you were the one to sit with!"

Somewhere along the road, he threw in that both his grandmother and grandfather were Jewish, but became Catholics. (Did he also "know" or sense that I was Jewish, I wondered)

He had long been estranged from his devout Catholic parents and fundamentalist sister who disapprove of his ideas. Now his mother had asked that he come for Thanksgiving, and he said he feared he might be making a mistake in going.

Suddenly it began to dawn on me that his family could be considering hospitalizing him as insane, and that he himself was questioning his own sanity.

We had reached the airport.

"Do you think I'm crazy?" he said finally, seemingly reading my thoughts, and asking for a diagnosis.

"No I don't," I said. "I *do not.*"

He got up to leave and I followed. At the bus exit he turned, smiled and faced me squarely for the first time. "I'll *remember* this ride," he said, and stepped off the Airporter bus.

Chapter Seventeen

UFO, NDE, and the Metaphysical Relationship

"It seems that once one breaks-through the normal dimensions of space and time, either through an NDE or alien abduction, one may be open to various paranormal phenomena."---Kenneth Ring, PhD

Interestingly, Dr. Ring, author of The Omega Project, has found startling similarities between the experiences of "near death" and alien contact, including after-effects—the most profound being a heightened spirituality and sense of mission. Furthermore, his research leads him to hypothesize that the real significance of extraordinary NDE and UFO encounters may lie in their evolutionary implications for humanity."

Raymond Fowler also writes of UFO and NDE encounters. In *The Watchers II* he notes that UFOs and their occupants are paraphysical in nature like NDEs, with the ability to enter and exit our world seemingly from another space time continuum. He compares Betty and Bob Luca's UFO experiences and NDEs—in which both involved "being in an OBE state—traveling toward a bright light, being greeted by a loving being, experiencing Oneness, seeing beings of light, being transformed into light, communicating by telepathy, being brought 'home,' having a feeling of timelessness, exhibiting extreme reluctance to leave the place of light, returning with a sense of love, and showing extreme concern for earth's ecological state." He also notes that both have precognition in common, especially regarding the death of someone.

Fowler feels that so-called aliens, rather than being extraterrestrials—that is, from other planets might be from another dimension, another plane, coexisting with us. (However, I don't see why there couldn't be both.) He goes on to say, "Could it be that the UFO phenomenon and NDEs are controlled by an advanced civilization in another dimension peopled in part by human beings who have entered that dimension through the death process? Could it be that the human-like Elders (seen in both UFOs and NDEs) are what we will evolve into in a future existence?"

UFO contactees have had NDEs and vice versa. Shirlè at the age of eight, while looking in the mirror, had an experience that resembled a NDE. Raymond Fowler and Kenneth Ring find that contactees (or abductees) and NDE subjects have similar make-ups, called an "encounter prone personality."

***

I went over Shirlè's story and was struck by the sheer number of paranormal experiences. I began to count and categorize them. I had already noted their continued presence after her association with Frank, and realized that each one indicated the presence of an entity. Next thing I knew, I found myself summarizing them.

Signs of Possible Alien, Angel, or Spirit Presence
A Summary—From Shirlè's Own Experiences

Artifacts from Frank:
Two disks, one retrieved by Frank; one in her possession
One bracelet in her possession with Frank's writing on it, photocopied before being lost
One belt in her possession with special magnets
A two-page letter (no copy) of Frank's writing in strange symbols
Eight copper plates in her possession, each with Frank's "hieroglyphics"

Entities from Another Dimension or Another Planet:
The **"Angel Story"** of mother in labor with Shirlè, given orange juice and told her child would be special. (Was the woman an alien, angel, extraterrestrial or interdimensional, or are they the same in some cases?)
ET entity showing she omitted his neck appendages.
The aliens of the **"scuba divers"** incident
Entities in the **initiations** of air and water
Woman (ET, angel) by her bed, comforting her
"Danny Kaye" ET, angel who came to heal her back
The two **vibrating entities** at the foot of her bed
ET or departed soul teleporting Shirlè and stuck car
ET, departed soul--telekinesis (moving canvasses)
ET, departed soul materializing a quill into her thigh
Spirit of the dead in astral form: Hymie
Spirit of the dead in solid form: Hymie's dead mother
Entities from another dimension: Nickelodeon dancers
Solid spirits of mother's departed friends
The **ghost** of a little boy
Voice of departed soul: Hymie's dead sister Libilla
Astral form of Yannish in **bilocation**

People Holograms:
1) Shirlè and friends at Stonehenge. Was it a hologram projected by aliens?
2) A psychic says a UFO is outside; they see a huge color hologram of a man.

UFO Holograms:
1) Shirlè is shown a UFO (in a vision) that others actually saw physically.
2) UFOs in all shapes, colors (birthday present from Frank) seen while awake

Scenes in a Parallel Universe, or Another Dimension:
Appearance of 1) Flowers, 2) Sculpture, 3) Horses running

Electronic Outage: (frequently reported by contactees with UFOs nearby)
1) Outage while giving a lecture
2) New car wouldn't start on Las Vegas trip; entire day of missing time

Missing Time: Indication of probable abductions
The "scuba divers" story
The "Reno-Las Vegas" story
The "clock" story
The "red bands" story

Hospital "missing time"
Gaining Time: possible hospital visit abduction in Arizona/Nevada in 2001
Beam of Light: At three years of age, being enveloped by a beam of light from above
Under Hypnosis: Abduction at age five, possible missing time

Implants: Seeing needle being withdrawn from back of head

Nose Bleeds and Possible Implants in New Mexico Motel
Nose bleeds can sometimes occur with implants. Had she been given another implant?

Bleeding Cuts: (same motel), Shirlè (as well as author) woke up with bleeding cuts

Buzzing in the Ears: Then she'd see a spacecraft. Was it an implant/UFO connection?

Invisible Marks on Shirlè's Back (seen under black light UV): At a Contactee Conference

Marks on Clothing: At Iceland UFO conference Shirlè and Icelanders had same "stamp"

Red Band of Skin Circling Each Wrist: Abduction? 1999 UFO Conference in Laughlin

Smells
1) Orange smell at Shirlè's art show
2) Delicatessen smell – possibly "departed" friend Zellinger
3) Cooking smell in Roswell and New Mexico motel

Hebrew Writing:
1) Vision in which a bearded man reprimanded Shirlè with message in Hebrew letters
2) Star of David and Hebrew writing on hand and wrist (aliens or spiritual realm?)

UFOS Visible in Australian photos after development: Frank pointed them out.

Genuine UFOs?
1) In 1967, Shirlè and girlfriend saw their first UFO—a light zigzagging in the sky

2) On Reno trip she spotted a craft high above the earth with revolving colored lights
3) On the last night of the Laughlin UFO Conference UFOs were seen as lights

Huge Light Diving into the Ocean:
Shirlè saw a light, larger than full moon, hover, then dive into the ocean (Hologram or alien underwater base?)

Large Globe of Blue Light: Appeared as she said she missed a special dog named "Blue"

Lights in the Sky in Safford AZ: return flashlight signal sent by Shirlè and friend

Animal in the Wild: Shirlè pet a wild fox from the woods. (Aliens can use animals to show their presence.)

UFOs as lights appeared in the sky in formation after appearance of the fox.

Hearing Voices:
What to study: when not to go when dangerous; when to go to Iceland: where to find ideas for murals; warning not to hit her father; told to ask Mary to go with her to Iceland (Aliens or angels?)Telepathy or Strong Intuition:
1) Being drawn to Frank's store (telepathy, hypnotic order, or implant given earlier?)
2) Shirlè on her way to party (Intuition or mind control?)
3) Strong feeling of being observed. "Are you an alien," she asks. The woman nods

Materialization: Porcupine quill, missing from a locked glass case, materializes into Shirlè's thigh

Scoop Mark, Electronic Beeps: Can also be indicative of abduction, and were the only ones that Shirlè did not experience. They were the author's.

Chapter Eighteen

Realizations
Teaching While Out-of-Body
Spiritual Love

"Be humble for you are made of earth. Be noble for
you are made of the stars"—Serbian proverb.

"Being desirable means being comfortable with your own ambiguity. The
most ambiguous reality is that we are flesh and spirit at the same time. Within
everyone there is light and shadow, good and evil, love and hate. In order to be
truthful you must embrace your total being. A person who exhibits both positive
and negative qualities, strengths and weaknesses is not flawed, but complete."
--Rumi, scholar, artist, poet – 1244

Realizations

By now Shirlè was giving occasional UFO lectures but preferred
interacting one-on-one. She was living a quiet and simple life,
despite the turmoil and travail of being an "Indigo", "Wanderer", "Star
Child" contactee. She had matured and mellowed. She had already
initiated peace with one sister and come to terms with her mother with
compassion.

In 1999 she attended classes and lectures at The Institute for the
Research of Human Happiness, and went with some of her classmates on
a trip to Japan. At the Institute she gained more psychological and
spiritual insights. At the same time, delving into her life for this book,
she had a chance to really look into things, get feedback, and see her

childhood and later life from other perspectives.

The following is a condensed compilation of her notes at the Institute:

"When you're happy with yourself, they say, you can give off happiness to others. And I faced myself dead on. At one time I had a sense of failure, an inferiority complex, a negative self-image, belittling myself and blaming others, at times feeling suicidal. It all comes from my childhood. I have done wrong, hurtful things that almost destroyed me, thinking that only my parents were at fault. It was wrong. I was to blame as well.

"I had to heal the inner child that I had neglected, pushed away. My parents were novices in bringing up children, and I was a novice to my children as well. And I suddenly realized I had done to my children some of the hurtful things my parents had done to me!

"I also had to learn not to be so sensitive. I can't live on this planet being so sensitive, or I'd be hurt day and night, and wouldn't be able to function. And I realized that their role was to make me aware of what this world was all about, and to accept rejection without having my world fall apart. But every now and then something brings me down, because I still haven't reached that strength where nothing can affect me so much. So I still have work to do. But I mustn't be too hard or insensitive, or I won't be able to feel for other people as well. It's a thin line. Being hurt is all right as long as you look into it and understand why.

"And I did look into it. I had some reservations with the Buddhist group, some differences of opinion, and felt hurt. But it taught me a lot, and I'm thankful to them for that."

The Buddhist group was a humbling experience for her. Only later did she realize that without the work she did on herself there, she may not have met a Tibetan monk two months later who made a powerful impression on her with his spiritual knowledge. At the time, however, all she had was the familiar strong intuitive feeling to make another trip to Iceland—that there was more than just her strong feeling about the country, its people, and a possible past life there. She longed to return to Iceland to find out.

Spiritual Love

"O hidden Life, vibrant in every atom, O hidden Light, shining in every creature, O hidden Love, embracing all in oneness, may all who feel themselves as one with thee, know they are therefore one with every other."-- Annie Besant

It was 1999. Shirlè had waited so long. Maybe Iceland held the next step in her mission. She arranged her airfare. Upon arriving, she stayed at the home of her friends Elizabeth and Ollie, and happily visited everyone else she knew. She felt really at home in Iceland—so many of the locals were psychic and believed in aliens. One day, coming home from an outing, a smiling Elizabeth related an incident.

"You know," she said, "I was watching television, and suddenly a tall figure of a man came out of your room. Then he vanished into thin air. He was completely solid. I wasn't shocked, just surprised. I feel it was an alien."

Shirlè feels it was her protector. (It wasn't the first such story. A visitor in Shirlè's home once said he saw a man in a dark suit come down the stairs of her house, then suddenly vanish before his eyes.)

It was through Elizabeth that she received a call the next day from Elizabeth's nephew, Albert Edelson, (coincidentally Shirlè maiden name), asking Shirlè to lecture to his group. When? Now. In fifteen minutes a taxi was waiting.

Shirlè arrived at the meeting hall and was introduced to Albert Adelson, He was slender, dark, and serious. She figured he was about twenty-five years younger than she. He told her that he was a Tibetan monk and his Tibetan name was Phubten Lekshe. He worked for various companies checking vitamin production. The conversation was short and mundane.

"I didn't know that monks worked outside."

"Yes," he said, "they do, everywhere."

Shirlè gave a great talk. The audience, mostly in professions or in the art and literary world, gave her rapt attention and received her warmly in the socializing period afterward. As he took her home he offered ideas regarding her artwork.

"I knew of you before, but you weren't ready"

At nine the next morning the phone rang. "Would it be alright," he asked, "if I come over in about an hour?"

He entered with a suitcase full of books. They talked and talked. "I'm surprised," he said finally, "at all your present knowledge. *I knew of you when you came three years ago but I didn't bother to see you. You weren't ready for me then, but you are now.*"

She figured the constant reviewing of her life for the book, and the certain psychological issues she had faced at the Japanese Institute for the Research for Human Happiness had helped to make her ready. (Her contact, Frank, had also told her that he had come for her in previous lifetimes, but each time she wasn't ready—she was "sitting on the fence," so he had chosen not to make contact.)

They talked for a few hours, and then went out to eat at a soup-and-sandwich place. In nervous expectation, she didn't eat much. They returned, and he imparted still more spiritual knowledge.

The next ten days of teaching were intense. They went over *A Treatise on Cosmic Fire* by Alice A. Bailey (in which are mentioned planets in decaying solar systems whose people are forced to find a new home), and they discussed various highly spiritual people. He spoke on his work in the field of health, and about his experiences in Tibet as a monk, having left Iceland as a young man to study spiritual doctrines in a monastery there. It was not a typical monastic life, he told her; he was free to travel and work.

He believed the writing on her plates was in the language of Lemuria of 40,000 years ago, and that Shirlè was once a scribe there. The interpretation of the inscriptions on the eight thin copper plates that Frank gave her are already *in her mind*, he told her, and when the time is right, the aliens will reveal the meaning.

The next day, Albert brought Shirlè along on his visit to his mother who was to go in for surgery the following day. Immediately his mother hugged and kissed her.

"Do I know you?" Shirlè asked, perplexed, for they had never met.

"I know *you*," she answered. "You come to Iceland often."

Shirlè was stunned. "You mean I come out of body?"

"Yes," the woman replied, "and when I go to different planets, you are there too, greeting me."

Then Shirlè remembered that Frank had said that she works on many levels, and in many places, and is taller in some places. At the time, however, she didn't understand.

She thought, too, of a recent similar experience. She used to teach three or four artists at the Eckankar group. One day she got a call from one of them she hadn't seen for some time.

"Shirlè," she said, "thank you for teaching me how to do eyes."

"You haven't been to my classes lately," said Shirlè. "How can I be teaching you?"

"Well," she said, "we happened to be in the same place. By the way, are you doing a large mural now?"

"Yes," said Shirlè.

"Well," she said, "what you are doing here, you've already done before, in the astral. When I went into that realm you were there, teaching me."

Apparently, this happens while Shirlè is asleep. Her soul goes astrally and teaches while Shirlè's personality or ego is unaware. In dreams we visit other levels of existence, and even gain needed skills. Each of us has counterparts in other systems of reality (probable realities), developing abilities in a different way than we are here. So, if we know something or have a particular strong talent, we have already known it or done it somewhere else. Could this be why she was already artistic as a child? Was she, as Frank had said, Botticelli in another life? Or, does she have, as discussed in *The Seth Material*[54], a counterpart in another system of reality, in its own time system, developing different abilities? (Or could both be true?)

One evening, while dining in a restaurant with Albert, her thoughts reeled. "He was so knowledgeable and the way he spoke, he elevated me to such a height... We were totally one, unconditionally loving one another, soul with soul. HaShem, I said, I can't believe this is happening to me. It's a miracle."

He took her back home, gave her a hug, said good-night, and left her. But she couldn't sleep.

"HaShem," she said aloud to God, "I can't believe it. Never in my life could I believe there is such a thing as a total bonding with another human being without having sex—the intense warm feelings being reciprocated. If ever there was love[55] this was it."

***

When she returned to Vancouver she was still full of inspiration from her contact with the Tibetan monk, and found herself scribbling:

"Gently, gently goes my heart as it beats with all of you—you gentle souls. Hand in hand we must go from the third into the fourth and fifth dimensions. We are all soul travelers. Together our souls will shine brightly like a beacon. We send you our love. Come join us. We will lighten your load and show you how beautiful this world can be."

---

[54] Probable selves and probable systems of reality in *The Seth Material* by Jane Roberts, 1970.

[55] This non-sexual love has been reported by others revering a spiritual teacher.

Afterword

What's It All About?

A Global and Personal Transformation

"It's about more than UFOs and ETs. It's about our essence,
about human destiny, soul evolution."--Scott Mandelker, PhD.

"Life is the only game in which the object of the game is to learn the rules."
--Ashley Brilliant

Working on this book I learned a few things from Shirlè's story. I learned there are *infinite* dimensions in the Universe—parallel worlds, and the veils that hide them can be pierced. I learned to trust more in God the Creator or "spirit within," as I became more aware of the part synchronicity plays in life. I learned how to notice these "coincidences" and how I can use them to shape my purpose in life. And finally, I learned that God the Creator may work not only through angels and the spirit within, but in synchronicity with other humans, spirits of the dead, or extraterrestrials—all for the purpose of helping us evolve spiritually to the *next dimension.*

And that's what it's all about.. Shirlè's story is not only about a particular alien with his message and warnings, nor is it just about Shirlè's travails as an Indigo, Wanderer, Star Child contactee—with her many paranormal[56] experiences (though the metaphysical is an integral part of the UFO and alien phenomenon)—*it's more importantly about our spiritual growth and the cosmic plan.*

It's About the Transformation of Earth and its Inhabitants:

Earth and its souls are at the end of the third, moving into the fourth vibratory phase, in readiness for the coming of the fifth[57] dimension. As we do so, our bodies reach a higher frequency and we become bodiless—invisible, yet alive. As an embryo's heart is entrained to the heart of the mother, we humans are entrained to Earth, and Earth is entrained to the sun. But the sun is *changing.* So *we* must change.

Meanwhile Earth will be going through earthquakes and floods of great magnitude, from natural and man-made causes. There will be parts of the Earth that will be uninhabitable. Because of these events, various alien races have come here to influence or control Earth and human evolution.

"Alright," you say, "so aliens *do* exist on other planets, even in other *dimensions* or parallel worlds—*and some are here on Earth,*—so what? Will it make my *personal* life any better?"

What the Aliens Can Mean to You Personally:

Spiritual evolution of the species begins with the *individual.* The aliens are telling us we must examine ourselves, be more grateful, more compassionate, more forgiving. They can affect us personally by raising our consciousness to understand that we are all One and that Earth is a school— **we're here to learn** *compassion*—**and compassion is required to evolve spiritually.** Of course, one can arrive at the same conclusions from various known disciplines—but the study of the UFO and alien phenomenon can be an additional tool.

It can make you aware of the existence of many other *dimensions,* which you may learn to pierce. It can prepare you for eventual *communication* with entities from other dimensions for personal guidance; raise your consciousness about astral and parallel worlds and get you on a spiritual path—perhaps by studying the best channeling

---

1. Abilities we all have to varying degrees.
2 This transition to the fifth dimension or fifth world, is said to have been preceded by four cycles of about 25,000 years each.

from an alien (RA, *The Law of One*).

You may ask for and receive help for *medical problems* from aliens in another dimension who do this work (*Cured by Aliens* by Adrian Dvir).

And politically—*Being informed on UFOs and aliens can be vital in influencing our government in its handling of it.* We should have a say on the why and wherefore if we are suddenly told we are in "Star Wars." We should know of the benefits and "curses" of a mass landing of aliens—how it could affect the economy, politics, and religions of our world.

Reports from UFO activists can inspire you to do your own investigation and study of the subject—so that you can be informed enough to make an intelligent evaluation for possible future action on your own—should our government decide to do something regarding them that would not be in our best interests.

PART IV

To Do a Study of UFOs

Chapter Nineteen

The UFO and Alien Presence

"Everyone has gifts, but the greatest gift is inspiration, for with it,
one can have the desire to do anything." -- Alien Frank

A Few Points to Consider Before You Begin

To start with—the subject is complicated and involved—you have to at least believe in *possible* life on other planets in our galaxy. Then you find that there are an *infinite* number of *galaxies*—in universes past ours, with intelligent life on planets in those far galaxies.

Then you have to accept the possibility of aliens traveling past the speed of light—playing around in our skies by manipulating space and time, coming to Earth for thousands of years (explain, please, those medieval era religious paintings with UFOs in the background.)

Then there's the possibility of these extraterrestrials landing or crashing on Earth and leaving alien bodies, with "Roswells" not only in America but China, Russia and other countries.

Next you have to get past the idea of alien crafts changing into various physical forms, appearing as lights or orbs—some even producing and operating their vehicle by *thought*.

You discover there are Grays, *varieties* of Grays, some working with very human-like beings. There are also the Reptilians, Insectoids, Humanoids, Nordics, Giants, and pure energy Lights. And in each there are those that are "good" or "bad," just like people on Earth.

You find that 30% to 50% of physical UFOs are most likely our own military's secret crafts, which have been back-engineered from UFOs downed accidentally, or otherwise.

About abductions—you learn there's the possibility that *some* abductions are done not by aliens, but by part of our own military "Black Ops"!

Then you have to understand that while some abductees report positive, spiritually rewarding contact with aliens, astrally or in person, many others have been traumatized by medical examinations. Women have been made pregnant with genetic manipulations, and their hybrid fetuses removed from the host or natural mother (missing fetus syndrome). Have these hybrids who look similar to us but with paranormal abilities come to live amongst us to help us and our Earth or mainly to control us?

And you have to wonder about the meaning and significance of the messages and prophesies given to abductees and contactees.

Also you have to consider that an alien or extraterrestrial *soul* could come here by entering a fetus, or an adult human body, (remember we are first *a soul that inhabits a body)* and so there is the possibility that *we* are all "aliens" here on Earth. The aliens may have "seeded" us here, in various DNA and genetic experiments and continually tended their "garden" Earth. There may be reincarnation not only back to Earth, but possibly to *other planets.*

You then have to come to the premise that *some* aliens may not even be extraterrestrial, but rather from other *dimensions* (which are many), or even our future.

Then there's the animal mutilation connection to aliens, and with investigation you soon find that some may be the work of our own government (for study of pollution) and some (however rare) are even human mutilations. If you are not yet confused or disillusioned, you find out that *some* crop circles which you are convinced are alien-made, are actually man-made hoaxes.

Then there is the Bigfoot, Chupicabra and Men in Black connection to extraterrestrials or other dimensions for particular study.

You learn too, that we humans have already communicated with aliens (today and for thousands of years) with signs and lights, and received responses (CSETI today); humans have been inside UFOs consciously and physically, or in the astral state, and have received communication through channeling and dreams.

Then you hear that while some aliens may be here living in the physical—others able to become invisible may even be walking around our Earth *undetected*! You learn that some in the physical may look alien, some may appear human (either their natural state or they have shape-shifted—that is, changed their appearance). Some have made themselves known in person to ordinary citizens such as Shirlè. But some could also possibly be working in various places and in various capacities—even in cooperation with our own military (area 51). And you wonder, what's their agenda?

You will also have to wonder about the psychological, political and religious implications of the UFO phenomenon, positive and negative— as well as the spiritual implications—what it's really all about—for it's *the spiritual evolution of humanity*. Then you have to ask yourself what it all really means to you *personally*. And if it does, what you're going to *do* about it.

If you've gotten this far, you have to weed out all the disinformation (a few falsehoods mixed with the basic truth) if you can, that comes from our government, UFO researchers, NASA, or the aliens themselves—and come out of all this with your head still on.

But for those who persevere, it can be rewarding as well as challenging.

To see the total picture, I had to first sort it all out under headings, and it became my list of UFO and related subjects which follows.

***

UFO and Related Subjects:

Nuts and Bolts: appearance, shape, size, colors.
Alien Technology: How they operate, use energy.
Science: How do they go faster than light, interstellar travel
     use wormholes, black holes?
Humanity's Origins: Where do we/they (ET) come from?
     Ancient civilizations: Sumerian, Egyptian, their connections to ET.
Possible ET Bases: Various alien races seen by remote viewing
     on Earth, the moon, and Mars.
Alien Agenda:
The various races and their origin
     Other planets, parallel universes, our future, or all three?
     Are they extraterrestrials, time travelers, angels, or all three?
Monitoring humans
     For earth ecology? Samples taken of skin, eggs, sperm, DNA
     For saving their/our species—or controlling ours?
     Hybrids, Genetic engineering
For communication?
     Implants, channeling, and with our military remote viewers
     For raising our awareness
     Paranormal—increase of extrasensory perception.
     Soul reincarnation and life between lives
Spiritual evolution
     ETs, science and religion
     Medical science and the spiritual
Men in Black
     US government agents or aliens--perhaps hybrids?
Warnings
     Regarding Earth and human disasters
     The need for new energy, new behavior
     Through personal contact and/or channeling.
     Aliens' Prophesies, Bible Code
Contacts & Abductions
     Abductees, Contactees and Support Groups
     Similarities between Near Death & Contactee experience
     Regressions, leading to existence of Soul and spiritual?
Crop Circles, Animal Mutilations, Sasquatch: (ET involvement?
     UFOs, lights near crop circles. Magnetics high. Node change.

Bluish vapor filmed beside carcasses. Bloodless laser incisions
Sasquatch (Bigfoot)- UFOs seen nearby

Seeking Physical Evidence:
From actual UFOs and bodies of aliens—Roswell & MJ 12
From back-engineering of downed UFOs
From surgical removal of implants of unknown material & origin
Marks on body; elements, radiation in soil after UFO departure

Evidence for UFOs and Aliens:

Debunkers and Skeptics:

Government Military Cover-up:
Retired witnesses testifying
Military personnel who have come out of the closet
Remote viewers of UFOs & ETs
Air forces and NICAP – astronauts talking

Social and Political Activists:
Working for government exposure, sane interaction with aliens,
the teaching of spirituality, and the prevention of possible "Star
Wars" against "hostile" aliens

***

Next, I compiled what I think is basic UFO knowledge as of today
into a concise UFO review. However I want to emphasize that not
everything referred to is necessarily proven *fact*. For example, I may
quote certain aliens and channelers of aliens; the content may be colored
by the receiver's own personality and beliefs—or the alien may be more
technologically advanced, but not necessarily more spiritual or have our
best interests in mind. I may mention certain government witnesses, for
example Bob Lazar, who claims to have worked in Area 51 with back-
engineered UFOs. Physicist Stanton Friedman, after researching Bob
Lazar's education and employment, pronounced him a fraud. Remote
viewers have claimed that where Lazar worked and what he saw was
true—but how can that be proven?

Clifford Stone, who claims to have witnessed and taken part in the
Roswell incident, is another whose veracity has been questioned. When
records cannot be found, it does not necessarily mean he was fraudulent;
they could have been destroyed. Shirlè and I both had a talk with him
while he was writing his book in Roswell. I had no reason to doubt his
story.

I could go on and on; the MJ 12 papers are still being questioned for authenticity. (Stanton Friedman believes *most* of the papers are genuine.) Another case that is still disputed is the Billie Meier story. I won't go into it here. It's too convoluted. I leave it to the reader to figure out. Many other testimonies are considered inauthentic. The reader must come to his own conclusions on these, as well as on the chapters that follow. I can only give my own unprofessional view; I am not a scientifically trained investigator—and a true objective scientific approach to the UFO phenomenon is vital.

However, at the same time I feel that *sometimes* this approach rules out as flaky, some experiences of witnesses and experiencers that should be looked at more seriously and accepted as genuine.

The UFO and Alien Presence

"We are not machines that have learned to think. We are thoughts that have learned to create machines."—Alien Frank

The average person will have heard of UFOs and abductions from the media, and will perhaps have seen a UFO. However, they are no more than curiosities to him. And there is so much more to the subject. The following are three less known aspects worth emphasizing:

The Metaphysical and Alien Connection:

In order to understand the UFO phenomenon you need to accept the metaphysical phenomenon as real and see its connection to the UFO

Indigo, Wanderer or Star Contactees:

Parents, teachers, psychologists and social workers should be aware of the traits of "Indigos, Wanderers, and Star Children" to better understand and help their children and clients.

They are here among us and always have been:

There have been "Roswells" in China and Mexico but some land safely and stay awhile.

According to researcher Warren Aston, there are perhaps twenty or more different alien groups visiting our planet and involved with us with various motives and agendas. He firmly believes that some of these races live among us here undetected. To complicate the picture, some may be extra-dimensional as well as extraterrestrial in origin.

Their warnings for us, and their hope for us:

Natural and man-made catastrophes are in store for us, which we can avert by tending to the ecology of the planet, and learning the art of compassion. This is nothing new. Many contactees have received the same message, but world events today make the message more cogent, more compelling.

Now To Start at the Beginning

Our Ancient History:
Some aliens claim (via telepathy or channeling) that in the far distant past (before the Flood) various extraterrestrials had come to Earth, and some had mated with the then highest naturally evolved beings on Earth—creating the first humans. (In Genesis we read "the sons of God" mated with the "daughters of men.") It should be noted, however, they only manipulated, added, subtracted, changed, what the Supreme Creator, the Source of all life, had caused to be present on Earth and in the Universe.

Alien Races:
They are all technologically far superior to us (from other planets or other dimensions). An alien may come here physically in a space ship, be born here as a hybrid, come here in spirit and enter a human fetus (wanderer), or take over a willingly relinquished body (walk-in). Some aliens can materialize, dematerialize, pass through walls, and communicate by telepathy. Some can be physical or non-physical (invisible to us) and can shape-shift (change looks).

Some types:
"Nordics"—6-7 ft tall, blond, blue-eyed, friendly, helpful, could be living on Earth undetected.
Reptilians—scaly-looking skin, well-built and appear aggressive
"Insectoids"—resembling a praying mantis 7-14 ft, long arms. They supervise research.
Giants –(seen in Israel)—8-10 ft tall, leave giant footprints
Grays—3-5 ft tall, large eyes and head, and a thin body (biological robots?)
"Orientals"—4-5 ft tall. Zeta Reticuli grays interested in neurochemicals for emotion
Humanoids—in various sizes and shapes, such as the Pleiadians, interested in human behavior
Non-physical entities of pure energy—invisible or as lights, acting with intelligence

Alien Bases:
Some aliens are said to be from planets in our galaxy with bases on the dark side of our moon; underground and undersea on Earth; on Mars

and Venus, as well as on satellites in space

Abductions and Contacts:

Some aliens do abductions to monitor our health and that of the planet; some do them to remove hormones they need; some are studying our emotions; some are done to impart technological information, warnings, and prophesies to us; some occur for genetic engineering of hybrids for their (and our?) planet.

Aliens Living and Working Among Us:

If you can accept seeing UFOs and accept their existence, how come you (most of you) can't imagine that the UFOs could be manned, and if so, they could land—and why would they not stay awhile to study Earth and strange humans? Is it so hard to fathom that aliens could be living, even working right here among us? Retired military personnel believe it. However, not much real serious discussion on it can be found in books or papers.

Implants:

Some aliens insert implants on any part of the body, nose, ear, hand, foot, leg. Its purpose is probably to monitor health, communicate, raise our consciousness, (and perhaps to do mind control?) Dr. Roger Leir has removed implants of unknown origin—but with no actual *proof* of their *extraterrestrial* origin.

The Zeta Grays—(One theory according to **Channeled Alien Information** in *Visitors From Within* by Royal & Priest:— (paraphrased):**

The planet Apex was ruined with radiation. Unable to bear children, the descendants cloned themselves and altered their genetics to adapt to living underground—restructuring their bodies to change light to heat, food to nutrients, oxygen to chlorophyll. Sexual organs gradually disappeared. To eliminate wars and crime, emotions and diversity were bred out, and their mental bodies became dominant. Now they would like to bring back some of the traits they lost.

Another interesting channeled alien view on abductions (paraphrased):

In short, as the abductee works on the integration of fear and victimization, the negative ET experiences change. Probes or implants in the brain are not for control; being organic they absorb neurochemicals which are studied for the purpose of providing emotions the aliens feel they lack. The abductions are so that they may learn about emotion and diversity, but primarily they are done to save their species from extinction, and to teach us about fear and unity.

On the other hand, the author asks, perhaps we should fear preprogrammed zombies given posthypnotic commands to obey an unknown or evil master plan.

Warren Aston on Nanno Technology of Alien Origin:

At the 1998 UFO Conference in Laughlin, Nevada, Australian researcher Warren Aston made a few points in his talk that I thought were worth mentioning here—that our scientists were working on nanotechnology—similar to that of aliens (manufacturing at the molecular or atomic level), and have already produced the strongest and lightest material that springs back when crumpled. Aston went on to list all the benefits of nannotechnology:

Storage of information at the non-localized molecular level; manufacture of powerful small super-computers containing all knowledge interfacing with our brain, making us geniuses; manufacturing without conventional tools, without seams, rivets or joints; machines designed to restore habitats to their natural state, remove nuclear waste, toxic chemicals, make deserts fertile; molecular machines programmed to destroy or repair diseased cells within the body, rebuild damaged organs, restore missing limbs and defective organs, have us breathe in different atmospheres, create intelligent biological robots to perform menial tasks; locate, read and store genetic information of every living species; accomplish tasks in a fraction of the time it takes now, without dangerous byproducts and pollution.

The resultant economic revolution would mean the elimination of the economic, environmental, and social problems that plague our planet. But this nannotechnology could also be abused by amassing arsenals of weapons with far greater potential than our current nuclear and biological weaponry. A nation or a small group could develop this technology to dominate all others. There is mounting evidence that the military/intelligence/industrial cover-up of UFO activity in recovered alien technology has been orchestrated in part by using nanno-engineered devises far in advance of anything known elsewhere.

Good Guys

It has been claimed they have "given" us inventions, inspired us to higher technology and consciousness—even healed illnesses. However, they are not allowed (by their superiors) to actively interfere with our destructiveness. They say their purpose is to raise humanity's evolution without resorting to *direct intervention*. However should Earth become uninhabitable due to human or natural causes, some races say they would transfer some humans to another planet.

Bad Guys

In my view, if their intentions were to take over and negatively control our world, they could have done so long ago—with their advanced technology. But perhaps they are restrained by other aliens or it is not their purpose at this time when their agenda is that of rejuvenating their race with human hormones, genetic engineering, and producing hybrids. They take what they need from us, and do their job of abductions without any seeming compassion. Just as we try to save endangered species, tagging, taking samples, and removing them to another place, without thought of the psychological damage done to them, so they traumatize abductees, leaving them with a fragmentary memory, and the feeling of being violated, disrespected, and treated like an animal.

Other negative aliens, some researchers believe, hope to "conquer" us by slow genetic manipulation or by putting mind-controlled hybrids on Earth. Gene and mind control are already being done by our scientists. More important are the motives—ours and theirs.

How Do You Tell Them Apart?

First of all, they are not black and white; they are mixtures, just like humans. Like us, they live in a world of polarization of consciousness (positive and negative orientation—good and evil), and like us, can be at varying levels of spirituality or wisdom.

"So not only do you have to determine if the contact you had was negative," says Dr. Mandelker, "but what was the relative maturity of the source? There is a Brazilian saying: 'Just because he's dead doesn't mean he knows anything. Just because he walks through walls doesn't mean he is a Buddha or loves you. And just because he's real doesn't mean he's going to help you, no matter what he says.' Let's have discernment."

A rule of thumb, according to Dr. Mandelker, if contact leaves you feeling good, empowered for service to others, it's positive; if it's fearful, full of doom, it's negative. Some abductees, however, have mixed feelings.

For and Against the Existence of UFOs:
The Strongest Evidence:

Reverse engineering of "captured" UFOs by witnesses in Area 51; nuclear physicist Stanton Friedman on his research of the Roswell incident; retired US military, pilots and astronauts coming "out of the closet" reporting UFOs; remote viewing by our military—alien bases seen; multiple UFOs seen by many, videoed and reported openly in Mexico, China, and the USA; astronauts Gordon Cooper and Scott Carpenter reports of seeing UFOs; high-ranking Air Force officers in Russia, China, Brazil, Mexico, and France reporting it's real; reliable military personnel testifying regarding downed UFOs and alien bodies; signaling and mental telepathy between humans and UFOs and aliens (e.g., J. Gilliland); abduction and contactee reports by reliable reputable people, (e.g., the late John Mack, M.D.); the 1978 UN report on the reality of UFOs; Italian researcher Georgio Bongiovano's video of a Russian general admitting that UFOs are real, and would report to the UN, if the US and China do likewise; knowledgeable UFO activists, like attorney Peter Gersten, Daniel Sheehan, and others; the 2002 Disclosure Project by Stephen Greer; the 2001 Cometa report made in France; NASA's own films of UFO's; papers supporting the belief that Truman, Eisenhower, Ford and Reagan were informed of UFOs and aliens.

Debunkers and Skeptics

They believe UFOs have a psycho-social explanation—that is, they are all in the mind or inter-dimensional, and not extraterrestrial, or they are concocted by hoaxers. Regarding regressions, they believe (rightly) there is the danger of leading questions. Always, their argument is: no actual *proof.*

And If They're Real...

People keep asking, "If they are really here, why don't they just show themselves on the White House lawn?" They don't land there, but many have seen them over our Capitol. And *fleets of UFOs have been seen by thousands over cities in Mexico, China, Russia,* to name a few countries—but if governments don't give them credence... They have been attacked by weapons of our military, and they subsequently counteracted our radar. The governments of the world are not welcoming them. We are busy with wars, and the more spiritual aliens are not allowed to actively interfere, but only guide.

Stanton Friedman had this to say in 1977: "The only hope for this planet, before some idiot puts his finger on the button, is for us to think of ourselves not as nationalities, but as earthlings. I am not surprised that they (the space people) don't make contact with us on the White House lawn. It's perfectly obvious to any intelligent visitor that we are a primitive society whose major occupation is tribal warfare."—Stanton Friedman, physicist, 1977 International UFO Congress.

Their Fears of Us and For Us

The positive aliens say our reckless use of nuclear bombs can send reverberations into space, affecting other planets, as well as causing earthquakes on Earth—and our biological and chemical weapons can wipe out our civilization. They want to make sure we do not go into far space before we are ready to abide by the rules of law already in space, for their good as well as ours. And so they prefer to interact little by little, with people such as scientists, artists, writers and just ordinary people who are "open"—so that they and their information are *gradually* understood by the general public. The negative ones—may have somewhat self-serving motives.

Chapter Twenty

Actions by Prominent People
UFO Activists

"Our deepest fear is not that we are inadequate. Our deepest fear is that we are powerful beyond measure. It is our light, not our darkness, that frightens us."
-- Nelson Mandela.

S hirlè's life story, though partly as an artist with a mission, is mostly on the connection of her metaphysical experiences to her contact with an alien. It does little to convince the reader of the reality of aliens. It's impossible to do so, for there *is* no proof. Nevertheless, I have added the endeavors of prominent people and organizations that do not take the UFO and alien subject as fad or hobby, but as the serious subject it is.

The United Nations Conference

As far back as November 28th, 1978, an attempt was made to get the UN to take serious notice of the UFO & alien presence. One hundred people attended the meeting in Room 4 of the UN building, arranged by Lee Siegel, (Chief of Field Investigations for the UFO Review). Sir Eric Gairy of Grenada opened the meeting.

Speakers

Dr. J. Allen Hynek, astronomer and scientist: "The UFO phenomenon is real and not the creation of disturbed minds; it has both grave and important implications to science as well as for the political and social well-being of the people of the Earth."

Dr. Jacques Vallee, MA in astrophysics and PhD in computer science: "The phenomenon is increasingly affecting the lives of people around the world."

Col. Larry Coyne: "There is a need for worldwide cooperation and an international code for pilots contacting UFOs."

Stanton Friedman, nuclear physicist: "After twenty years of investigation, the evidence is overwhelming—impressions on the ground after landings, sightings confirmed by radar, witnesses in the air and ground, and UFOs maneuvering in any direction at thousands of miles an hour, using clean, free energy."

The Cometa Report on UFOs and Potential Defense Implications

Gildas Bourdais, UFO researcher in France reported on the Cometa Report of 2001. Though not put out officially by the French Government, it was composed by generals of the Navy, Air-Force and Army along with France's leading scientists, a doctor in political science, an attorney, the national police superintendent, and the former director of a military think tank. The foreword was written by Dennis Ledding, former head of CNN (French equivalent of NASA).

The report states that UFOs are real. That is, they are an actual technological phenomena, possibly originating from off the planet, and *not merely psycho-social* (a product of the mind). The French press discussed it; the American media did not even report it.

Steven M. Greer, M.D. and the Disclosure Project

Washington, DC. Press Conference, 2001

The Disclosure Project claims there is a secret shadow government within the government regarding ETs; and that not only Washington, but the Vatican as well, has been hiding the truth about extraterrestrials for over fifty years. The Disclosure Project's counsel, Daniel Sheehan, had been constitutional attorney for the Silkwood, Three Mile Island, Pentagon, and the Iran-Contra cases. The conference was attended by 20 reputable individuals, a fraction of the 400 people willing to testify under oath who claim to have eyewitness testimony about UFOs. They included a former NASA astronaut, retired senior military officers from several nations, decorated pilots, scientists, and even a cardinal from the Vatican. They have tracked UFOs on radar, filmed them when they have landed, examined a craft and its technology, and handled alien life forms.

First to be briefed by Greer were President Clinton and CIA director James Wolsey in 1993. Then in 1994 and 1995 he addressed the Senate and the House. He also had meetings at the Pentagon with the head of the Defense Intelligence Agency, and the head of the Intelligence of the Joint Chiefs of Staff. Both related that they were not told the truth when they made UFO inquiries. Even Carter as president was unsuccessful. The CIA director at the time, George Bush Sr., had him inquire at the Congressional Research Service where he was again unsuccessful.

"What we're asking the public to do now," said Greer, "is write a letter to your congressman, senators, and the president, asking them to hold an open hearing, ban the weapons in space before it's too late, and allow these fabulous technologies that could give us a pollution free and abundant society to be declassified for peaceful application." (*American Freedom News*) www.disclosureproject.org.

Greer's reasoning and approach has been applauded by some and reproached by others, as can be expected.

Bud Hopkins and David Jacobs

Two long time researchers in abductions, Bud Hopkins, author of *Sight Unseen,* and David Jacobs, author of *Threat,* have a more negative view of the aliens' true motives. The hybrid program, they feel, has dangers; it could be used to gradually infiltrate Earth with the transgenics (humans or aliens with altered genes so that they look perfectly human but have paranormal abilities), with subsequent loss of some freedom for us. Hopkins and Jacobs wish to stress that more discernment is needed.

Bud Hopkins and Carol Rainey in *They Are Among Us Sight Unseen—Science, UFO Invisibility and Transgenic Beings* write: "If the UFO occupants' agenda includes preparation for eventual co-existence with us humans, *is there any evidence that right now, at this very moment, beings allied with them are already here, living covertly among us?*"

Well, I'm sure they are here and some are among us, but I feel Hopkins and Jacobs are emphasizing too much fear and negativity.

Abduction Study Conference at M.I.T. in 1992

The five-day conference at the Massachusetts Institute of Technology was chaired by physicist David E. Pritchard and the late Harvard psychiatrist John E. Mack, author of *Abduction: Human Encounters with Aliens*. The book report on the conference, *Close Encounters of the Fourth Kind--Alien Abduction, UFOs and the Conference at M.I.T.* by C.D.B. Bryan is 475 pages.

Dr. John Mack: "The intelligence that seems to be at work is subtle; its method is to invite, to remind, to permeate our culture from the bottom up as well as the top down, and to open our consciousness. It is for us to embrace the reality of the phenomenon and take a step forward appreciating that we live in a universe different from the one in which we have been taught to believe."

Colin Wilson in *Alien Dawn*: "If, as that M.I.T conference on abduction seemed to imply, that something new and strange is going on, then perhaps the human race ought to be looking for the answer with far more persistence and interest than we display at present."

Timothy Conway, PhD

A quote from one of his lectures:

Physics as we know it is only the most elementary way to understand and influence matter. There are said to be many other intelligent beings able to shape and control matter using nothing but conscious ideation, and that is the source of the seemingly bizarre UFO encounters. It is actually a latent ability of ours as well, feebly manifesting at present as psi phenomena—but for some reason, probably related to our own evolution, it was necessary for the human race to explore matter and develop a mastery of physical processes on this level, and this could best be done by becoming oblivious to the existence of non-material realities and the true nature of creative consciousness.

However, we have now come to a level of mastery of physical matter and technology that is dangerous to the ecosystem of the entire planet Earth—and the time has come for a reawakening from this materialist-reductionist delusion.

Daniel Sheehan, attorney

He was a defender of Karen Silkwood and the late Dr. John Mack, attorney on the Pentagon papers case and the Iran-Contra case, general counsel to the Jesuit office of social ministry, as well as founder of the Christic Institute in Washington, D.C.

Ten percent of his working time was spent on the study of the implications of the UFO phenomenon. He warned of: global warming—the melting of polar ice caps inundating coastal areas with salt water contamination of free drinking water; the missile confrontation with China; and major "Black" operations seemingly preparing to fight "hostile" technologically superior aliens, and he was concerned we have no program to prepare our consciousness for the latter.

At a recent UFO conference he voiced his feeling that we live in a world of hopelessness, yet there is hope. As he saw it, if we can get energy developed where every home in the world can be running without polluting the environment, the world in a generation can witness a time free from want, and free from war. But, he warned, it has to be combined with leadership based in a conscious awareness of our place in the universe, and we have to vow that these and related technologies are only used for the common good, and not for weapons of war.

Sitchin and a Vatican Theologian Discuss Extraterrestrials and the Origin of Man

A high official of the Vatican, **Monsignor Corrado Balducci** sat down with a Hebrew scholar, **Zecharia Sitchin** to discuss the issue of extraterrestrials and the creation of man and they came to these conclusions:

"Extraterrestrials can and do exist on other planets, they can be more advanced than us—and materially Man could have been fashioned from a pre-existing sentient being."

The following is from an actual meeting in the Vatican on a most controversial subject:

Msgr. Balducci: "That life may exist on other planets is certainly possible. The Bible does not rule out that possibility, and in spite of what some people think, we would be in a position to reconcile their existence with the Redemption that Christ has brought us. I can bring up the view of the great theologian, **Professor Father Marakoff,** who is still alive and is greatly respected by the Church. He formulated the hypothesis that when God created Man and put the soul into him, perhaps what is meant is not that Man was created from mud or lime, but from something pre-existing, even from a sentient being capable of feeling and perception. So the idea of taking a pre-man or hominid and creating someone who is aware of himself, is something that Christianity is coming around to. The key is the distinction between the material body and the soul granted by God."

Sitchin: "In my writings I deal with the physical evidence, but in my first book *The 12th Planet,* the very last sentence of the last paragraph raises the question: If the Extraterrestrials 'created' us, who created *them* on their planet? From this, and the contents of my subsequent books, my thinking evolved to the spiritual or 'divine' aspects. My second book dealing with Man's aspiration to ascend the heavens, is titled *The Stairway to Heaven*. It seems to me that you and I are ascending the same stairway to heaven, though from different steps."

© Z. Sitchin 2000 Reproduced by permission.

***

World-Wide International Conferences

There are many conferences nationally and internationally, all with excellent speakers. Take one conference for example: the seventh International UFO Congress in Laughlin, Nevada, which I attended in 2000 for eight days. It was almost overwhelming in scope and intensity.

Besides the US researchers, there were those from China, Russia, Brazil, Mexico, Venezuela, Germany, Italy, England, Australia, New Zealand and Israel who gave presentations. They spoke on UFOs and every related subject, but I have chosen to list only the following speakers, simply for their international prominence.

Chinese researcher Professor Sun Shi Li showed videos of a group of UFOs over Beijing being viewed by thousands. It was interesting to hear that China offered to be a bridge between Russia and the US to get world attention, and did this by subsequently hosting an international UFO conference in Hong Kong. China has the largest UFO organization in the world, with 300,000 members, eighty percent of them graduate aeronautical students working with university professors and scientists.

Russia's researcher Valery Ouvarov, PhD, showed an important document—a video of Major General Vasilji Alexeev, chief of the

Center of Space Communications, acknowledging the existence of UFOs and aliens.

Italy's researcher Giorgio Bongiovanni also had a video of historical significance (since the US and Russia have a pact of silence regarding UFOs). He interviewed the highest ranking officer of the Russian Air Force who agreed to come out and speak the truth before the U.N. if at the same time the US and China did likewise.

Jaime Rodriguez of Ecuador (a very active area along with Brazil, Peru, and Mexico) was a speaker. He heads a team of UFO researchers consisting of an M.D., psychologist, psychiatrist, attorney, and scientists of various disciplines.

Germany's full time researcher Michael Hesseman showed films of the latest UFOs. He has investigated in forty-two countries, lectured in twenty-two, and made documentaries.

Peter Gersten, a New York criminal defense attorney, invoked the Freedom of Information Act in his suit against the CIA, NSA, and the military, for refusing him papers relating to UFOs.

At this particular conference, the theme seemed to be the determination of all researchers internationally to get the truth out in unison to the U.N. and heads of governments, with a demand for immunity for breaking so-called security codes. At the same time, through meetings and any non-suppressed media, they would work to raise the public's awareness of ETs. They would also emphasize the need for spiritual growth—recognized as necessary for adequate survival through the coming earth changes.

***

SOME UFO ACTIVISTS: (alphabetically)

I was especially impressed with the books and tapes by courageous activists such as:

—**Warren Aston,** Australian researcher, for emphasis on the need for researchers to be more open to contactees' reports (from the 1940s to today,) of *aliens living among us.*

—**Nick Begich PhD**, European Parliament Subcommittee on Security and Disarmament panelist, for warning of an arms race of hidden new technologies, with no debate on safety

—**Georgio Bongiovanni,** Italian Catholic contactee and UFO researcher, for obtaining on tape, Alejeiev, a Russian three-star general stating "I will tell the UN the UFOs are real, if the US and China do also," and for helping Catholics deal with the reality of ETs.

—**Gildas Bourdais**, journalist and researcher in France, for bringing to the world public *The Cometa Report* (on UFO's and potential national defense) stating that UFOs are real.

—**Gregg Braden**, scientist, author, for bringing UFO knowledge in his talks to wide audiences, and especially for promoting world peace through the power of planet-wide group prayer.

—**Delores Cannon**, regressionist, for her many books translated into foreign languages on past lives, channeling of aliens and departed souls, including prophesies from Nostradamus.

—**Former President Carter** for trying to get UFO information from CIA Director Bush.

—**Timothy Conway, PhD**, author, scholar, lecturer on politics, philosophy, ecology, religions, and *engaged spirituality* for courage to include advanced, scholarly classes on UFOs and aliens.

—**Robert Dean,** retired army sergeant major, for revealing in 1972 secret 1963 NATO reports of alien involvement; for winning a lawsuit in 1992 for job promotion loss due to his UFO interests; and for his work as president of Stargate International, a research/educational organization.

—**Stanton Friedman**, physicist, for lengthy research on MJ12 papers, educational website on UFOs, and frequent media exposure as a reputable authority on UFOs.

—**Peter Gersten,** ex New York criminal attorney (President of CAUS) for suing the CIA and NSA for freedom of information

—**James Gilliland** (Self Mastery Earth Institute), for promoting alien communication and the raising of consciousness.

—**Steven M. Greer, M.D**. CSETI-Center for Study of ET Intelligence)

for his talks with top US officials, in order to get them to openly tell the truth about UFOs and aliens.

—**Budd Hopkins** founder of Intruders Foundation (although I consider his over-all views too negative) for his research and support organization for traumatized abductees; for bringing UFOs to the general public on TV and radio; and for bringing awareness of aliens or hybrids living among us in his book *Sight Unseen*.

—**J. Allen Hynek,** for his groundbreaking research on Project Blue Book; creation of the Center for UFO Studies (CUFOS), and for devising the "Close Encounter" identification system

—**Michael Lindemann,** author, lecturer, researcher, for co-creating The Institute for the Study of Contact with Non-human Intelligence, a UFO education website.

—**The late John Mack, M.D.** for risking psychiatry career by disclosing research on abductions.

—**Scott Mandelker, PhD.** for his detailed research on "wanderers," his discernment regarding negative ETs, and his initiation of spiritual study groups on the channeled RA Material

—**Jim Marrs**, for urging researchers to pressure the President and Congress to reveal cover-ups

—**Peter Paget,** for disclosing that the U.S. uses drug money to finance "black" UFO projects

—**Kenneth Ring, PhD.** researcher and authority on near-death-experiences, for his courage in tackling the link between NDE and UFO encounters in his scholarly *The Omega Project: Near-Death-Experiences, UFO Encounters, and Mind at Large*

—**Jaime Rodriguez** of Ecuador, for his work as head of a team of researchers from disciplines such as physicians, psychologists, attorneys and scientists

—**Michael Salla, PhD.** President of the Exopolitics Institute (promotion of scholarly research, ET disclosure, and the Citizen Diplomacy Program for promoting world peace.) Also for bringing to our attention the ramifications of extraterrestrials **living among us,** interacting with us and infiltrating clandestine organizations embedded in our and other governments.

—**Marcia Schafer**, for leaving the corporate world to promote detailed aliens' channeled teachings in her informative book *Confessions of an Intergalactic Anthropologis*
t

—**Daniel Sheehan** (John Mack's attorney) for warnings together with hope regarding ecology, politics and energy—"Stop bickering, and prepare for galactic federation"

—**Steven Spielberg** for directing the movie "ET", as well as the 20-hour miniseries *Taken* by writer Leslie Boehm, and his latest--*War of the Worlds.*

—**Leo Sprinkle, PhD**, "Father" of regression and contact therapy, for risking his career.

—**Wendelle Stevens**, for being a groundbreaker—one of the first UFO researchers and founders of the UFO community—with the largest collection of photos of UFOs

—**Jacques Vallee**, who co-founded CUFOS with Dr. Hynek, for the awareness that UFOs may have psychic origins (from other dimensions) as well as physical origins (other planets)

Chapter Twenty-One

Implications of the UFO Phenomenon

"The UFO and ET phenomenon is not about "little gray men". It is about the marriage of consciousness and science--about learning how unknown universal principles can explain what is thought to be impossible. Most importantly, it's about our human spiritual evolution and relationship to a higher consciousness."
Marcia Schafer, *Confessions of an Intergalactic Anthropologist.*

"The only way we can help mankind is through truth—
and the truth is that life is about love, God is love."—Alien Frank

Possible Reasons for Cover-up

First of all, if there are government cover-ups, and it appears so— why, we may ask. If the US already has UFO technology from back-engineering downed UFOs, or received technology from certain aliens in exchange for allowing research of abducted humans—the government would want to use that technology for military weaponry, and as such would consider it highly secret for use in "Star Wars" against another country or an alien race deemed hostile to us.

The Vatican has a large library of knowledge and research on UFOs that, understandably, they will not divulge. The US government is also very knowledgeable on UFOs but is not ready to reveal to the public they have no control over aliens, especially those they consider enemies; they not only fear being controlled by the aliens, but losing control of leadership of the world. And of course, they can't tell the public they are *working* with some aliens when they have lied about it.

Then too, perhaps they feel that ending secrecy would panic the public against an "enemy alien" (the projected image) and the public is not ready for it. The possibility also exists that *some* aliens come *only* to influence us and our civilization in negative ways, and the government may believe it is best to keep it secret until all of our weaponry is ready for use against them.

The *truth* about the aliens would bring chaos to organized religions; aliens claim they initiated them, and "seeded" humanity. There is reluctance to give up oil money for the aliens' free no-pollution energy that would destabilize the world economy. Poor countries would get free energy and no longer need oil.

So, it's easier to put out disinformation (a lie mixed with the truth). An "intelligent" public would then disbelieve the existence of UFOs— while the government secretly goes about researching aliens, working with some, and building up the military for possible defense against those they deem hostile.

Michael Salla, PhD recently posed some questions for consideration (paraphrased):

What if the public learns that our military has been cooperating with alien races for years in exchange for their superior technology? What if our military is in a long-standing "cold war" with one group of extraterrestrials? What if our military has been shooting them down, and we have lost our own aircraft and pilots? How can the military undo a lie this big? What if this secret UFO military group goes private and even more secret?

There are over 57 different races of aliens. How do we deal with them when some don't get along with each other? What if one group is in a position of power over the others and over us?

What if they offer us non-polluting free energy—what would happen to our oil economy and civilization?

What if the people learn that their ancestors have "seeded," created us humans? That they have been doing genetic manipulations on humans and created hybrids, with agendas that are unknown? What would that do the major religions?

What if people learn that aliens who look like us are living and working among us—how will they feel, react to their presence? How will it affect our culture, politics, etc.?

Finally, to what extent does the US have control of the UFO phenomenon secrecy in the world? What would open and free disclosure be for the entire world--very good or very dangerous?

Negative Implications

We could unwittingly give ourselves over to aliens having their own agendas (the use of people and natural wealth), so that our culture and values gradually disappear. Or we might be considered inferior, even as slaves, just as humans have done to other humans on Earth.

We could possibly be used by them for replenishing their race's genes, or for making hybrids for their own planet or to place hybrids on Earth to become our masters.

Negative aliens could continue to abduct people for their own purposes, and cause humans emotional harm by not understanding people's reactions or not caring.

Aliens with higher technology but little spirituality would naturally be feared. These major fears could cause our government to make "star wars" against perceived hostile aliens all more advanced than us technologically. This could be disastrous to the world.

Positive Implications of the UFO Phenomenon

With the revealing of the truth that we are not alone, an open and more comprehensive study of the UFO phenomena throughout the world would be possible, and a truer picture of various alien agendas may be obtained, making better discernment of those deemed hostile.

Some aliens have given our scientists nannotechnology—technology to manufacture goods that last forever, and that can also be used to clean up the environment. They have shown us a pollution-free energy source, which we can put to use.

With their superior medical knowledge, they can teach us how to prolong our lives. Aliens from other dimensions working through and with humans on Earth, have healed people of illnesses (*Cured by Aliens* by Adrian Dvir).

They have already helped contactees physically, psychically and spiritually; they can help us to evolve spiritually, while strengthening our psychic sense. Even abductees have received benefits such as an increased spiritual sense and psychic ability. We can learn from those more spiritual, how to live in peace with one another; we can learn from the negative ones what ultimately, does not work. And if we align ourselves with the positive aliens, our *personal* lives would improve. They help us raise our consciousness; they teach us about spiritual evolution.

Most importantly, they make us aware, not only of the danger for our planet of nuclear warfare, but the danger reverberations of it reaching into other dimensions.

My Own Particular View on Aliens

There are some negative aliens, but we should not rush to fight them off. We should be discerning as we would be with people here on Earth. There will be evil as long as there is free will. Good ETs in "The Vast Assembly of the Confederation of Planets in Service to the Infinite Creator" (if there really such an organization) would, I feel, in the final analysis, not allow bad ETs to attack us, but would *help* to stabilize the Earth as it goes through vibratory changes. However, we cannot expect the more spiritual aliens to "fix" our world. They are allowed only to guide. We must clean up our own mess—wars, pollution, over-population.

We must prevent our government from *provoking* or *faking* a war with "enemy" aliens. Some questions: Is our government conditioning us for "star wars?" Should we worry about alien mind control, or worry more about our own government mind control (Black Ops) over its citizens?

And are we really ready to end the government secrecy and suffer the consequences to our economic, religious, political, and cultural life?

Chapter Twenty-Two

Aliens and Prophesies
What's A Good Attitude?

"What we are is God's gift to us, what we become is our gift to God."
-- Eleanor Powell

"We are connected with the universe and each other, and the world
is powerfully influenced by our thoughts."--Alien Frank

"Love is the highest expression of life. It comes from understanding without
judgment, not from emotions or sentiments. We all have this divine essence, and
it is our choice whether or not to use it, whether or not to love." --Alien Frank.

Various aliens have given abductees and contactees (such as Shirlè), prophesies warning of coming natural and man-made catastrophes due to our unloving attitudes towards Earth and each other. *Have aliens also been communicating through the Bible?*

***

Coded Bible Prophesies—*The Bible Code* by Michael Drosnin.
If the code is authentic, is it from God, or from beings from another planet or *dimension?* In 1950, rabbi Weissmandel of Prague noticed that

if he skipped fifty letters (with no breaks between words), then another fifty and still another fifty, the word "Torah" was spelled out at the beginning of Genesis, the books of Exodus, Numbers, and Deuteronomy. Much earlier, Isaac Newton learned Hebrew to seek the code and failed to find it. It had to wait for the invention of the computer. Recently, an Israeli, Eliyahu Tips, succeeded, his work verified by other mathematicians.

According to Michael Drosnin, author of *The Bible Code*, the code predicted the first Gulf War, a comet colliding with Jupiter, and the assassination of Rabin—the odds of the latter being about 3000 to 1. A prophesy[58] or a warning of a third World War, an Armageddon, is in the original five books of the Hebrew Bible. But now threats of nuclear and biological weapons are in the hands of terrorists all over the world. The Bible code does not clearly foretell *one* future only. It appears to suggest *many possible futures*. In the end, what *we* do determines the outcome.

Aliens' prophesies (including those of the alien Frank) and those in *Bible Code I & II* have two things in common—the inevitability of spiritual evolution no matter our pace or stage—and "prophesies" of destruction by natural and/or human causes which we have the power to modify or change. The Bible code is more of a warning, for "Will you change it?" is placed near the prophesy in the book.

Aliens have warned individuals in various ways—audibly, telepathically, and through channeling. The following are two other methods of prophesying—remote viewing and channeling from a departed soul.

Predicting the Future by Remote Viewing

Remote viewing is precognition by technicians trained by US military personnel who in turn were trained by psychic Ingo Swann with his strict procedures and protocol. At times it has not only revealed the presence of aliens and their whereabouts but has been used to predict the future. I quote an interesting excerpt from *The Ultimate Time Machine* by Joseph McMoneagle, former government remote viewer, regarding prophesies:

"***By our thoughts alone,*** we are capable of generating reality and

---

[58] Also in a separate scroll called a mezzuzh for fastening on the doorways of Jewish homes.

controlling what is going to happen to us. We have only to clean up our act and begin to envision the positive changes possible instead of focusing on the negative."

Channeled Prophesies From a Departed Soul

Regressionist and researcher Delores Cannon author of *Conversations with Nostradamus,* believes she communicated with the departed soul of Nostradamus through a subject in deep hypnosis, and that *Nostradamus* related the following paraphrased excerpt:

When a prediction is made, do we accept it with a resigned sense of doom and gloom, thinking it is set and therefore unchangeable? That would be a very morbid reason for wanting to know our destinies. Or do we want to know in the hope that this knowledge can allow us to change what is predicted? Without hope and free will, Man is nothing but a puppet, with no control over his life. *Nostradamus believed in a theory of probable futures.* The subject under hypnosis said that Nostradamus asked: 'If I show you the most horrible things you can do to yourself, *will you do something to change it?'*

Channeled Knowledge From the Alien Called Ra

Four books on *The Ra Material, The Law of One,* by Don Elkins & channeler Carla Rueckart

They contain channeled knowledge on extraterrestrials and the spiritual, and are transcripts of 104 question-and-answer sessions from 1981 to 1983 on various alien races and universal spiritual laws. Don Elkins, with channeler Carla Rueckart, had contact with the entity called RA who claimed to be one of a group of members of the Confederation of Planets in the Service of the One Creator.

Besides the workings of the Confederation, descriptions of the spiritual hierarchies and information on well-known entities on Earth, there is a good deal of information on negative aliens and how they might operate. I was impressed with the intelligent and sensitive questions of Don Elkins, revealing an already comprehensive knowledge of aliens and the spiritual, and I felt the calm spirituality of the entity Ra to be genuine.

Ra tells of a gradual transformation of the planet to a fourth density positive existence as humans evolve to fourth density predominately positive, with the majority returning to third density existence. Researcher

Don Ware on *The Ra Material*: ***"The reason for the human experience is to determine through our own free will whether we will orient ourselves towards positive service to others or negative service to self."***

Michael Drosnin's *The Bible Code*, Delores Cannon's *Nostradamus*, McMoneagle's *Ultimate Time Machine*, Don Elkins' *The Ra Material*, as well as the warnings of Shirlè's alien Frank—all remind us that it is in our power to lessen or change any prophesy or circumstance.

***

Prophesies, to my mind, are warnings, not predictions of the future. We now know there are natural changes that Earth and Earthlings must go through—a pole shift and sun changes that are cyclical for Earth, but which added to man's actions, can bring disaster to Earth.

We have free will, and the power to change it with good works; that is, stop wars, protect the ecology and engage in active prayer. Doom is not inevitable. However, a mass landing to "help" us is unlikely, because the majority of people on Earth do not want change, and the aliens have to respect our free will. If there *is* a landing it would be only to evacuate some people from a doomed planet. We will survive the changes either through reincarnation to another planet, or to Earth (when it is again inhabitable) or be "harvested" (their term) by being removed to a fourth density planet, should the Earth be uninhabitable for some time. According to *The Ra Material,* most will repeat the cycle on another planet to further learn the art of compassion.

So What's a Good Attitude?

I liked what psychologist **Dr. Leo Sprinkle,** had to say in his book *Soul Samples*: "My own bias is to minimize the significance of the doom and gloom, conspiracies and control scenarios. My view is that the human spirit can learn and evolve from various interactions with both good and evil entities, both angels and devils. The purpose of the ET encounters seems to be an initiation for the individual, and a stimulus to society, so that human development moves towards a merger of science and ethics, a union of technology and spirituality, a balance of masculinity and femininity, and a transition from Planetary Persons to Cosmic Citizens."

A wise note from **Marcia Schafer** in *Confessions of an Intergalactic Anthropologist:* "We can control whatever reality comes our way. We are not to dwell on catastrophic Earth changes and economic demise; if we do, we will draw these things to us. If we stay conscious and guide our thoughts, they will catapult us into a desirable reality and we will have controlled our destiny."

Some advice from **Bud Hopkins and David Jacobs**: "We must seek the truth about aliens' motives and not be gullible. We need discernment. They are already here among us.

Daniel Sheehan's closing UFO conference speech: "We have a fundamental challenge: We must become an adult and mature civilization at peace. New energy technologies cannot evolve properly in any other setting; yet if they are not disclosed to the public, the public won't know how important it is that we evolve in that direction."

Robert Dean, retired NATO Army Intelligence analyst and UFO researcher said it well: "The time has come to leave behind racial, religious, and ethnic bigotry. We must be prepared to step up and out into the universal community of life as one people, from one small planet, with one future. Or sadly, we may not go at all."

I like what **James Gilliland** (creator of The Self-Mastery Institute in Oregon), was told in his near-death experience. "How can I serve?" he had asked, after receiving so much love and compassion. The voice replied "What do you want to do—what brings you joy?" And he understood that all the "Source" wants him to do is be happy. The highest vibrational thought, he realized, is of pure unconditional love, joy and service to the Creator and all creation. And when you align yourself with that, you align yourself with the Creator—the Source. And the Source is right here—in all of us.

Some simple advice from **Dr. Scott Mandelker**: "Let go of the need for controlling inner process, and let go of the need to exert our will over others." For "wanderers" like Shirlè (one to two percent of earthlings), he had this special message: "A big issue for wanderers is the existence of so much negativity on Earth. Well, love is not enough; love must be complemented by wisdom—first, by acceptance of negativity, no matter how painful, knowing its causes—then by *compassion*. Only then can energy rise up to do something positive about it. We don't have to get stuck in rage, in powerlessness. Know yourself, accept yourself, become the creator."

Yes, we are here to learn about love—compassion for ourselves as well as others. Scientist **Greg Braden** gives a thorough understanding of the subject in his *Walking Between the Worlds –The Science of Compassion.* He tells how we can meditate and pray.

Braden, in *The Isaiah Effect:* "Prayer is to us, as water is to the seed of a plant, and we are in constant prayer as we sense, perceive, and express ourselves throughout our day."

So, as I see it, our thoughts have the power to manifest into the physical, and are therefore the real cause of the present state of the planet and the life on it. According to Braden, when we use the power of our thoughts with intent, feeling, and emotion, it is *active* prayer—its power greatly magnified as more people participate together. Only about twenty percent of earthlings or aliens have negative agendas. The other eighty percent have positive intent, and *if synchronized in their thought vibrations, can wield a much more powerful influence on the world and the universe than can the negative.*

Okay, I hear you say, we don't want war, we'll have thoughts of peace—does that mean turn the other cheek to the terrorists—to evil aliens? We had Jesus, Gandhi, Martin Luther King Jr.—and the world is *still* full of violence. And there is no end to it. Will it take a million years to be ready for *another way*? …Maybe.

"Another Way" by Terry Dobson, is exactly the title to a story I found in *Chicken Soup for the Soul* the other day. The following is a paraphrased version:

A young American tourist in Japan is on a suburban train, when a very belligerent and dirty inebriated laborer gets in, cursing and shouting. He terrorizes the occupants, especially a woman holding a baby. As she and others run for safety, he is furious. The occupants are frozen with fear. The American, with three years of intense aikido training, but no actual combat, recalls what he has been taught. If you fight or try to dominate people, you lose your connection with the universe. Aikido is the art of reconciliation. It studies how to *resolve* conflict, not how to start it.

Though the American has always abided by this teaching, at the same time he secretly yearns for a chance to save the victim. He gives the drunk a look of disgust and signals a kiss to antagonize him so that he can act only in defense. The drunk roars he will teach the foreigner Japanese manners and is about to rush him when someone shouts "Hey" in a light and happy tone, as though to greet a friend. The drunk spins around. A tiny old Japanese man in a kimono, smiles warmly and asks him what he's been drinking. The drunk answers angrily he has been drinking sake and it is none of his business. The old man engages in light conversation with the drunk who soon sobs that his wife has died, he has no job and no home, and he feels ashamed.

To make a long story short, as the American steps off the train at his stop, he looks back and sees the inebriated laborer sprawled on the seat with his head in the lap of the old Japanese man who is stroking his filthy matted hair. He realizes he has just seen Aikido in action, and the essence of it is *love*.

***

We must learn to get along with each other, learn to love, and pray for peace. Idealistic perhaps, but we have to start somewhere, sometime—Why not now?

Because, many believe, we are living in *special* times. Dr. Scott Mandelker in his book *Universal vision* explains: "It seems the aliens are here *because* of this time of transition—the evolution towards unity; towards freedom from duality (good and evil)."

Until then—until we live and act with love and compassion—with the knowledge that unity or God is within each of us—we earthlings may experience a sense of separation.

Visionary **Barbara Marx Hubbard** cautions: "The individual cannot flourish in a dying world, and the world cannot evolve if its members are alienated and in despair. Let the flame of expectation ignite us—to do more, to be more, to know more, and above all to connect with each other, to discover what we can do *together* that none of us can do isolated and alone."

The spiritual cannot be separated from the UFO perspective. The highest teaching is the realization of unity—we are all One. "Humankind has not woven the web of life. We are but one thread within it. Whatever we do to the web, we do to ourselves. All things are bound together. All things connect[59]."

---

[59] In the 1970's, screenwriter Ted Perry reinterpreted Dr. Henry Smith's 1887 translation of Chief Seattle's 1854 speech, and the publisher/producer attributed it to Chief Seattle-- including this inauthentic saying.

Suggested Reading

An excellent list of UFO books is the **Readerware Book Catalog** on the internet. There is also Timothy Conway's **UFO Bibliography and Resource material** (in private circulation). I also recommend **"UFO Book Review"** (http:/www.mactonnies.com/ufobooks.html). His concise book reports are excellent—well written and fair-minded.

To better understand the personality and experiences of a contactee like Shirlè, I have first listed those books that especially pertain to her story. Other UFO and related books follow (under topic) together with some personal impressions.

Indigo Children, "Wanderers" and "Star Children":

I recommend Carrol and Tober's *Indigo Children and Indigo Celebration*, already touched on in the Introduction.

The best books on "wanderers" are Scott Mandelker's two books: *From Elsewhere –Being ET in America* and *Universal Vision—Soul Evolution and the Cosmic Plan.*

Star Children—The True Story of Alien Offspring Among Us by Jenny Randles, and *Visitors from Within* by Royal & Priest are also full of material to consider.

Synchronicities:

For understanding synchronicities in everyday life I recommend *The Purpose of Your Life,* by Carol Adrienne, Depak Chopra's *Synchrodestiny* **tapes** and his book *The Spontaneous Fulfillment of*

Desire—Harnessing the Infinite Power of Coincidence.
And there is *Synchronicity—The Bridge Between Matter and Mind*
by F. David Peat., a scholarly search for the unifying principle behind
meaningful coincidences, and *Synchronicity as Spiritual Guidance* by
Mark Thurston, PhD.

Art: For readers who are artists, *The Spiritual in Art* edited by
Maurice Tuchman is excellent.

On the Link Between the Paranormal and UFO:

There is the thought provoking *Perils of the Soul—Ancient Wisdom
and the New Age* by John Ryan Haule. On the paranormal there is
Exploring Psychic Phenomena:-Beyond Mind and matter by D. Scott
Rogo. There is the excellent *Miracles and Other Realities* by Lee Pulos
and Gary Richman which relates the amazing feats of Brazilian psychic
Thomaz Morais. Another very good book, well researched and
informative, is *Angels and Aliens* by Keith Thompson.

**Aliens and Hybrids From Other Planets and Other Dimensions,
LIVING AMONG US:**

Ruth Montgomery's *Aliens Among Us*, published in 1986—human
contacts with aliens from other planets and other dimensions, walking
among us. Much good information.
Bud Hopkins and Carol Rainey's *They Are Among Us—Sight
Unseen—Science, UFO, Invisibility and Transgenic Beings*. I
wondered if Shirlè's alien "Frank" could possibly be a hybrid, a
transgenic. Both authors fear the motives of these "negative" aliens.
Helen Littrell and Jean Bilodeaux's *Raechel's Eyes*. A true story of a
young hybrid girl attending a US college—one of a few hybrids from
another planet here in exchange for a few of our people to *their* planet—
in our so-called government "humanization" program for hybrids.
On alien/human hybrids and inter-dimensional beings: James L.
Walden Ed.D. *The Ultimate Alien Agenda*—the re-engineering of
humankind. Interesting and thought-provoking.
On our military (and other nations' military) working with alien
races living and working on Earth : *Exopolitics: Political Implications
of the Extraterrestrial Presence* by Michael Salla, PhD.—political
analysis and activism in extraterrestrial affairs. A book with important

and disturbing information.

Enrique Castillo Rincon, engineer, rare contactee and UFO researcher, author of *UFOs—A Great New Dawn for Humanity* (English translation in 1997). Three years after his four month friendship (listening to music, going to movies etc.), with a man he met in Caracas, Venezuela, Enrique meets the same man in uniform, descending from a UFO, and on five different occasions from 1973-1976, he is given messages and education while traveling with him in a UFO.

Exopolitics

On the study of key individuals, institutions and political processes associated with extraterrestrial life—*Exopolitics: Political Implications of the Extraterrestrial Presence* by Michael Salla—a thorough presentation on the motivations and agendas of various alien groups, and the ramifications internationally, politically. A must read on the political management of the extraterrestrials **living and working on Earth** within clandestine organizations in our (and other) governments of the world.

Extraterrestrial Friends and Foes by George C. Andrews, is another book on the subject—and equally disturbing.

Rare Contactees:

Ida Kannenberg's guide book for contactees, *UFOs and the Psychic Factor—How to Understand Encounters with UFOs and ETs*, and her latest, *Reconciliation,* are honestly and humbly written. I personally interviewed this remarkable contactee in her home in Oregon. She claims her aliens could technologically hear through her ears, and see through her eyes.

I found the book *The Contact Has Begun* by Philip Krapf, *LA Times* journalist, to be believable, not only because he lost his job after revealing his two days on an alien ship, but he impressed me as a humble and honest person as he related his experience at a UFO conference.

Abductions:

Most people have read Whitley Streiber's 1987 *Communion.* In 1998 he published *Confirmation:The Hard Evidence of Aliens Among Us.*

Dr. John Mack in *Abduction* sees alien motives as predominantly positive.

Budd Hopkins in *Missing Time, Intruders,* **and** *Sight Unseen* is predominantly negative.

Others on the subject: *Close ET Encounters,* by Richard Boylan, and *Visitors Within,* by Royal & Priest. Another is Colin Wilson's *Alien Dawn,* filled with interesting and conflicting information in his attempt to piece together the contact experience.

Thomas E. Bullard, *On Stolen Time: A Summary of the Comparative Study of the UFO Abduction Mystery,* FUFOR, 1987—a good analysis of the abduction phenomenon.

Abductions by Interdimensional Beings:

James L. Walden, Ed.D. author of *The Ultimate Alien Agenda* relating his experiences with *inter-dimensional* beings. Food for thought.

Jim Sparks author of *The Keepers.* Being taught an alien language. I couldn't put it down.

Channeling:

I was very impressed with Marcia Schafer's *Confessions of an Intergalactic Anthropologist,* (channeling from aliens and entities), for the amount of serious spiritual and intellectual knowledge –all given in a professional manner.

Psychic Greta Woodrew's book: *Memories of Tomorrow* of channeled conversations with extraterrestrials from another dimension, was fascinating.

Ruth Montgomery's *The World to Come—The Guides' Long-Awaited Predictions for the Dawning Age—*How to survive the coming "Shift".

I skimmed over *You Are Becoming a Galactic Human* by Essene and Nidle—the channeling of Washta of the Galactic Federation, on the Sirius civilization and the origin and transformation of Earth.

On other dimensions, parallel universes—I was intrigued with the channeling received by some of Delores Cannon's subjects in her book *The Convoluted Universe.*

But the most information on races of aliens and the spiritual, and the best of channeled material, seemed to be in the four books of *The Ra Material: The Law of One* by Don Elkins, channeled by Carla Rueckert. Even though much of it was beyond me, I learned a good deal.

Between Lives:

Michael Newton's **Destiny of Souls** and other books on life between lives were most fascinating. I was absorbed with all of Dolores Cannon's books on past lives and channeling of aliens, including **Between Life and Death, and The Custodians.**

Psychology, Reincarnation and UFO:

Soul Samples, by Leo Sprinkle, PhD. This book is for the lay person as well as researcher. It includes enjoyable personal stories and insights—tells it like it is, and with optimism.

On Spirituality:

I found **The Seat of the Soul,** by Gary Zukov, easy to understand, and **How to Know God** by Deepak Chopra thought provoking. **The Seth Material** and **Agartha** are also good.

Spiritual Evolution:

A few good books—**Walking Between the Worlds, Awakening to Zero Point** by Gregg Braden, and **Becoming Gods I & II,** by James Gilliland.

Medical Science and the Spiritual:

Where God Lives, by Melvin Morse, M.D. A must read.

Seeking Physical Proof of Extraterrestrial Origin of Implants Through Surgical Removal:

The Aliens and the Scalpel (revised second edition). Actual proof still considered elusive and controversial. I, having no technical knowledge, found the lab results confusing. But the work is intriguing.

On Ancient Civilizations:

For information on ancient civilizations, read **The Twelfth Planet** and **The Earth Chronicle Series,** by Zacharia Sitchin, **Chariots of the**

Gods, by Eric Von Daniken, and *Our Cosmic Ancestors,* by Maurice Chatelain, former NASA expert.

I found *Humanity's Extraterrestrial Origins—ETs Influence on Humankind's Biological and Cultural Evolution,* by Dr. Arthur Horn, to be overly negative with its strong belief that certain aliens' main desire is to control and manipulate us.

On Atlantis:

Shirlè's painting *Atlantis* hangs in my home. Books: *Atlantis the Antiluvian World* by the father of Atlantology Ignatius Donley. Searching for newer books on the subject, I found *Lemuria and Atlantis: Studying the Past to Survive the Future* by Shirlèy Andrews. There is also *Imaging Atlantis* by Richard Ellis, and *Atlantis and the Power System of the Gods* by David Hatcher Childress and Bill Clendenon.

There are many theories as to its demise. I found the most interesting to be the channeled material obtained by Delores Cannon from a few of her regressed subjects in her book *The Convoluted Universe.*

On Alien Intervention in Human History:

Gods, Genes, & Consciousness, by Paul Von Ward; also books by Zacharia Sichin.

NDEs and UFOs:

It was good to see a book on the similarities between near-death experiences and UFO encounters, *The Omega Project: Near-Death Experiences, UFO Encounters, and Mind at Large*--Kenneth Ring, PhD.

Other books that cover both experiences are *The Watchers II – Exploring UFOs and the NDE* by Raymond Fowler, *Sacred Encounters* by Janet Colli and Thomas Beck, and *Children of the New Millennium* by P.M.H. Atwater.

For a Beginner on UFOs:

I would recommend the excellent *UFOs & The Alien Presence: Six Viewpoints* edited by Michael Lindemann (despite the questioned testimony in it of Bob Lazar). It's the book I suggest for those who need some convincing of the reality of UFOs.

Analyzing Aspects of the UFO Phenomenon:

An excellent over-all book for beginners is *At the Threshold— UFOs, Science and the New Age,* by sociology professor Charles F. Emmons, PhD revealing the UFO phenomenon to be varied and complicated. Dr. James Deardorff: "This is a book for the interested, thinking person who wishes to be brought up to date as quickly as possible." I found the book to be very helpful. However, it has little on the subject of government disinformation.

Written in a predominantly scholarly approach is *The Lure of the Edge: Scientific Passions, Religious Beliefs, and the Pursuit of UFOs* by Brenda Denzler PhD and published by the University of California Press. The detailed research and bibliography should satisfy the scientifically minded.

Extraterrestrials Among Us by George C. Andrews gives a balanced overall view of negative as well as positive aliens. Good detailed book.

Nuclear physicist Stanton Friedman's thorough research for his book *Top Secret Majic* strengthened my belief in the reality of a UFO crash at Roswell, and in a government cover-up.

But for scholarly facts and figures, regarding implications, evidence, disclosure, CSETI, government documents, refer to *Contact—The Evidence and Implications,* by Steven Greer, M.D. Very detailed good information.

And for an easy to read very detailed report on the M.I.T. Conference on Alien Abductions, there is *Close Encounters of the Fourth Kind* by C.D.B. Ryan.

Connecting the Dots—Making Sense of the UFO Phenomenon. Italian journalist Paola L. Harris. By interviewing top UFO players (from various disciplines) she reveals information on researchers and their work not otherwise known.

Remote Viewing:

Some of my education on remote viewing and its part in the picture of government cover-up came from *Penetration* (by the "father" of remote viewing Ingo Swann), *Cosmic Voyage,* and *Cosmic Explorers (various alien races)* by Courtney Brown, PhD, and from cassette tapes of talks by former military men such as Skip Atwater, Forest Crawford, and Joe McMoneagle, who were trained by the US military.

Crop Circles:

The Circle Makers, by author Colin Andrews. Despite the hoaxing in England, he believes there is enough evidence of non-human cause (radiation and genetic effects on the plants).

The book *Vital Signs—Guide to Crop Circle Mystery, by* Andy Thomas is good,

However, the best overall video I have seen is *Crop Circles—Crossover from Another Dimension* by Terje Toftenes of Norway, for both narration and crop circles.

Cover-Ups:

So many good books: A few are *Above Top Secret,* by Timothy Good; *Dawn of a New Age* by Philip Corso; *Covert Agenda,* by Nicholas Redfern; and *Top Secret Majic,* by Stanton Friedman. *The History of ET Cover-up II,* by Richard Dolan has been very well researched.

Debunkers, Skeptics, and Mixed Views Believers: (interesting, conflicting information)

UFOs—The Public Deceived and *UFO Reports*, by leading debunker Philip Klass

UFOs Psychic Close Encounters – The Electromagnetic Indictment, by Albert Budden

ET Friends and Foes, by George Andrews

Alien Intent, by Raymond Robinson

Alien Contact-- Top Secret UFO Files Revealed, by Timothy Good

Captured by Aliens – A search for life and truth in a large universe, by Joel Achenbach

Saucers Illuminati, by Jim Keith

The Abduction Enigma, by Randle, Estes and Crone

Alien Intervention – the spiritual mission of the UFOs, by Paul Christophe

Resource
Information

UFO & Metaphysical

The largest UFO organization in the world is CURO in China, and the first truly international organization was conceived and set up in 1997 by a working committee[60] of international researchers. It was The First International UFO Festival/Conference between the East and the West, sponsored by the China UFO Research Organization, the Hong Kong UFO Club, and the USA UFO Photo Archives. It took place at the Hong Kong Stadium with 40,000 seat capacity. To cover the five-day events there was prime time TV in Hong Kong, satellite TV over China and worldwide, live TV programs, videos, and international media contacts.

Each country has its UFO conferences, calling itself international because it has speakers from all over the world. And each area or state in a country has its own UFO conferences. Besides the general UFO conferences, there are separate conferences for contactees to share their experiences with others who have had like experiences.

J.ALLEN HYNEK CENTER FOR UFO STUDIES CUFOS
2457 West Peterson Ave., Chicago, Illinois 60659, USA
312-271-3611

THE CENTER FOR THE STUDY OF CSETI
EXTRATERRESTRIAL INTELLIGENCE
Dr. Steven Greer, PO Box 15401 Asheville, NC 28813
704-274-5671, fax 704-274-6766

---

[60] Director: Moon Fong. Associate directors: Henry Chen, Hong Kong. Prof. Sun Shi Li- China, Wendelle Stevens- USA, Prof Lui Yin Chung –

THE SEARCH FOR EXTRATERRESTRIAL INTELLIGENCE SETI
NASA, Washington, D.C., 202-358-1547
MUTUAL UFO NETWORK MUFON
103 Oldtowne Road, Seguin, Texas 78155 USA, 515-379-9216

ALIEN-HUMAN HYBRID ASSOCIATION AHHA!
Christianne Quiros, PhD., 909-825-8587 etahha@aol.com

INSTITUTE FOR UFO RESEARCH IUR
1304 So. College Ave, Fort Collins, CO 80524

THE INSTITUTE FOR UFO CONTACTEE STUDIES IFUFOCS
1425 Steele St. Laramie, Wyoming 82070,
307-745-7897

CENTER FOR UFO STUDIES CUFOS
1955 St. John's Drive, Glenview, IL. 60025.

AERIAL PHENOMENA RESEARCH ORGANIZATION APRO
3597 West Grape Drive, Tucson, AZ 85741

SOCIETY FOR THE INVESTIGATION OF THE SITU
UNEXPLAINED P.O. Box 265, Little Silver, NJ 07739
201-842-5229   Publishes *Pursuit* (Good)

CITIZENS AGAINST UFO SECRECY c/o CAUS
Lawrence Fawcett, 471 Goose Lane, Coventry, CT 06238
Also P.O. Box 20351 Sedona, AZ 8634-0351, Peter Gersten

CLOSE ENCOUNTERS RESEARCH ORGANIZATION CERO
Abduction Research and Support Group
Box 131, Verdugo City, CA 91046

UFO RESEARCH INSTITUTE UFORI
P.O. Box 958, Houlton, ME 04730-0958

FUND FOR UFO RESEARCH FUR
P.P. Box 277, Mt. Rainier, MD 20712, 703-684-6032
Publication: Quarterly Report

THE COMMITTEE FOR THE SCIENTIFIC INVESTIGATION OF CLAIMS
OF THE PARANORMAL ("anti" UFO) CSICOP
P.O. Box 229, Buffalo, New York 14215
Philip Klass 716-834-3222, 716-834-0841
skeptinqaol.com, Publication: The Skeptical Inquirer

SOCIETY FOR SCIENTIFIC EXPLORATION SSE
P.O.3818, University Station, Charlottesville, Virginia 22903
804-924-4905, fax 804-924-3104
Also P.O. 5848,Stanford CA.94309
ERL 306 Stanford University, Stanford, CA 94305
415-593-8581, fax 415-595-4466
Publishes The Journal of Scientific Exploration and the Explorer.

INSTITUTE FOR UFO CONTACTEE STUDIES IFUFOCS
1425 Steele St. Laramie, WY 82070.

INTRUDERS FOUNDATION IF
P.O. Box 30233, New York, N.Y. 10011
212-645-5278 Budd Hopkins, founder
Publishes Bulletin of the Intruders Foundation

PROGRAM FOR EXTRAORDINARY EXPERIENCE RESEARCH PEER
1493 Cambridge St. Cambridge, MA 02139
John Mack, M.D. P.O. Box 390707, Phone 617-497-2667

ASSOCIATION FOR PAST LIFE RESEARCH AND THERAPY APRT
P.O. Box 20151, Riverside, Calif. 92516
909-784-1570, Fax 909-784-8440
E-mail pastlife@empirenet.com

INTERNATIONAL ASSOCIATION FOR NEW SCIENCE IANS
1304 South College Ave., Fort Collins, CO 80524
970-482-3731, Fax- 970-482-3120, E-mail science@ians.org.

ORGANIZATION FOR PARANORMAL
UNDERSTANDING OPUS
AND SUPPORT, Dr. Eugene Lipson, President
P.O. Box 273273, Concord, CA 94527, Phone 510-689-4198

AMERICAN ASSOCIATION OF ALTERNATIVE HEALERS AAAH
P.O. Box 10026, Sedona, Arizona 86339-8026
415-452-2603, Fax 415-333-4645
E-mail aaah@cris.com, Website www.cris.com/-Aaah

THE COMPUTER UFO NETWORK CUFON
Seattle, WA. 206-776-0382

THE EXCEPTIONAL HUMAN EXPERIENCE NETWORK EHE
Rhea White, Director, 414 Rockledge Drive, New Bern, NC 28562
919-636-8734

INTERNATIONAL ASSOCIATION FOR REGRESSION IARRT
RESEARCH AND THERAPIES, P.O. 20151, Riverside, CA 92516
909-784-1570

INTERNATIONAL SOCIETY FOR THE STUDY OF ISSSEEM
SUBTLE ENERGIES AND ENERGY MEDICINE
356 Golden Circle, Golden, CO 80403, Phone 303-278-2228

NEW BEING PROJECT NBP
P.O. 1657,Guerneville, CA 95446, Phone 707-869-1038

THE INTERCONTINENTAL UFO GALACTIC SPACECRAFT
RESEARCH AND ANALYTICAL NETWORK ICUFON
35-40 75th St. Suite 4G, Flushing, New York 11372, 718-672-7948

THE NEVADA AERIAL RESEARCH GROUP NARG
Box 81407, Las Vegas, Nevada 89186-1407
The Leading Edge publication

THE SOCIETY OF EARTHBOUND EXTRATERRESTRIALS SEE
2140 Shattuck Ave, Suite 2329, Berkeley, California 94704
Voice 403-426-3134; Fax 403-429-4926

THE BORDERLAND SCIENCES RESEARCH ASSOCIATION BSRF
Box 429, Garberville, Calif. 95542, Phone 707-986-7211
Publication: The Journal of Borderland Research

CALIFORNIA UFO
1800 South Robertson Blvd. Box 355, Los Angeles 90035
213-273-9409, 818-951-1250, Publication: UFO

PROJECT IDENTIFICATION
Dr. Harley Rutledge, Dept of Physics, SE Missouri State University, Cape
Girardeau, MO 63701

INTERNATION UFO CONGRESS
9075 Wadsworth Parkway #K2-274, Westminster, CO 80021, 303-543-9943,
fax-543-8667
THE SOURCEBOOK PROJECT, P.O. Box 107 Glen Arm, MD 21057

EXOPOLITICS INSTITUTE, Michael Salla PhD., President
P.O. Box 2199, Kealakekua, HI 96750, USA
Phone 1-808-323-3400
www.ExopoliticsInstitute.org
ARCHAEUS PROJECT, 629 Twelfth Ave. S.E. Minneapolis, MN 55414

CENTER FOR TREATMENT & RESEARCH OF
EXPERIENCED ANOMALOUS TRAUMA
PO Box 728 Ardsley, New York, 10502

AMERICAN SOCIETY FOR PSYCHICAL RESEARCH
5 West 73rd St. New York, N.Y. 10023, Phone 212-799-5050

THE COMMUNION FOUNDATION, Whitley Strieber, 5928 Broadway, San
Antonio TX 78209

ACADEMY OF CLINICAL CLOSE ENCOUNTER
THERAPISTS
2826 O St. Suite 3, Sacramento, CA. 95816, Phone 916-455-0120

THE NEWSLETTER FOR SPIRIT RELEASE THERAPY
Free Spirit Center for Human Relations, P.O. Box 4061, Enterprise, FL 52725,
407-322-2086

THE AMERICAN ASSOCIATION OF META SCIENCE P.O. Box 1182
Huntsville, AL 35807

CENTER FOR UFO STUDIES, 2457 West Peterson Ave. Chicago IL, 60659

THE EYES OF LEARNING (STAR PEOPLE GROUP) Elaine Resnick,
Director, Joanne Steele
60 Autumn Lane, Hicksville, NY 11801, Phone 516-661-2424

* * *

INTERNATIONAL

BRITISH UFO RESEARCH ASSOCIATION BUFORA
BM BUFORA, London, WC1N3XX, Great Britain.
Or Suite 1, The Leys, 2c Leyton Rd, Harpenden
Herttfordshire AL5 2TL
Or 1 Woodhall Drive, Batley, West Yorkshire WF17 7SW
England. Also London, WC1N 3XX England
e151@Qial.pipex.com Publishes UFO Times

THE INTERNATIONAL COMMITTEE FOR ICUR
UFO RESEARCH
P.O.314, Penn, High Wycombe, Buckinghamshire,
HP10 8DH, England. (Important multinational organization.)

ITALY: CISU; DENMARK: SUFOI; SWEDEN: Project URD; AUSTRALIA:
VUFORS

NORTHERN UFO NETWORK NUFON
England and Scotland

NORTHERN ANOMALIES RESEARCH ORGANIZATION
NARO
37 Heathbank, Rd., Stockport, Cheshire, SK3 OUP

FSR REVIEW FSR
P.O. 162, High Wycombe, Bucks, HP 13 5DZ, England

CANADIAN UFO RESEARCH NETWORK CUFORN
Box 15, Station A, Willowdale, Ont.M2N 5S7

CANADA - UFO RESEARCH INVESTIGATION CENTER UFORIC
Dept.25, 1665 Robson St., Vancouver, B.C. V6C 3C2
CANADIAN UFO RESEARCH NETWORK, INC. CUFORN
592 Shephard Ave. No, Box 77547, Downsview, Ont.M3H 6A7

AUSTRALIA – UFO RESEARCH AUSTRALIA UFORA
PO Box 1894, Adelaide, South Australia 5001
Or – PO Box 229, Prospect, South Australia 5082

AUSTRALIA–THE VICTORIAN UFO RESEARCH SOCIETY, INC. VUFORS
P.O. Box 43, Moorabin, Victoria, Australia 3189
Voice 61-3-6076849, fax: 61-3-6076198
Publication: Australian UFO Bulletin

IRELAND – Irish UFO & Paranormal Research Assoc. IUFOPRA
PO Box 3070, Whitehill, Dublin 9, Eire

FRANCE – OVNI PRESENCE , BP 324, OVNI
13611 Aix-en-Provence, Cedex 1, France

BELGIUM-SOCIETE BELGE D'ETUDE DES SOBEPS
PHENOMENES SPATIAUX
74 Ave Paul Jansson, B 1070 Brussels, Belgium

SWEDEN – Scandinavian UFO Investigation SUFOI
PO Box 11027, S-600 11, Norrkoping, Sweden

THE NORTH AMERICAN INSTITUTE FORCROP CIRCLE RESEARCH NAICCR
Box 1918, Winnipeg Manitoba, R3C 3R2 Canada
REPORTING CENTERS and ARCHIVES

THE UFO REPORTING AND INFORMATION SERVICE UFORIS
P.O. Box 832 Mercer Island, WA 98040, 206-721-5035

THE UFO CONTACT CENTER INTERNATIONAL UFOCCI
3001 So. 288th St. #304, Federal Way, WA 98003, 206-946-2248
Publication – The Missing Link

THE UFO INFORMATION AND RETRIEVAL CENTER UFOIRC
3131 West Cochise Drive, #158 Phoenix, Arizona 85051
602-997-1523, 602-870-3178
Reference for outstanding UFO sighting reports

THE NATIONAL SIGHTING RESEARCH CENTER NSRC
P.O. Box 76, Emerson, New Jersey 07630

THE NATIONAL SIGHTING RESEARCH CENTER NSRC
P.O. Box 76 Emerson, New Jersey 07630
Publication The National Sighting Yearbook

COLLECTORS OF UNUSUAL DATA-INTERNATIONAL COUD-I
c/o Raymond Nelke 2312 Shields Ave., St. Louis, Missouri 63136
314-388-0087. Publication Research Kit –Anomalous Thoughts

UFO PHOTO ARCHIVES- Wendelle C. Stevens
P.O. Box 17206, Tucson, AZ 85731, 520-296-6753, fax 721-9025

ISLAND SKYWATCH
164-22 77th Road, Flushing, New York 11366, 718-591-1854 (24 hr hotline)
Publication: Skywatch Journal

THE ARCHIVES FOR UFO RESEARCH
Postfack 11027, 5-600 11 Norrkoping, Sweden
Publication: The AFU Newsletter (English)

THE NATIONAL UFO REPORTING CENTER Peter Davenport
www.nwlink.com/-ufocntr
P.O. Box 45263 University Station, Seattle, WA. 98145, 206-722-3000

PERIODICALS

UFO MAGAZINE
P.O. Box 6970, Los Angeles, CA 90066-6970
5455 Centinela Ave., LA 90066
Tel. 310-827-0505, 1-888 836-6242, 310-652-6990
Website www.ufomag,com

or P.O. Box 1053 Sunland, CA 91041
818-951-1250, fax 818-951-0098

INTERNATIONAL UFO REPORTER
J.Allen Hynek Center for UFO Studies,
2457 West Peterson Ave, Chicago, IL 60659

CNI NEWS, an electronic new journal
CNINEWS@ aol.com

INTERNATIONAL UFO LIBRARY MAGAZINE
11684 Ventura Blvd. #708, Studio City, CA 91604, Phone 818-769-2917

STRANGE MAGAZINE
Box 2246 Rockville, Maryland 20847, Phone 301-460-4789, fax 301-460-1959

UFO NEWSCLIPPING SERVICE
Box 220, Rt.1, Plumerville, AR 72127, 2 Caney Valley Drive,
Plumerville, 501-354-2558

INTERNATIONAL UFO REPORTER
2457 West Peterson Ave. Chicago 60659

GLOBAL COMMUNICATIONS
GPO 1994 New York, NY 10001, 212-685-4080
Publication UFO Universe; Unsolved UFO Sightings

UFO UNIVERSE
1700 Broadway, New York, NY 10019

SEDONA JOURNAL
2020 Contractors Road, #4, Sedona, AZ 86336, Phone 1-800-450-0985
www.sedonajo.com, sedonajosedonajo.com

MUFON UFO JOURNAL
103 Oldetowne Road, Seguin, TX 78155-4099, Phone 217-382-4502,
dconnell@ccipost.net

WORLD UFO JOURNAL
16 Newton Green, Great Dunmow, Essex CM6 1DU, UK

FATE
P.O. Box 1940, 1740 Future Way, Marion, OH 43305-1940
DISCOVERY TIMES
270 Sandycombe Rd, Kew, Surrey, TW9 3NP, England

UFO MAGAZINE (ENGLAND)
66 Boroughgate, 1st floor, Otley Near Leeds, England LS21 1AE

UFO TIMES – BUFORA
Suite 1, 2C Leyton Rd. Harpenden, Hertfordshire, England

CROP WATCHER
3 Melbourne Court, Tavistock Close, Romsey, Hampshire So 51 7TY, UK.

FORTEAN TIMES
Box 2409 London NW5 4NP England

FLYING SAUCER REVIEW
Snodland, Kent ME 65HJ , England, m
or PO Box 162 High Wycombe, Bucks HP 13 5DZ

UFO AFRINEWS – Cynthia Hind
PO Box MP 49, Mount Pleasant, Harare, Zimbabwe

BULLETIN OF ANOMALOUS EXPERIENCE (BAE)
614 South Hanover St. Baltimore, MD 21230-3832, USA
IN CANADA – Dr. David Gotlib, 2 St. Clair Ave. West
Suite 607, Toronto, Ont. M4V 1LF, Canada

THE NEW ENGLAND BIGFOOT RESEARCH CENTER
21 Benham St, Apt. F, Bristol, CT 06010, Phone 860-582-4752

OMEGA COMMUNICATIONS
Box 2051, Cheshire, CT 06410, Fax 203-250-0501

CONTACTEE
Box 12, New Milford, New Jersey 07646, Publication: Contactee

WEBSITES

SCIENCE AND UFO DEBATE www.primenet.com/-bdzeiler/indez.html

SCIENCE FRONTIERS www.knowledge.co.uk/frontiers

JOURNAL AND SOCIETY OF SCIENTIFIC EXPLORATION www.jse.com

CNI NEWS www.cninews.com Michael Lindemann
ART BELL WEBSITE www.Artbell.com

THE FBI FREEDOM OF INFORMATION UFO WEBSITE
http:/www.fbigov/foipa/ufo.html

UFOs and EXTRATERRESTRIAL ALIENS, CENTER FOR UFO STUDIES, UFO NET GLOBAL

VIDEOS

There are too many to list. I recommend checking Paradigm Research Group Video Archives on the Internet

UFO RESEARCHERS

–See "List of UFO researchers—Wikepedia, the free encyclopedia."

UFO CONFERENCES

—See "Lost Arts Media Online"

In Conclusion

My education on UFOs and aliens is continuing and evolving. Beginning as curiosity, it has become for me a compelling desire to **inform the ordinary general public (rather than the knowledgeable UFO community)** of the following:

There are many races besides the negative "grays" who abduct; there are also positive ones who guide and care for us. And some aliens are living and working among us. They are far superior to us technologically, but they are only our neighbors and like us, have originated from the one Creator God. To understand UFOs one must acknowledge the paranormal as in "Indigo, Wanderer, Star People"—the UFO/metaphysical connection. UFO knowledge is necessary for understanding the psychological, religious, financial, social, spiritual implications of alien/human interaction—and how it can affect us personally. We need it in order to intelligently influence our government—perhaps to prevent a possible trumped-up "star wars."

All aliens have the same message: Earth will experience many natural and man-made disasters as it and its inhabitants go from third to fourth and fifth dimensions in our inevitable spiritual evolution. Prophesies are only probabilities; we have free will to change them. It is imperative we save the ecology and show compassion for each other as the Earth goes through the "Shift".

About the Author

Dena Blatt was born and raised in a small town in Canada of immigrant Jewish parents from Russia. She has had varied careers. In each her talent has been to analyze, whether as head medical lab technologist; the owner of an electronics business; an investor in real estate; a graphoanalyst writing a "Dear Dena" newspaper column; a student of Holocaust studies; a collaborator on Holocaust writings—or as a "self-styled journalist" interviewing subjects in the following countries: **Germany**—SS Karl Frenzel, mass murderer, acting commandant of death camp Sobibor at the time of the revolt. **Israel**—Thomas Blatt, survivor of Sobibor, author of *From the Ashes of Sobibor*. **Russia**— Sasha Pechersky, Russian Jewish officer, leader of the 1943 Sobibor revolt; **Switzerland**—Simon Wiesenthal and family, author and world famous Nazi hunter;. **England**—Egidia Bochetta, amazing Italian psychic, and her children. **USA**—Ida Kannenberg, "walk-in," rare UFO contactee, author and antique dealer. **Canada**—Shirle Klein-Carsh, "wanderer," rare UFO contactee and cosmic artist.

Personal experiences growing up influenced the author to seek books on the Holocaust, psychology and the metaphysical. She had no knowledge of "wanderers," Star People, aliens from other dimensions— or ETs looking like us, living and working among us—until meeting Shirlè.

Dena Blatt is a grandmother and writer, living in California and Washington State. E-mail address: denawrites@comcast.net

About the Artist

Shirlè Klein-Carsh was born and raised in Montreal of immigrant parents from Poland. She received her Fine Arts degree at Sir George Williams (now Concordia University) in Montreal; completed studies at the Museum of Fine Arts, Montreal under Dr. Arthur Lismer (one of the Canadian Group of Seven Artists); and studied at the School of Fine Arts, Saidye Bronfman Centre, Montreal.

She calls herself as a cosmic surrealist fascinated by the symbolic language of the subconscious and the mysteries of the Universe. A prolific painter and a master of color, she has had many shows in Canada and the USA, as well as exhibits in Australia, France, Russia, and Bulgaria, since 1965.

Shirlè continues to paint and is a great-grandmother living with her husband Fred in West Vancouver, B.C.

To view photos of her paintings in color, go to her website: www.nsartists.ca/shirlekleincarsh

***

"Shirlè is a surrealistic painter whose talent reaches deep into the cosmic realm of the infinite, to create images and impressions of both magical and mysterious worlds outside the realm of the ordinary. Her strong sense of colour and unique style of presentation make each of her paintings a rare find in today's art world. Shirlè has held many exhibits of her art around the world since 1965."
—Frank Lewis Morton, Poet and Metaphysician, White Rock, B.C. Canada.

Shirlè in Studio

Artist Shirlè Klein Carsh and Author Dena Blatt

Printed in the United States
90570LV00007B/1/A

9 781432 712853